Urban Anthropology

Urban Anthropology

*Perspectives on 'Third World'
Urbanisation and Urbanism*

by PETER C. W. GUTKIND

Professor of Anthropology McGill University

BOOKS
10 East 53d St. New York 10022
(a division of Harper & Row Publishers. Inc.)

Published in the U.S.A. 1974 by
HARPER & ROW PUBLISHERS, INC.
BARNES & NOBLE IMPORT DIVISION

ISBN 0-06-492610-9

Printed in the Netherlands by Van Gorcum, Assen

Preface

To set out ideas with clarity, and brevity, is no easy task. Few men have the ability to set to paper a view so important and so clear that minor flaws fade into insignificance. This monograph is not of this order. It was a struggle to attempt to bring together some of the ideas which have guided my work in Urban Anthropology since 1953 when I began research in urban Africa.

Few of the ideas set out are my own. I owe an enormous debt to all my fellow Urban Anthropologists be they Africanists or otherwise. I cannot say whether I have contributed anything new, anything creative.

My debts are legion to all those with whom I have been in contact at universities, conferences, in industry and government, and in the field; to all those of my colleagues everywhere, who have put up with me – but in the process have stimulated me to try again. My debts are legion to the thousands of Africans whose life I have tried to understand. I have admired them for their tenacity, their versatility and their enterprise, all in the face of frustration, humiliations and no small degree of physical suffering. But their future will change.

My debt is also very great to my late father, Professor E. A. Gutkind, who, for sixty of his eighty-two years, was completely devoted to the study of urbanism and whose visions of a less ugly world have influenced my own. The testimony to his intellectual brilliance, which I cannot match, is enshrined in his eight volume work, recently published, of *The International History of City Development*.

And, as always, I owe much to my own immediate family who have suffered along with me in the preparation of this small book. Their tolerance far exceeds any legitimate expectations.

The idea of writing this book stems largely from a conversation which I had with my teacher and friend, Professor Andre Köbben, whose calm and reasoned intellectual life has set very high standards. Had it not been for the fact that my close colleagues at McGill University, Bruce Trigger and Richard Salisbury, allowed me undue use of our Department Secretaries, who did much of the typing, I would still be pecking away at my own typewriter – or making life miserable for my wife.

Over the years I have received support from various agencies which allowed me to go into the field and gather material. Such support has been provided, at various times, by the Canada Council, The Wenner-Gren Foundation for Anthropological Research, the Centre for Developing-Area Studies at McGill University, and the Social Science Research Council.

I must conclude with a question posed by one of my four children, a boy of nine, who asked me one day whether the book I was writing would be as interesting as the book on trains and planes he was then looking at. I could only whisper to him saying: I hope so.

P. C. W. G.

McGill University
Montreal.

Table of contents

I   *Why study African towns?*

1. *Urbanisation: An Overview*

It has frequently been suggested that the history of civilisation is really the history of urban life. The archeological record indicates that the cradle of urban development was located in the lower Middle East – the "Fertile Crescent" – and its beginnings have been dated between 9000 B. C. and 6000 B. C. in the Neolithic age. Whether or not it was from the Middle East alone that this important "revolution" spread to other parts of the world, or whether there were other independent centers of urban growth, is still a matter about which we cannot be certain. However, somewhat later in time very important centers of (urban) civilisation appeared in Northern China, in the Indus Valley of Northern India and in the lower Nile Valley. What was the thrust behind the slow development of these communities in which a large number of people lived in units much larger than a village or scattered homesteads? Is it appropriate to refer to these communities as towns? Were they perhaps no more than large-scale peasant settlements? After all, when does a village become a town? The last two questions in particular have relevance to the history of urban life in Africa.

Though the archeological record is still not complete, urban development has its roots in inventions and discoveries of very great magnitude: the change from food gathering and hunting to food producing, from being preyed upon by animals to the domestication of many, from the uncertain existence based on a subsistence economy to the production of a food surplus. In short, urban development was rooted in the agricultural revolution which in turn eventually gave rise to yet another transformation, perhaps of even greater significance, the industrial society.

The systematic cultivation of grain crops did not immediately bring people together in larger settlements. Agricultural skills had to be learned, storage facilities for the harvest had be provided and the technology of irrigation had to be mastered. But as men slowly became masters over their environment the basis of their social life began to change. Of course, even in pre-neolithic times men achieved a considerable measure of adaptation and control over many different kinds of physical environments ranging from the harsh deserts and the arctic cold to temperate regions of the world. But in the days before the agricultural revolution the energies of young and old alike were wholly devoted to the day by day needs, to gather food, build shelters and seek protection. Much time was taken up by the need to move in search of food and water and away from, perhaps, hostile neighbours. To facilitate this need for mobility, the number of people who lived together was generally very small. Probably several families, perhaps extended family units, would hunt and gather food together. During difficult times, when food was in short supply, these "bands" would in all likelihood break up into yet smaller units, to facilitate the search for subsistence and to eliminate the potential of conflict which might arise over competition for scarce resources. But, no doubt, periods of nomadic seasonal migration were interspersed with periods of a settled existence – but almost invariably in small units. Perhaps, at times for political and ceremonial reasons larger numbers of people who considered themselves members of the same "tribe", of the same ethnic community, or the same political and cultural group might gather together. But generally circumstances were not favourable to either prolonged contact or a large number of people living together. Yet it is important to remember that all the time these small-scale communities were moving in the direction which eventually made a settled existence of larger groupings possible (Cohen 1968).

It is also important that we do not think of these groups as wholly undifferentiated. There clearly was an internal division of labour, between men and women and young and old, and some specialisation of skills and duties. Whereas men did the hunting, the women searched for berries and roots and collected water and firewood. While the women looked after children, the men protected their families. Yet it is more than likely that these soci-

eties did not go much beyond this simple specialisation – to the point that
some people would not be engaged in food gathering. Every man was both
hunter and craftsman. Probably, there were a few priests, a few "doctors",
but no scholars who devoted themselves *exclusively* to the pursuit of these
activities. As far as we know there probably were few, if any, full time "specialists" such as traders, soldiers or administrators. These, and many other
types of specialisations, only became possible when people had learned to
produce a surplus of staple foods. When this was achieved, however, the basis for larger social groupings had been created. This transformation was of
such magnitude that culture historians have not hesitated to call it a revolution (Childe 1936). It is no exaggeration to suggest that the history of technology, the systematic knowledge applied to manufacture, and the history
of science, the systematic collection of knowledge, are deeply rooted in
these early beginnings.

It might be desirable to apply a little conceptual shorthand to label and
identify the main characteristics of this great transformation. It might be
useful to do this because some scholars have suggested that the basis of urban
life in Africa is so very recent, in an historical sense, that we are still able to
detect some of these early characteristics in many of the towns of contemporary Africa. Whether this is a really creative approach to an understanding
of African urbanism is a matter which we shall deal with later.

The change from a subsistence economy to one which rests progressively
on the ability to create a surplus of food can also be described as a change
from a nomadic-band society to a village-based society. For the sake of shorthand we can say that this is a change from hunters and gatherers to peasant-
ry; from a high degree of mobility to settled village life.

To identify a form of human settlement as a village is to suggest an important intermediate step in the movement from band societies to urban life. Of
course this is partly an abstraction and should not be interpreted to mean that
there is a pre-determined evolutionary sequence involved. We know very
well that people can, and do, leap from a subsistence or simple agricultural
base to an urban way of life, and that an ever larger number of people are
doing just this. But even with this caution in mind, it is probably more realistic to identify these early incipient urban settlements as large village com-

munities. Nor should we assume that it is only in a city or town that we can point out the unique features of urban life. Thus some villages might be very large indeed, perhaps comprising several thousand people, yet everyone living there obtains their living by means of agricultural work, let us say by means of growing cash crops. Such villages despite their size might have very little specialisation of skills and offices as these are supposed to be a reflection of a clear urban style of life. On the other hand a very *small* settlement, which is tucked away in a rural area, might have most of its people work in a nearby factory who buy their food from local farmers or a general store. The wider implications of these contrasting possibilities, i.e. that urban areas (at least in size) can have rural characteristics and vice versa, is a matter to which we will have to give some attention. It is a problem of definition which has complicated the work of culture historians, of social geographers and, more recently, of urban anthropologists.

It is common to think of villages, hamlets, and small towns, having a population which is more concentrated than dispersed rural homesteads, and living within an area which is administratively and politically defined. Yet size of population alone may not be the most important distinction we should make between rural and urban, or semi-urban. The distinctions which we might more usefully employ are those which point to the *scale*, the *complexity* and the *functions* of various kinds of settlements (Wilson and Wilson 1945).

By *scale* we mean the area covered, its size, population density, and its degree of isolation or contact with other settlements both in a regional and national context. *Complexity* refers primarily to the internal characteristics of the settlement such as economic specialisation, social differentiation, political diversity and ideational diversity. By *function* we mean a documentation of the history of the settlement, how people make their living and the "services" which the settlement provides both for its own residents and for those living elsewhere. Taking these three variables into account, we can then order and appreciate the significance of what are considered the main characteristics of urban areas. But what is more important, by this means we can also maintain a three dimensional approach, i.e. what is the relationship between scale and complexity, between complexity and function, and between function and scale. The study of urban areas in Africa, indeed the study of any human settlement anywhere, and at any moment in time, will only yield results if we constantly see the relationship between these variables.

As we have indicated earlier, the transformation from pre-village life to village organisation, and eventually to an urban-industrial society, has been very slow. The agricultural revolution produced a situation which made new demands on the population to develop new social forms, to institutionalise and internalise these so as to achieve order, coherence and stability. At first, no doubt, these agricultural-village settlements were quite small and the way of life of the people was probably not very different from the immediate past. The agricultural surpluses which could be produced were not of such a high order that a significant percentage of the population had endless time on their hands. But certainly the foundations had been laid for a greater diversification of interests and activities. It is more than likely that several new occupational groups began to appear fairly rapidly, such as traders, scholars, religious leaders, administrators and craftsmen. The settlements became the centers not merely of technological innovation, and its diffusion, but also assumed a collective political importance which was translated into influence and power. The way this power was expressed varied greatly. Thus in the valley of the Lower Nile immensely powerful autocratic and dynastic empires eventually emerged, while in strong contrast the much later Greek settlements were centers of major participation by citizens in public affairs; and the Maya settlements excelled in the emphasis they gave to religious thought and ceremonial activity. Still other settlements, as those on the Mediterranean fringe, and those in Northern China, became important centers of trade and commerce. But the power which radiated from these new settlements had to be both enforced and protected as people outside the village walls were made servants of the newly powerful and as conflict arose between one settlement and another. Thus the history of organised military might is rooted in the cross currents of new collective motivations, objectives and desires and a search for rewards which unleashed a new dimension of inter- and intra-societal relations. In short as the size of the settlements grew so did the competition, sometimes positive but more often negative, between them.

As the technology became more efficient, as food surpluses increased in magnitude and as occupational specialisations became more established the new village settlements became attractive to rural migrants. Then, as now, but presumably on a much smaller scale, those beyond the boundaries of the new settlements began to look upon these as centers of influence and opportunity at first to be sampled and later, perhaps, to actively be part of. Then, as now, the move away from the purely rural area was selective. Not all men had either the opportunity or the initiative to migrate. Perhaps, then, as now, women were less free to move. The old tended to stay behind while the young were prepared to plunge into a new world of considerable uncertainty. Again, as now, the transition was one from relative isolation, from relative societal homogeneity, to one of new and close contact in a context of a diversity which had no exact parallel in any previous experience of the migrant. The overall result of the new movement of people was to transform the diversified agricultural settlement into a small town and, what was perhaps even more important, the severance from the land of a small part of the population.

However, at this point we need to proceed with some caution. At least we need to ask ourselves certain questions the relevance of which will become clearer as we begin to study African urban life. As settlements become larger, do they necessarily become urban? When is incipient urbanism transformed into "urbanism as a way of life" – if we may borrow from the late Louis Wirth (1938). Whatever the answer, the balance tips slowly from one direction to the other. The old does not always yield readily to the new, at least not during the historical time when this next transformation took place.

We cannot now deal with yet another controversial matter which is closely linked to the discussion so far, namely that the transition from village to town life is frequently equated with the origin of civilisation, the appearance of writing, the application of rationality to technology, and different philosophical and cosmological perspectives. Yet we need to bear in mind that the roots of urban life, anywhere, are deeply implanted in this transition. At the same time we need to be careful before we suggest that something of the past is always brought forward into the present and the future. Nor should we assume that the study of more recent urban development in Africa can help us to reconstruct those processes which were allegedly responsible for the change from rural to urban life because we cannot easily isolate them under contemporary conditions. While we should keep our conceptual options open, and accept the premise that industrial urban life has its historical roots, the view we shall develop in this presentation is that the link between tradition and modernity has been all but severed in African urban life. What we must recognise is that what we call tradition, be it in the realm of material or non-material culture, must be nurtured and reinforced by a total complex, i.e. habits, ideas, behaviour and by social, economic and political institutions which reject any alternative to tradition. Because this is not the case in Africa today, despite the subsistence economy which still prevails over most of the continent, we must apply to the study of urban life in Africa a rather different set of premises. If we fail to do this our insight into both the historical development of towns in Africa and into their contemporary structure and the problems they face will be gravely distorted.

We are not suggesting that we should irrevocably reject any link between the past and the present, or that some "traditional" ideas and practices of the more recent past do not play some part in the present. No observer could fail to be impressed by the startling differences between Timbuktu with its deep roots in medieval Islam and the City of Nairobi which was established no more than seventy years ago. Rather we might work with the premise that when and where we are able to detect traditional practices and ideas, it is because these are appropriate, or seem appropriate to some category of the urban population, in some situations and on some occasions. But even then we must recognise that if we make an effort to see these traditional practices in the total (urban) context in which they take place, we will find that this alleged tradition has been substantially transformed. If that is so, are we still talking about tradition? Thus, we should not confuse tradition with history. Ancient city walls, an old mosque, a local shrine, the use of a hoe rather than a tractor, the use of a gourd rather than a glass or basin, the use of a "native" doctor rather than a modern medical practitioner, a house built of sun-dried mud rather than cement blocks, the use of spears rather than rifles, the importance of kinship rather than an emphasis on individuality, to work on the land rather than in an office or a factory, all this and much more is no indication that custom is king and that modernity has not reached into the furthest corners of a society. Traditions are long established conventions as these determine or influence the behaviour and shape the ideas of people. Tradition is a point of reference, a measure and a guide. A real traditional society is impregnable. Its members will fight to keep it traditional. The non-conformist, or the heretic, is put to death or is expelled or shunned. Tradition, when custom really is king, will not compromise with alien influences and pressures. Any external pressures against its boundaries agitate the traditional society.

Of course, these are generalisations and abstractions, but they also serve to highlight the implications of the use of the concept of tradition. In modern Africa, and in particular in urban Africa, we cannot get very far if we apply this concept too frequently. Social anthropologists, who are beginning to take an interest in urban studies in Africa, tend to concentrate their attention on what they consider to be traditional. This is so, Professor Gluckman has told us, because anthropologists have "been reared on the rural tradition of the tribe." But if the anthropologist were to give greater thought to what is really implied when he talks about tradition he might come to the conclusion that the institutional fabric of African societies was radically transformed when the continent fell under the impact and control of colonial domination. To be sure, the anthropologist is cognisant of the fact that changes have taken place, but the basic premises he brings to his research have more often been a denial of this recognition. While this is not the place to debate this matter further, we can say that anthropological tradition might not be the most suitable perspective when applied to the study of urban communities in Africa (Gulick 1963).

We have said that tradition and history are not the same. Traditions are conventions which change, while history is the constant presence of the ideational, institutional and material roots of a society – of a living people, sharing a recognition and, perhaps, a pride in their past. It is this past which is often important to (some) people rather than, as we have learned over the years, the conventions – the traditional practices of a people. Whereas history is not compelled to adjust itself to the present, it being no more than a view of past events and ideas, conventions are concerned with behaviour, everyday behaviour, everyday demands, hopes, failures and successes.

We have made some brief comments on the historical roots of the city, its multiple roles, form, and structure. At best these comments have been designed to encourage the reader to recognise the relevance of this perspective. Because it is quite impossible to overstate the importance of the "Urban Revolution" in historical perspective, the student of urban life should penetrate this subject in far greater depth. We have also offered some thoughts to guide our approach to the study of urban phenomena in Africa, where it started, what it is, and how to study it. We must now take a closer look at the main characteristics of urbanisation and urbanism as a way of life. We shall then be ready to concentrate the rest of our attention on African urbanism and, by inference, "Third World" urbanism.

2. *Urbanisation in Africa: Some Historical Considerations*

We still know very little about the history of urbanisation in Africa, at least in Africa south of the Sahara. The main reason for this is that much archeological work remains to be done particularly in "Middle" Africa, the vast region south of the Sahara and north of the Limpopo. Thus far archeologists have concentrated on the history of urban settlement in the Nile Valley and the important trading centers on the north coast of Africa, the "City States" on the East African coast, and the Zimbabwe complex in Southern Rhodesia. Important as these have been for the African continent as a whole, we need to give a great deal more attention to the history of (urban) settlements in the forest and savannah belts of West Africa, Southern Zaire and the region between the Zambezi and the Limpopo.

Although Africa is the least urbanised of the continents, and its urban history is less well documented than that of Asia and Latin America, it has the fastest rate of urban growth in the world. Thus, between 1850 and 1950, the United Nations estimates (on the basis of centers with a population of 100,000 and over) the annual rate of growth as at least 3.9 per cent compared with 2.6 per cent for the world as a whole. Since then, this figure has probably reached almost 5.0 per cent per annum, although Thomas (1970) has predicted a falling off of growth rates. Only Latin America can boast that its rate is almost as high. It is therefore no exaggeration to say that the

"Rise of the Cities" is probably one of the most significant events behind the great transformation of contemporary Africa. Yet despite this it is important for us to recognise that a very small proportion of the population of Africa lives in cities today. Only about 11 per cent (made up of Africans and non-Africans) live in cities of 20,000 and above and only about 8 per cent in cities of 100,000 and above. Clearly, if we were to define urban as towns with a population of 10,000 and above, which in the African context might be a more realistic definition, the percentage living under urban conditions would be substantially higher. But because there are significant national differences in how urban is defined, when studying comparative urbanisation of the world it has been generally agreed to standardise definitions. Thus the word urban is applied to towns of 20,000 and above, or 100,000 and above. It is questionable whether the assumptions underlying these definitions have as much meaning in Africa as they do in Europe, North America, Asia and Latin America. These considerations are important to remember before we make some brief comments about the history of urbanisation in Africa.

While Africa remains the least urbanised of the continents, its urban history is not insignificant. So far our evidence is taken from three areas which pre-date European colonisation. These are: the valley of the Nile in Northeast Africa which for reasons (eventually) of cultural history can be combined with the North African lowlands; the savannah and forest regions of West Africa and parts of the East African coast between Lamu in the North and Lourenço Marques in the South. Another area will be found in Southern Africa but, with the exception of Zimbabwe, the foundations of urban life there are primarily European.

The first major urban centers in Africa emerged, probably around 3500 B.C., in the floodplains of the Lower Nile, as a result of the efforts by the Pharaohs to exert their influence, and to centralise their administration, over the population of the Nile Valley. Their attempts were successful and for nearly 3000 years their control and hegemony prevailed. Their political efforts created such towns as Memphis, Thebes and Tell-el-Amarna – all of which grew up, and declined, as the capital cities of successive dynasties. Other and smaller urban centers grew up which were, however, strictly subordinate to the capitals of the Pharaohs. Whether the traditions of these towns were carried westward and south-westward to the savannah and the forest belt is still a matter of some speculation. The towns of the Lower Nile were complex structures containing a fairly wide range of people such as priests, traders, craftsmen, shopkeepers, administrators and members of the dynastic elite. However, all categories of the population were severely subordinated to the theocracy of the Pharaohs who enforced their will completely. Thus it is likely that there was little in the way of a civic spirit rooted in a measure of autonomy.

Somewhat later in time, commencing perhaps in 1200 B.C., small-scale, but important, trading centers began to develop, and eventually flourish, on the North African coast. The fathers of this urban development (and the appearance of an "urban culture" under the Romans) were the Phoenician and Carthaginian traders who dominated life on this stretch of the Mediterranean coast for nearly 100 years. When the Romans occupied and destroyed Carthage in 146 B.C., their influence on the life and the economies of these towns was considerable and lasted for about 700 years. No doubt the Romans were the first "exploiters" of Africa as their interest was primarily in the export of wheat to other parts of the empire. However their strictly commercial efforts meant that their own strongly rooted urban culture impressed itself strongly on the towns on the North African coast. Although Carthage had been plundered and destroyed by the Romans, it rose from the ashes to become a town of between 75,000 and 100,000 people with an influence which penetrated deep into the hinterland and over its satellite small towns.

There is no need to dwell on the internal structure of the Carthaginian and Roman towns – suffice it to say that they were complex social, political, and economic systems with a considerable division of labour and a distinct "urban culture", in as much as virtually all the residents were engaged in non-agricultural activities. The most important aspect of their function, as far as West Africa is concerned, was the fact that these coastal towns had close and vital ties with the inland centers which connected the North African coast (and hence Southern Europe) with the areas to the south of the Sahara. What the exact nature of this contact was still remains to be explored. Could it be that urban development further south in West Africa owed its origin to this contact with Northern Africa, or are we dealing with a case of independent development?

The Roman control over these towns came to an end in the fifth century A.D. The immediate result was that as trade relations declined so did the urban culture on this Northern African coast. The Vandals destroyed the cities, showed little interest in urban life, and until the arrival of the Byzantium period the importance of these once vital centers declined seriously. But much of this changed when in the 7th century the whole of the North African coast was overrun by a vast migration of Arabs from the east. But as the Arab people had their cultural roots in a nomadic way of life, what remained of the Carthaginian and Roman towns had, initially, little interest for the invaders. However, by the late 8th and early 9th centuries trade contacts with the interior were re-established, a development partly attributable to the introduction of the camel. From this period onward, the towns of Northern Africa have an almost unbroken record until the present day.

While the towns of Northern Africa were "African", in the sense of being located on the African continent, they were certainly not populated by negro Africans. For evidence of this we must turn further south, into the Sahara and beyond. In the Western and Southern Sahara, and in the savannah belt, there emerged some important and large kingdom states whose leaders centralised their political and economic power in central capitals and regional towns. In some cases the power of these important empires, as they rose and fell in conquest and internal decline, rested on trade relations, on exports and imports, with both the Northern and the Western coasts of Africa. Gold was a prime commodity for export as were ivory, hides and skins. For example "Moroccan" leather was exported from Sokoto in Northwestern Nigeria. Thus the towns of the Western Sudan became perhaps the first urban areas in Africa which, while not populated by true negroid Africans, had close contacts with the southern part of West Africa – that area from which the European slavers eventually removed millions of Africans to the West Indies, Brazil and America.

But the cities of the Western Sudan were not merely important trade and communication centers which bridged the Islamic north and the pagan south. Such important towns as Timbuktu on the banks of the river Niger as it penetrated deeply into the heartland of the Southern Sahara were also centers of a flourishing intellectual life which was centered around a university. Other towns of equal importance, each with a particular history and functions were those of Gao, Lirekka, Kumbi and Tadmekka. Further south were towns whose importance is still great today as they have become major centers in the new nation-states of Africa. Such are the towns and capital cities of Kano, Katsina, Bamako, Ouagadougou, Djenne and Segou. Some of the towns no longer exist or have declined in importance such as Kong, in the Ivory Coast, a market town of over 10,000 people in 1888 which was destroyed in 1895, or Beyla, in Guinea, established in the twelfth century but today of little significance. Some towns were of substantial size at an early stage such as those which form the present cluster of Yoruba towns or those of Ghana such as Kumasi or Benin City to the east of Lagos. From the fifteenth to the nineteenth centuries numerous coastal towns developed in West Africa such as St. Louis, Monrovia, Lagos, Freetown, Goree and Dakar, Cape Coast and Accra, the latter two tracing their origin to a string of slave castles on the Guinea Coast. Today, each one of these towns still bears the evidence of its ancient past, their morphological features are such that it is possible to reconstruct, with a good measure of exactitude, the composition and the activities of the population. There is no question that these centers were towns by almost any definition (including that of size which only has become an important measure during the last two hundred years) and with very distinctive urban cultures.

Our first contact with what are clearly all-African towns comes when we turn a little further south in the forest belt of West Africa. Here important kingdoms developed such as those of the people of Dahomey, Yoruba, Ashanti and Ewe. The exact origins of these kingdoms still require further research. These ethnic groups probably migrated into the areas which they presently occupy between the 8th and 10th centuries either on their own free will or because they were driven south by those living further to the north. The forest gave the protection they needed and provided them with conditions which made settlement possible, although conditions were so harsh that they could be overcome only by a superior technology (Smith 1969). As these groups pushed into this area they probably conquered, or otherwise displaced, people whom they found in the forest. Thus far the best documented case of the conditions leading to the rise of these kingdoms is probably that of Yoruba

(Smith 1969) and Dahomey. The Yoruba, linked loosely by language and a certain homogeneity of customs, were really a set of independent kingdoms each of which attempted to exert influence and power over their neighbours, and each of which translated their aspirations into warfare and conquest. However, the immense complexity of the agriculturally-based kingdoms, with their advanced technology, their art, their ceremonial and ritual, their political hierarchy, their ability to put large armies into the field and their trading and craft activities, all were centered on the core of the kingdom's power, the town (Mabogunje 1962). Each of these towns, be it Old Oyo, Ile-Ife (regarded as the cultural mainspring of Yoruba society), Oshogbo, Owo, Ijebu-Ode, Ogbomosho or Ondo, trace their origins to having been important centers of political power at one time and another. More recent events, during the 18th and 19th centuries, gave rise to the important towns of Ibadan and Abeokuta and, more recent yet, to such vital coastal towns as Lagos. Whether these towns were large or small, whether their roots were deep or shallow, each one of them imposed upon the residents an elaborate and viable administrative system with ultimate power in the hands of a hierarchy of chiefs who themselves were subordinate to a local ruler. Urban as these settlements were, then as now one of their unique features was that a large percentage, up to recently probably the majority, of the residents were engaged in agricultural activities. While men and women lived in tightly-knit lineage-based compounds, on land considered the property of the lineage, their lives were deeply rooted in the land. Besides, we must not give the impression that all the Yoruba people were urban-based. The vast majority lived in the rural areas although their ties to the towns were then, as now, close and visits back and forth were far from unusual. We shall have occasion to turn to the Yoruba towns to illustrate features of contemporary urban life. But at present their importance for us is simply to indicate that the history of urban life in true black Africa is not as shallow as the uninitiated might have suspected.

Finally, we must briefly turn our attention to the coast of East Africa where some measure of urban concentration also developed, although once again the archeological record is as yet far from complete. However, there is evidence to suggest that this coast was a meeting place for people from

Southwest Asia, India and perhaps the Far East, as long ago as the first century A.D. (Mathew 1963), thus placing early trading settlements in about the same time span as urban developments in West Africa. The East African coastal region came strongly under the influence of waves of Arabs who fanned out from their homeland sometime in the 7th century A.D. Many of these Arabs selected the East African coast for permanent settlement from which they eventually conducted their slaving activities into the East African hinterland. Perhaps the best evidence of how important this coast was can be seen to this very day in the extreme diversity of its peoples among whom one can detect, easily, Arab, African, Indian and even Malay strains all of which came together, very slowly, into the Swahili speakers as we know them today. Perhaps the most unique feature of the towns along this coast is their root in a "city-state" structure seen most clearly in the dynastically organised community of Kilwa (Oliver and Mathew 1963) which was established towards the end of the 10th century A.D. The influence of Kilwa reached far beyond its own boundaries, at least for a time, although we shall have to wait for further information to understand what the relationship was between this important center and other states whose economic powers were also of considerable significance.

In these few paragraphs we have set out a rough time perspective of the main historical features of urban development in Africa. We still know far less than we ought to know, and until such a time when both the archeological and the oral tradition records are more complete we must be satisfied with little more than an enumeration of often speculative dates, and an even greater uncertainty about the nature of urban life in Africa. But even with these shortcomings, we have established, it is hoped, the simple fact that Africa does have an urban history and, further, that the past can and does have an important bearing on the present if in no other context than African urban history is an important part of the total history of the African continent.

While the historical record is still to be filled-in, our knowledge about urban life in more recent times is both more extensive and more exact. The first significant distinction is between the old, pre-colonial towns, and those towns which commenced their life during the colonial era. The former are primarily to be found in West Africa, particularly among the Yoruba, and have been described by Bascom (1955, 1959), Mabogunje (1962), Schwab (1965), Krapf-Askari (1969) and Lloyd (1959) plus a large number of the West African explorers such as Bowen (1857), Lander (1854), Denham *et al* (1826), Clapperton (1829) and Barth (1857-8). When the English and French established themselves in West Africa as the major colonial powers they found a number of well established small towns forming a strong contrast with the prevailing type of village and scattered settlements. When Clapperton reached the interior of Yoruba country in 1825 he visited Katunga (Old Oyo) and other sizable towns, although the Portuguese explorer d'Aveiro had visited the city of Benin in 1485. Almost all these West African towns, in the region of what is now within the boundaries of Nigeria, Dahomey, Togo and Ghana, were the political and administrative centers of powerful kingdoms and chieftainships and engaged in extensive trade and warfare with each other. In the course of conquest towns were frequently moved; new settlements were created as kingdoms grew in size and older towns were destroyed.

The significance of these pre-colonial towns is that many of them are still in existence today and that their present day functions do not differ very significantly from those of the past although they are now part of regional and national units, linked by means of modern communication, trade and political union. The old core city is still a vital part of the newer developments which have been grafted on to the old towns. Thus there is Old Kano and New Kano and Old Ibadan.

The internal complexity of these old towns was as great when they were thriving as it is today. While a very large percentage of the inhabitants engaged in farming (as is true today of the inhabitants of Ibadan), alongside them lived the ivory and leather workers, the dyers, the weavers, the woodcarvers and the brasscasters. These specialists were highly organised in guilds (as they are today) and, together with the diviners, and those dispensing medicines and charms, exercised considerable political influence. Each town had its distinct political administration, usually hierarchically arranged, which culminated in the authority of a king, a chief or a leader endowed with sacred power. At lower levels were the heads of clans and the lineage heads, each contributing a specialist function to the welfare of the town as a whole. Social stratification and political segmentation was an important feature of the towns.

The influence of these towns then, as now, reached far beyond their boundaries as kings and chiefs held other towns under protective and/or tributary control. In due course, as a result of colonial control, the influence and viability of the kingdoms was sharply reduced and the towns began to serve as administrative centers and as nodal points to which export crops were despatched to be forwarded to the European capitals. While there were few censuses before 1910, the size of these towns remained fairly steady, probably in the 10,000 to 50,000 range. The population of Lagos Island in 1901 was estimated at 25,000 and by 1950 had risen to 87,000. Ecologically, the towns often covered considerable areas, ranging from two to eight square miles, because political jurisdiction frequently included the agricultural areas farmed by inhabitants of the town.

On the whole, the towns were more homogeneous than they are today. Foreigners who lived in these towns were either itinerant traders, captives or slaves. While diversity of behaviour and values was perhaps less than it is nowadays, political relations probably generated much the same kind of conflict extant today. In this regard the towns reflected the political, social and economic complexities of the powerful kingdom states.

We still know very little of the physical layout of these towns. In most cases, however, there was a central core occupied by the ruler or other leading political personalities. Thus the *kibuga* of Buganda, the royal capital of the Ganda kings, was reserved for the residence of the king and his most senior chiefs, and commoners had to seek special permission to visit. The *lubiri,* the royal enclosure, was surrounded by a woven reed fence some ten feet high and the entrances were guarded by the royal bodyguard. As the *kabaka,* the king, and his chiefs were frequently not very secure in their office, elaborate escape arrangements were designed (Gutkind 1963). As in some of the Dahomean capitals, and in Benin, the royal enclosure of the Ganda kings was lavishly laid out and approached by means of at least one well constructed and wide avenue. This was not always the case in some of the Yoruba towns where the ruler's enclosure was ringed by densely settled residential areas. This is still clearly evident in Old Lagos where markets and small enterprises crowd the residence of Oba of Lagos, while the palace at old Oyo is not crowded in this manner. In Dahomey (Arensberg 1968 : 12) the palace compound must have covered a considerable area.

Thus the royal city, the capital, of Dahomey, at least, was simply one village among many in its form. It was one village, that of a king and his royal sib and household, grown great. Thus it combined the palace, the residences and family lands of the royal lineage and its ancestral shrine, itself grown to be a temple seat within the palace of the royal cult celebrated by all the kingdom. The palace also had its own market, like any village, but it was the royal market. It housed a household, like any village compound, but it was a household hugely expanded into a "patrimonial bureaucracy" of Max Weber's kind ... In every particular the city was a combination of the usual dispersed institutions of the countryside and like them in essential form. But in function it was a gathering in of them into a single center, a node of ruling power. The reach of that rule was the extent of the kingdom.

Paths, rather than streets laid out symmetrically, joined the various zones and neighbourhoods. Unlike more recent urban growth, food plots were attached to each homestead giving the appearance of a "garden city". Only the specialists, the non-agricultural workers, lived on the surpluses produced by local or rural foodgrowers. Markets, often under the control of the ruler, served not only the needs of the urbanites but also those in the surrounding rural area. As markets today, they functioned both as centers for purchase and exchange for general and specialised goods, and as meeting places for the population as a whole. While some of the markets were held daily, others were held periodically moving to different locations, within a defined territory, according to a regular schedule.

These few comments give some idea of the major features of the pre-colonial African town. Compared to the new towns of Africa, possibly the most significant contrast between the towns of West Africa and those of East and Central Africa, is the fact that the former are wholly African in make-up. While the large trading companies in the West African towns are almost wholly in non-African hands, there is a vast amount of small-scale and middle-range African enterprise. Literally thousands of African traders, the majority of them women, crowd the sidewalks, the alleys, the public squares, the bus parks, the industrial areas – indeed it seems that in West African towns every available space bristles with traders from the very young to the very old. For several generations, and particularly since the end of the Second World War, this has been one of the outstanding characteristics of West African towns. It is this which gives these towns their distinct character.

A visitor to Nairobi, Salisbury, Kampala and any number of small towns in Central and Southern Africa cannot fail to notice that the layout and make-up of these towns follows a European and North American rather than an African pattern. Not only is the street system akin to Western towns, but the core of the town comprises modern shopping centers and arcades. Streets and avenues are frequently tree-lined with a center grass strip separating the lanes. Few African traders clutter the sidewalks and there is little African small-scale entrepreneurship in the way of shops or services of one sort or another. Indeed, the most marked feature of these "colonial" towns is that their life is dominated by non-Africans. Unlike the intense congestion of Ibadan, these new towns are spaciously laid out and usually very well maintained by an efficient system of municipal services. While the Europeans control, and own, the major commercial enterprises, those of Asian and Middle Eastern descent own the retail stores. Expensive hotels and specialised shops dominate the commercial core of the town. African participation in commerce, in East, Central and Southern Africa, is still minimal although most menial jobs are held by Africans.

Even more significant, few Africans actually live close to the heart of the town. Nowhere else is the colonial imprint on these towns seen more clearly than in the racial distribution of the population. While Europeans and Asians tend to live in separate locations, but usually close to the center of the city, Africans live in housing estates which are often several miles from their place of employment. Such racial separation was either dictated by racial and/or colonial laws (Watts 1959) or, where this was not so, effective economic barriers prevented Africans from living in less congested areas and closer to the heart of the town. Since the middle 1950's, when most African colonial territories became independent nations, this urban racial ecology has changed little. The exclusive residential areas once occupied by expatriate Europeans are now occupied by the senior, and elite-minded, African civil servants and African housing estates are becoming more congested, therefore producing increased personal deprivation, frustration, and serious slum conditions.

Most of these new towns are rarely more than seventy years old; most of them started as small centers occupied by colonial administrators, traders, explorers of mineral resources, educators and missionaries. Others owe their origin to railway camps, such as Nairobi, supply centers for European farmers, such as Naivasha in Kenya, small mining communities such as Enugu in Nigeria or the large number of mining towns in Central and Northern Zambia and the Southern Zaire, harbour towns such as Lobito in Angola, or Mogadishu in the Somali Republic. Occasionally we find towns with a somewhat longer history such as Dar es Salaam, St. Louis in Senegal, Monrovia in Liberia and Addis Ababa in Ethiopia. While the latter does not fit into these categories, the others, despite their older roots are essentially colonial towns and bear many of the same features of their more recent origin. Unlike the West African towns, particularly those of the Yoruba, the new towns lack deep historical roots. There is little evidence to be found in towns such as Salisbury, Lusaka or Nairobi of the compounds of chiefs and kings or the remains of protective walls or fortifications. Instead what historical sites there are were erected by the colonial powers in honour of explorers or conquerers, such as the statue in memory of Cecil Rhodes in the heart of Salisbury, Southern Rhodesia. Such sites in the urban areas seem to be designed with a clear purpose in mind: to remind Africans that they continue to live under a colonial dispensation. Gradually, of course, such landmarks are being replaced by independent African governments' rather imposing, if often ugly, monuments to honour their leaders and the struggle for independence.

Despite these significant differences, both the old and new towns of Africa have a number of features in common. Practically all the towns in Africa are now a composite of a very considerable ethnic mixture. While it is not unusual for a town to be dominated by one ethnic group, in whose natal land the town is located, and who may also dominate particular occupational categories, it is not unusual to find between ten and fifty different ethnic groups represented in most African towns. From such a highly diverse base, it is not difficult to project the kind of social and political order which coalesces into an urban system. Thus one main feature of all the towns, to be discussed in more detail in the following chapters, is the function of ethnicity, both in negative and positive terms, in urban life. Much of the literature on urban Africa is dominated by an analysis designed to show the allegedly negative function served by ethnic sentiment, ethnic groupings and ethnically-based politics. Such a conceptualisation, as we shall see, obscures the understanding of how in fact the urban system works.

Also, old and new towns have in common certain basic demographic features such as the fact that the urban population is a very young one. At least sixty per cent of the residents are under the age of thirty-five; hardly more than ten per cent are over the age of forty-five. The social, economic and political implications of this need hardly be spelled out in any great detail. To perhaps sum up briefly, they are young, ambitious, and often frustrated young people, the majority recent migrants, in search of jobs and opportunities. Coupled to these demographic features are two further characteristics; the sex ratio is often weighed in favour of men and they are predominantly single. Again, not much imagination is required to see that these characteristics will produce certain social patterns of individual and group relations and in the organisation of the urban family. Not a few observers have seized upon these characteristics and interpreted the consequences in moralistic terms because of their inability to understand the purpose of particular, i.e. non-traditional, structures, institutions and social and personal arrangements. Indeed some African urban studies give us vivid descriptions of the imminent fall of man!

Certainly, a combination of social, economic, political and, not least, ideational characteristics give towns their distinctive flavour and make up their fabric. To suggest that we are in a "transitional" phase adds little to the conceptual approach which ought to provide us with a better measure of exactness than springs from such a label. Furthermore, the concept suggests not only the obvious in as much as Africa as a whole is undergoing very major changes, none of which have crystallised to the point where we can predict behaviour, but it also suggests that urban Africans do not shape the nature of their life and lookout according to their perceptions and preferred arrangements. Rather than being in a transitional phase, (in what direction we might ask), it is more exact to speak of a particular style of life, as particular as any other set of arrangements considered suitable, at a particular moment of time and serving particular ends. As we shall see in Chapter Four, our dif-

ficulties in giving an accurate account of the social structure and organisation of African towns are often methodological. As we cannot study the
whole town, except over a considerable period of time, we must make certain
decisions concerning the why and wherefore in studying certain areas, neighbourhoods, zones or districts. We still have to find answers to important methodological problems.

To summarise, both the old and new towns of Africa have many features in
common. Although the older towns differ in the sense that they have deeper
historical roots and because they are more "African" than the new towns, the
urban areas of Africa are, as it were, being homogenised with the result
that structures and organisational patterns reflect certain similarities. This is
so not only of African towns, but also of those in Asia and Latin America.
While we must never ignore their individual differences, as these are often
the key factors in making the towns what they are and what they might become, neither can we ignore the fact that towns are now part not merely of regional units and national units, but progressively they are being
linked to an international urban matrix. Air and shipping communications
give reality to this view. Nairobi and London, and Ouagadougou and Paris,
Beira and Lisbon, Kinshasa and Brussels are as intimately linked as New
York and London and Vancouver and Tokyo. To assume that such links are
merely lines on a map, or that London is a modern "swinging" city while
Ouagadougou is out in the wilds, will result in such constraints in our documentation and analysis that the true nature of African towns will escape
us totally.

3. Are Towns the "Pace-Setters" of the New Africa?

To predict accurately the course of social and political affairs in Africa
ought to be left to seers and prophets or to those who think they really
"know" Africa. The know-alls are satisfied to expound their "I-told-you-so",
while others appear baffled by what they hear, read and see. Between these
extremes, there is clearly a middle course to be followed.

From a demographic view, there is no question that Africa has experienced one of the fastest rates of urban growth among the Third World conti-

nents: about fifty per cent every ten years. Many major towns, particularly those in West Africa, have doubled in size in less than a decade. On the other hand, what also needs to be taken into account, is the fact that over eighty per cent of the African population continues to live in rural areas earning it's living by means of farming. The towns, therefore, bring together a very small percentage of the population.

However, as we have indicated, the importance and influence of the towns reaches far beyond their legally constituted boundaries. This is so not merely because migration to the towns is now very considerable everywhere in Africa, as the movement between rural-urban-rural areas indicates, but primarily because the urban way of life is viewed as the model of the good life, the new life, the urge and determination to obtain a living in a manner different from the past. This is not to say that Africans reject tradition or that they are determined to become urbanites. But it does suggest that they view the towns as centers for economic opportunities, diversity and self expression. While we know little about the latter, we can be certain of the determination to search for work, for wages and incomes, to trade and sell one's labour. In this sense, many observers have suggested that urbanisation is an important indicator of economic development. Here though we should watch out for contradictions. While some of the most urbanised countries rank among the poorest, Zambia for example, some of the least urbanised have the highest per capita income, Ivory Coast and Senegal. However, many of the poorest countries are also the least urbanised, i.e. Malawi, while some of the "richest" African countries enjoy quite a high level of urbanisation, i.e. Nigeria and South Africa (although the latter is a very special case). We could also say that some of the most economically active countries, if defined in terms of exports and imports, also have the largest and economically most active cities, such as Nairobi in Kenya or Lagos and Ibadan in Nigeria. But such contrasts and comparisons have many pitfalls. While carefully collected statistical measures do not lie, statisticians do! While there are many "primate" cities, whose annual growth rate today might be as much as ten per cent, many more small towns are struggling to remain viable. Besides, the very heavy unemployment rate, which seems to range from a minimum of ten per cent to a maximum of thirty per cent of males over the age of fourteen, makes life in the African towns one of struggle and tension. Indeed life for many African urbanites seems to have little to offer over and above congestion, lack of privacy, undesirable health and sanitary conditions, high rents and generally high costs of living. Are such conditions really compatible with economic progress? Are we to view them as a "stage" on the road to better conditions? Or are they virtually a permanent feature of the urban landscape? Professor Akin Mabogunje (1965) has clearly suggested that some forms of urbanisation are a constraint to economic development: Third World towns, particularly the primate cities are "over urbanised". But why, we must ask do rural Africans flock to the towns, and why is the influence of the towns so great?

Some answers were suggested above. But the reasons are more complex. In the first case, the transformation which has touched every part of Africa, a transformation which commenced systematically with the arrival of the colonial powers, has crystallised in the towns. Today the African towns are the most transformed segment of the society. This clearly makes the towns the catalysts of change, and it is in this sense that we ought to assess their importance. While the ruralite can, and does, listen to radio and can, and does, read newspapers and books, as a community of people they are not the innovators of change; yet neither are they so tradition bound as to be immune to change. The history of urban life, be it in Africa or elsewhere, has told us that towns are the centers of intellectual, spiritual and material innovation. They are the centers of the "great tradition", the seats of the *litterati*, the focal points of trade and communication. Because they comprise a high degree of ethnic, linguistic, social, political and occupational diversity, they also generate many alternative styles of life. It is these alternative styles of life which are the thrust behind the transformation. Urban life has both its optative elements and its own determinism. Urban life presents the rural migrant with alternative choices, and a limited range of these choices appeal to the wide range of persons who are resident in the towns. While each choice has its potential, and its failure, seen overall life in the town, it is thought, offers the kind of economic opportunities which can increase mobility.

Secondly, whether or not Africans are "achievement motivated" must be debated by those who design measures to test the impossible and project their own ethnocentricity on Africa. Whether or not Africans want to be "modern" men, whether or not they have the "will to be modern" is likewise a conceptualisation predicated on certain Western premises. But what appears more realistic is to ask what are the alternatives open to Africans (and other Third World peoples) to seek a more competitive and viable economic and political basis for themselves and their nations? A number of observers have declared that the African nations must invest their human capital in rural development. So they must. But rural transformation is only part of a more comprehensive national transformation. It is in this national transformation that the towns have played, and will continue to play, a major part. At this moment, the African nations are being carried along, as it were, on a dialectic and a strategy which has its own, particular modernisation momentum. While modernisation is not a very exact word, it nevertheless conveys the image of the inevitable and the purposeful. We are not suggesting that the people of the new nations are not masters of their own gains and follies. But we are suggesting that there is purpose behind the migrations, the willingness to brave hardships in the towns, and that this is treated as a stepping stone along the road to a better life.

The influence of the towns is therefore tied up with ideational changes which are taking place within the African nations as a whole and over the total continent. However deprived the urbanite is, however congested the towns are, to be an urbanite is a measure of achievement (in local terms). To be a settled and working urbanite is an even greater achievement, and to be so settled and at the same time to occupy the niche of country squire is viewed as a greater achievement yet. We are not saying that the implications of this are that Africans are becoming "Western", nor are we imposing on the urbanite a speculative interpretation of his outlook and desires. We are merely saying that in terms of practical alternatives, town life is viewed as one, albeit an important, alternative to occupational mobility. In economic terms Africans want a more viable base which many work areas do not provide. While Western economic aspirations were imposed on Africans throughout the colonial interlude, it is now too late to lay before Africans totally different models. While African leaders will modify these models, as President Julius K. Nyerere of Tanzania is attempting to do, the social, economic and political structure of African societies is progressively characterised by the rise of a privileged bureaucratic and elitist class as in Western industrial society. It is this elitist class which dominates the urban areas.

Although the power of the vote rests in the rural areas, bureaucratic power is concentrated in the towns. Not only are the towns the seat of national and regional governments, but they are headquarters of political parties, trade unions and non-governmental organisations, and all modern mass communications media are concentrated there. In the towns, therefore, are concentrated all accruements of the modern state, and with the consolidation of political power in the single-party state the fundamental problem of legitimacy of government is being contested.

The towns reveal, in dramatic perspective, the growing inequity between the few who are established in employment and the mass of the poor, the casually employed and the totally unemployed. While it is, perhaps, too early to suggest that the towns already harbour a discontented and politically socialised revolutionary population (Nelson 1970), an activist *lumpenproletariat*, there is little doubt that active political mobilisation is slowly taking place. Thus Dorothy Nelkin (1967) has pointed to the politically active role played by urban youth, mostly unemployed, in the military take-overs in a number of African countries. As economic and political demands increase from below, and the pace of economic development is not greatly accelerated, the conditions for conflict and confrontation are being readied. While observers such as Fanon (1966) have suggested that it will be the rural people who will form the spearhead of demands for a true transformation, it is not unlikely that similar pressures will be generated in the urban areas.

Towns in Africa, therefore, along with towns in others parts of the Third World, might be viewed as a "critical mass" with a high degree of sensitivity to the growing rigidity, the lack of occupational opportunities and mobility, within African society as a whole. This in turn should be linked to other more complex problems which have emerged as major by-products of the industrial, technological and educational revolutions which are so much the hallmark of the twentieth century.

Thus we cannot be sure whether towns in Africa are the "pacesetters" of a much needed transformation. All that we can say is that the apparent conflict between the African past, the legacies of colonialism and the demands of modernity have combined to form a set of characteristics and circumstances which are clearly manifest in both the older and newer towns of Africa. There is no reason to believe that the population growth of the towns will not increase and at an accelerated annual rate, although at least one observer has predicted a gradual falling off (Thomas 1970). It is also rather unlikely that job opportunities will increase and that fundamental inequities of income distribution will be ameliorated. While this is a pessimistic view, no evidence has been brought forward to suggest that this premise is not essentially correct. What economic development takes place creates some jobs (although the problems posed by labour versus capital intensive methods (Ardant 1964) have still to be resolved – if, indeed, these are realistic alternatives), although in statistically insignificant numbers in relation to present massive rural-urban migration.

We can do no better but to conclude this section with the comments of two African urbanites: the first was taken from an interview with a senior civil servant in the Government of Zambia, in Lusaka, and the other was offered by an unskilled and unemployed man of twenty-four who had been in search of work for seven months in Lagos, Nigeria.

Just look around. Don't you think that Lusaka is a beautiful town. Our shops are good, and our streets are clean and well laid-out. We have many entertainments and cultural facilities here and we must add more of these. Of course, I know, that we have many unemployed people here and many others who don't know how to make the best use of the town and its many opportunities. The Government of Zambia is doing its best to provide all Zambians with good work, but we cannot do this over night. It will take time. For this reason it is useless to rebel because no government can achieve these miracles. . . . But I tell you this, and you must believe me, if a man really wants to find work he can. . . . Do you know of any modern nation which does not have large towns? Our towns are part of our national life, they are a measure of what we have achieved and they will continue to be such a measure. . . . Don't forget that town life and civilization go together.

This is the City of God.

I have lived in Lagos for six years and work on construction places. Sometimes I can eat and sometimes I must go hungry. When I have finished one work [sic] I try to find other work. Sometimes I go to the Employment Exchange to ask for work but they can never help me. Sometimes I find other work because my friends tell me about work. . . . . I now live with a friend who works in a shop cleaning the floors and sweeping. He gives me a place to sleep and sometimes he gives me food. . . . Sometimes I am lucky when I am at the Bus Park to get six pence or a shilling washing a bus, but I have not done that for three weeks. . . . I sometimes go without food for two days, but I have other friends who might help when I say that I have not eaten for two days. . . . I think that the Government does not care for all the people well. There are many, many, many people in Lagos who are looking for work. . . . I sometimes go to the Government (to a Ministry) to see a friend and ask him if he can give me work. He may give me a letter to another man but I can never get work. . . . Last year I was marching with other men to see the Government but the police told us to go away . . . I do not think that the Government will help us. (Gutkind 1966)

And this is the City of Babylon: it is the City of Hell.

4. Towns and the Rural-Urban Dimension

Although many towns in the low-income countries of the Third World are of recent origin, or at most have grown more rapidly during the last twenty-five years than during the previous fifty, their impact on the region and the country as a whole is very marked. Indeed, because urbanisation and urbanism is relatively recent, so much has changed in such a short time, that the influence of township and city is even more marked in such countries than in the West where the growth of urban areas has been spread over a longer period of time and, further, where the various consequences of this growth have led to a gradual adaptation to the demands and the conditions set by urbanism. Furthermore, until very recently the towns of Africa grew in size primarily as a result of widespread and massive migration from the rural areas, whereas the industrial towns of the West and of Japan have been expanding as a result of a natural increase of the urban population. With the exception of South Africa, and the older Yoruba towns, few Africans have been born in the new towns. However, within the next twenty-five years vital statistics will certainly show that the percentage of urban-born Africans will have steadily increased. The implications of this not only for further urban growth but also for the rapidity of social changes generally are likely to be very far reaching.

Most African towns are a new feature of the physical and social landscape of the newly independent African nations. While their ecology, form, and functions, can perhaps be analysed in much the same manner as proposed by the urban sociologist, the particular perspective of urban anthropology gives added depth and dimension to Third World urban studies. Thus the anthropologist, if he is not encapsulated in a narrow definition of what anthropology (particularly social anthropology) ought to be about, can add the historical and cultural dimensions which need to be taken into account. Thus to study a Yoruba town without any knowledge of Yoruba history and tradition is a useless exercise. Even if we were to ignore the part tradition still plays in the social life of the African urbanite, the more recent colonial history of the new African towns, such as Nairobi or Lusaka, must be taken fully into account if the structure and function of social organisation is to be documented in detail. It is the anthropological dimension which can, or ought to, provide this information.

However, anthropologists must first overcome certain handicaps. Until about twenty years ago, social anthropologists were encapsulated in tribal studies – they were "reared on the rural tradition of the tribe" as Professor Max Gluckman (1960 : 56) has written. While this tradition might have some relevance, in the context of specific situations in urban Africa (the function of ethnicity in urban social organisation), the urban anthropologist must use new conceptual approaches and new methodologies when he applies himself to urban studies, be this in Africa, Latin America or Asia.

While to some observers urban Africans are merely "tribesmen in town", a closer and more penetrating analysis reveals that the use of the concept of tribe, an ill-fitted term invented by anthropologists, administrators and missionaries during the colonial era, fundamentally obscures the documentation of particular but recurring patterns of social organisation unique to urban life. These patterns are determined essentially by urban conditions which range from ecological criteria to social attitudes, perceptions and motivations. Surely, every observer of the life of Africans in towns comes to the conclusion that there is an urban "style of life". To be sure if we compare this with New York, London or Paris we are not likely to be convinced that some Africans too are urbanites. But merely to point to the continuity of selective aspects of African urban life styles which allegedly reflect the continuity of tradition is scarce proof that it is far too early to insist that "urbanism as a way of life" has established itself in Africa.

Urban anthropology is a very new branch of the general field of social anthropology; and the concept of tradition is considered by many anthropologists to be the key in unlocking our understanding of many facts of African culture. But tradition, in its most common usage, ceased to be (if ever it was) the key organising principle after African societies were subordinated to colonial authority and control. Urban anthropology, therefore, should begin with a new conceptual baseline: the urban system. To be sure, we are called upon to document the patterns of organisation of *African* towns which means that we cannot haphazardly use theories of urban social organisation derived from the study of non-African urban areas. But such a formulation is designed to test the level of magnitude and the significance of tradition in diverse contexts. The urban system will reveal many diverse features, the so-called traditional, the non-traditional, the contradictions and the harmony of a style of life of fairly recent vintage – at least in most cases. What remains of tradition in urban Africa is geared to meet the specific needs of town life and not of "traditional" life. Certainly there is obvious evidence, for all to see, that some urban Africans, under some specific circumstances, will have recourse to magic and witchcraft or adhere to habits and values which, superficially, have brought the rural past into the urban present. But such actions and beliefs are not only selectively practised – they must fit into what comprises the totality of life in an urban area.

To some observers it appears that the population of African towns can best be divided into two, virtually exclusive, groups: the conservative and "incapsulated", as Professor Mayer (1961) has called it, and the aggressive modernisers. This is a very abstract and simplistic typological scheme which completely obscures the fact that both the conservatives and the modernisers actively participate in a wide variety of distinctly urban institutions and practices. Alike they are wage earners; alike they must buy their food rather than grow it; alike they must live in congested conditions and alike they are part of an extremely mixed environment composed of many different ethnic groups speaking many different languages. Some observers have drawn a sharp distinction between the work situation and the non-work environment. But this too is an artificial distinction which separates the African urban dweller from the totality of his surroundings. In short, all these typological distinctions have limited analytical meaning because their points of reference do not start with the reality that, as Professor Gluckman (1961 : 69) has written, "an African townsman is a townsman, an African miner is a miner".

The concept of an urban system rests on the simple proposition that "urban life exhibits sufficient regularities for us to extract systematic interconnections which we can arrange to exhibit a structure, and we can study how this structure changes." (Gluckman 1961 : 68) Moreover, the use of the concept urban system more aptly describes the very rapid growth of urban areas in Africa, their progressive specialisations and internal complexities. While African urban studies range along a scale from small townships to towns and to cities, distinctions between them are those of physical features rather than composition of population or of sociopolitical and economic organisation.

It is not intended that urban studies should be contrasted with rural studies, although an institutional analysis of rurality and urbanity does reveal significant points of difference. Rather, urban and rural studies alike must become part of the study of change and modernisation as these affect districts, regions and nations. The interrelation between urban and rural areas is progressively giving rise to a more uniform style of life and patterns of economic, social and political organisation. This is so for at least two reasons. Firstly, the general impact of town life reaches well beyond the boundaries of township or city into the total fabric of African society. While the degree and consequence of this influence will vary, the transformation of rural areas is perhaps as far-reaching as the influence of towns *as towns*. Secondly, both in pre-independence and post-independence periods, new economic and political institutions came into being which created a web of spatial interdependence linking ethnic groups in new economic and political exchange relations, and tying rural and urban areas into larger regional and national groupings. While the nature of these interconnections are all too frequently based on very fragile foundations, a sharp distinction between ruralite and urbanite is no longer meaningful. To be sure when an African leaves his natal community, to migrate to a town in search of work, he is likely to take with him values and habits which reflect the life of smaller and less diverse communities.

The degree of contact the African urbanite maintains with his home community does not involve him in *less* participation in the life of the town but, frequently, in deeper and *more* persistent involvement. Visits to a rural home, or other regular links, are usually a reflection of a fairly high degree of commitment to an urban-based wage economy or to the perception by the migrant that life in town provides him with the potential of some degree of upward economic and social mobility which, if realised, in turn increases his stature in his rural community. Thus rural (traditional) influences rather than making a migrant less of an urbanite might actually involve him more deeply in the urban milieu. "Extra-town" ties are not only selective in nature, they serve specific and usually short-term objectives, but they may also be variously analysed and interpreted. Both Professor Gluckman (1960, 1961) and Philip Mayer (1961, 1962, 1964) have analysed rural-urban ties in terms of an "alternation model" in contrast to the "oneway change" model. A general critique has been published by Epstein (1967).

However, the alternation model has been applied both to extra-town links and to within-town links. In the latter, within-town links, such ties help to explain specific social structures and categories of interaction. Within-town ties coalesce primarily around ethnic solidarity (in face of competition for political office and economic opportunities), kinship obligations, "home boys" groupings, common district and town origins and voluntary organisations. However, it must be understood that these particular ethnic-based links do not invariably indicate an urban bridgehead built by those who do not wish to put down roots in an urban area. Far from it. These structures go far beyond "adaptive mechanisms" (Little 1957) in their functions, a concept which suggests an amorphous, fluid and rather unstructured response to urban conditions. Within-town ties, ethnically organised or otherwise, are highly complex, structured and recurring patterns of organisation designed to exploit, rather than to adjust to, urban circumstances.

African town dwellers do not move between two "social fields", i.e. one urban and the other rural, but rather within one social field which reaches out from the urban area and significantly transforms the hinterland (the district or region). While this hinterland differs in physical features, and in mode of livelihood of the population, in socio-structural and political terms, it is no longer realistic to speak of two basically different social fields. Far from alternating between two social fields, the African town dweller uses the contacts with his natal home to consolidate his foothold in the urban system. In exactly the same manner as in-town ties serve desired urban ends, so extra-town ties are selective (and often far more tenuous and infrequent than some observers have suggested) and calculated responses to particular objectives which originate in the context of urban residence. Thus at most, we might suggest that there are various sectors in an otherwise unified social field which is the product of many years of political and economic changes having their origin primarily in the imposition of colonial rule and African responses to this domination.

There is no better evidence in support of these assertions than the present massive migration to the towns, and the consequent determination by the migrant to become established. As Professor Plotnicov (1965) has repeatedly demonstrated, to visit or to return "home" remains a dream unfulfilled. Indeed, his data, drawn primarily from the town of Jos, Nigeria, indicates that in-town ties take precedence over urban-rural ties. On the other hand, the more successful an African urbanite becomes, economically, the more likely he will visit rural kin and friends, maintain a second rural home (because he can afford to), or lead the life of a country squire who supplements his rural income, from cash crops, with steady urban earnings. While it remains to be tested, the least mobile migrant is probably also the least successful urbanite. The reasons would be that he lacks funds for travel, that he cannot play the role of a successful migrant when he returns for a visit to his kin and, above all, that he is most reluctant to give up his very precarious perch in the town. For example, data from Lagos and Nairobi clearly indicates that unemployed men will circulate from kin to kin, and eventually from friend to friend, while they attempt to find employment, a process which often stretches over many years (Gutkind 1967). As work seekers they show a tremendous determination to root themselves in town. Not only do they perceive urban wage work as a major break with the past, because urban life is viewed as a catalyst to social mobility, but they also know that work is hard to find in the rural areas. Thus, to suggest that their hardship might be less severe if they left is emphatically brushed aside.

Not only are millions of Africans drifting into the towns, there is also a significant increase in inter-urban migration which incorporates the migrant into an urban field of mobility, of activities and style of life. Thus, for example, the expulsion in recent years of Nigerian workers and traders from Dahomey and Ghana, because of the severe unemployment in these countries, merely added to the pool of unemployed in the Nigerian towns. Within the African countries, migrants do, and must, respond to whatever opportunities for employment exist. Although there is some reluctance to move frequently, because established linkages are broken, there is an even greater reluctance to return to the rural areas.

5. *Urban Life, Social Change and Modernisation*

With such a background we can begin to understand the role of the city in social change and modernisation, be this in Africa, Asia or Latin America. While specific urban conditions will vary, according to particular historical legacies, the towns of the Third World are now clearly the "motors of development", the main agents of social change on a national level. Everywhere, town life is identified with the idea of progress – a rejection of the ancient regime. While for a very small percentage of Africans, rural life has opened an opportunity of cash earnings, the vast majority of them continue to subsist on an extremely meagre return for their agricultural labour. The era of "rising expectations" which was unleashed in the later pre-independence era has gradually given way to an era of "rising frustrations". The reasons for this are, of course, manifold but they rest primarily in the very slow rate of transformation during the colonial era.

In East Africa, the British colonial administrators, and the missionaries, considered town life unsuitable for Africans whose "natural habitat", it was argued, was the rural area. Thus the Report of the East Africa Royal Commission (1955 : 201), sitting from 1953 to 1955, which studied various problems of East African development reported:

The theory of indirect rule as well as the personal inclinations of many administrators led to a concentration on the development of rural tribal societies rather than the training of an educated urban elite, and also to the view that the town was not a suitable habitat for a permanent African society: there has, indeed, been a tendency to look on the westernized African with suspicion. The towns have, therefore, been regarded rather as bases for administrative and commercial activities than as centres of civilizing influence, still less of permanent African population.

While this view was widespread in colonial Africa, it does not apply to the same extent to the towns and cities of Asia and Latin America. These towns, particularly those of Latin America, are long established and have reached very considerable size, while in Asia there are now at least fifty cities with a population of over one million. The growth of Latin American cities, between ca. 1950 and ca. 1967, has been very considerable. Thus Mexico City's population has increased from 2.2 million in 1950 to 3.3 million in 1967; San Salvador from 162,000 in 1950 to 317,000 in 1966; Ciudad de Guatamala from 294,000 in 1950 to 577,000 in 1965 and Caracas from 495,000 in 1950 to 1.7 million for the Greater Federal District in 1966. What is perhaps even more significant is that the really large cities are getting larger while the growth of those under two million is somewhat slower. However a study of the demographic features of Third World towns, and of the magnitude of rural migration provides ample evidence of the force which is behind this particular transformation. But these demographic features must be set into a wider context to assess their overall significance.

As was indicated earlier, the importance of the towns in the developing nations lies in the influence they radiate beyond their borders. The towns must be seen as comprising a linked network, each with its rural hinterland, of economic and political interdependence; and in turn the towns, indeed all the Third World nations, are tied into an economic and political satellite-dependency network to the metropoles. Nowhere is this satellite relationship (Baran 1957) seen more clearly than in the towns which are treated as showpieces of the new African nations. Thus Peter Marris (1961 : vii) reported the Minister of Lagos Affairs as saying in the House of Representatives in 1958:

... [Lagos] is the mirror through which foreigners make their initial appraisal of Nigeria and many regard it as an index of the progress and prosperity of Nigeria.

What is less often discussed is that nowhere else is the economic, political, and social distance between the few rich and the masses of the poor greater than in the towns of the Third World. Keith Buchanan (1963 : 6-7) in a perceptive analysis of the basic structural features of Third World nations has this to say about the urban poor who make up the largest percentage of urban populations:

The decay of traditional society, the pace and haphazard character of city growth and the conditions of labour exploitation in some of the overseas territories have created a sizeable 'lumpen-proletariat', a mass of hungry, rootless and detribalized wretches living in the shanty towns and squatter settlements. These are the people described by Ahmed Mezerna: 'the bands of men, women and children and aged, almost naked, whom misery and fear of death has pushed towards the cities and who, each morning, search the garbage pails, disputing with dogs and cats the remnants of food, the rags and the empty tin cans.' Politically trained and organized, these groups can form 'an urban spearhead of the revolution' and the struggle for liberation can reassert that human dignity which colonial exploitation smothered in the filth of the shanty town. The classic example of this is provided by the Algerian war where the integration of the Casbah, the slum quarter of Algiers, into the FLN campaign marked the real beginning of the battle of Algiers. Disregarded or by-passed by the national liberation movement, this mass of starving and status-less beings may turn for salvation to what Hodgkin terms the 'confessional parties', to the various messianic movements or may be used as a weapon by the forces of reaction. In the Congo the anti-Lumumba mobs in Leopoldville were recruited from among the 'lumpen-proletariat', and the 'harkis', the Algerians used by the French against their fellow-Algerians, came from the same group. Political work among the masses, and all sections of the masses, is thus essential if the colonist policy of turning class against class and tribe against tribe is to be defeated.

The towns, then play a very special part in the total and complex process of change and modernisation. Towns and the urban style of life are, as it were, superimposed on older structures and values. While the impact of the towns sets before the population at large a model, the expectations inherent in this model are far from being realised for any significant percentage of the population. But this failure, for the present, should not be interpreted as resulting from a too rapid growth of Third World towns at the expense of a far-reaching transformation of the rural areas. Tensions, of an economic and political nature, between rural and urban areas, will prevail over most of the world for several more generations to come. These tensions will multiply as class lines become more sharply defined and as the ruralite begins to sharpen his sense of political consciousness which in turn might lead to a more determined sense of political and economic participation (Nelson 1970). But the same will be true of the urbanite who, being closer to the model of the "good life", will seek a larger slice of a rather small national cake. It is, therefore, not unreasonable to suggest that the towns of Africa, Asia and Latin America might become the arena of major class confrontations. What part the rural people will play in this remains somewhat uncertain. While classical Marxist theory would suggest that the urban proletariat, in cooperation with farmers and peasants, will be the spearhead of agitation against exploitation and major inequity, Frantz Fanon (1965, 1966, 1967) has suggested that the towns (of Algeria, at least) are already filled with a bourgeoisie whose make up and ideology puts constraints on its political activism.

The future that the towns will play in the Third World nations will be largely determined by factors and policies external to these nations – although the relationship between these external factors and the internal conditions which they generate and support is clearly very close. Whether the Third World nations are still in the tight grip of neo-colonialism, or whether they are in the grip of an exploitative indigenous class, is not a subject to be treated in this monograph. But the fact remains that transformation and socio-economic mobility have not materialised for the vast majority of people of the New Nations. And the clearest manifestations of this will be found in the urban areas. How might these conditions be ameliorated?

Certainly not at the expense of the urban areas. Nations with run down cities and towns are as badly off as nations with an urban population living on the fat of rural labour. Much more needs to be done to bring rural and urban areas into a true symbiotic relationship whereby there is a mutual exchange of skills and resources (Dumont 1966). Yet the urban areas always will be the centers of intellectual thrust and innovation. While this gives them no right to exploit the rural hinterland, neither should governments take measures which do not encourage the towns to achieve a true florescence. As long as millions live in utter misery and abject urban poverty (which might be more debilitating than rural poverty), a true restructuring of society, at least a change from misery to decency, will be impossible.

To break the vicious circle of poverty and dependency, and the easing of tensions between the rural and the urban areas, requires first and foremost a major intellectual and ideological breakthrough of various kinds by leaders in the New Nations. While the will might not be there, there is great need to experiment with new premises of development designed to achieve a greater degree of economic independence and political autonomy. Difficult as this will be, in the context of a serious division of the world into rich nations and poor nations, it must be achieved if resources, skills and wealth are to be more evenly distributed both among the rich and poor nations and within the latter.

As indicated earlier, in such a context the towns of Africa, Asia and Latin America ought to play a leading part. To achieve this employment must be found for the urbanite – although this will turn out to be the most intractable of problems – so as to achieve a greater degree of social and economic stability and a sense of civic consciousness and participation. Under the highly diverse and complex cultural backgrounds and sociological conditions of the population, aspirations can be brought into line with reality and urban and rural areas can join together in the common task of restructuring the social and political fabric. What is needed is genuine progress. This cannot be achieved by means of ad hoc decisions, development plans which basically aid the few and not the many, piece-meal planning, or mere rhetoric without implementation. But as migration to the towns increases, as unemployment rises at an ever accelerated rate, inequity, poverty and misery steadily increase. Squatter settlements rise faster than they can be removed by governments offended by urban blight, and under these conditions the towns become tinder boxes of discontent. Thus far, as we shall see, this discontent has largely been absorbed by a still flexible social structure which has allowed for incorporation, but within distinct limits, of the masses of the poor into various structural niches. We can only guess how much longer these safety valves will operate.

The urban anthropologist has thus placed before him a set of unique circumstances related in a manner still largely unknown. Every town in the New Nations provides us with an almost infinite variety of organised social, economic, political, cultural, historical, and sociopsychological complexity. If we can arrive at an understanding of this complexity, how it is ordered, what its parameters are and how the parts which make up the whole hang together, we will have gone a long way towards an analytically more precise definition of modernisation and social change. Urban life, social change, and modernisation clearly hang together in some manner.

All definitions are experimental. They need to be discarded if they lack conceptual clarity and analytical precision. For the purpose of our discussion, social change might be viewed as a continuous process whereby a total and cultural configuration is gradually rearranged, a process which has no terminal point. While the speed of social change varies, it is a constant in all societies for it is part of the dialectic and strategy of political and social relations. The social fabric changes as social positions change, as they do in all societies, as the criteria for the distribution of wealth change and as political relations change.

Modernisation, on the other hand, is here used as "The Will to be Modern", to achieve change through new ideas and actions, to select from a wide range of alternatives and to create new structures and new institutions which have no direct antecedents (for many parts of Africa towns are a totally new phenomena). Martin Kilson (1963 : 426-427) defines modernisation (a term "not merely political in content or connotation") as

those social relationships and economic and technological activities that move a social system away from a traditional state of affairs in which there is little or no 'social mobilization' among its members. More specifically, the term 'modernization' refers to those peculiar socio-economic institutions and political processes necessary to establish a cash nexus, in the place of a feudal or socially obligatory system, as the primary link relating people to each other, and to the social system, in the production of goods and services and their exchange.

To achieve this, a shift of power positions is involved which gives rise to new groups (Professor George Blanksten (1963) has usefully described these as "ascendant" interest groups, a conceptualisation which might have particular applicability to urban studies) with new functions – a process which usually gives rise to class categorisation (while not absent in the rural areas in Africa, it is clearly visible in the towns) usually on the basis of non-traditional forms of social and economic differentiation.

Thus the link between social change, modernisation and urban life is that the towns generate not only a new range of institutions, activities, structures and values, particular to the local situation, but that they reflect national transformation as a whole. Thus, our unit for analysis is no longer the "tribe" or village but a larger, very differentiated, unit which is rooted in a new political and economic matrix. It is this matrix which concentrates in the towns, the districts, regions and nations of which they are a part, the processes and patterns of change and modernisation. The towns, therefore, are symptomatic of change and transformation; the study of an African town is a study of change and modernisation.

6. *The City and the Behavioural Sciences*

Although the number of students who have studied cities and towns of Africa has greatly increased in recent years (*African Urban Notes*), a small number of anthropologists have done such research for almost thirty years. Thus Ellen Hellmann published her account of *Rooiyard: A Sociological Survey of an Urban Native Slum* in 1948 (although the research was done several years earlier). While this is probably the first scientific study of African urban life, missionaries and travellers have contributed a great deal of information about life in African towns. To this we must add a large number of unpublished surveys and more specialised accounts by colonial civil servants.

The reasons why research workers have had, and increasingly do have, an interest in African towns are manifold.

Firstly, and the simplest explanation, is that the towns are there; they are established, growing very fast and hence part of the total social, economic and political fabric. It is in the towns and cities that a style of life is slowly developing which is being copied by many Africans as the basis of their aspirations, values and goals. Certainly, the older towns of West Africa have played an important part in the culture history of that region. Indeed, the towns, apart from the oral tradition about them, are sometimes the only surviving evidence of extensive empires, the movement of peoples, trade routes and the political centers which existed in Africa.

Secondly, during the period of colonial rule, from about 1800 to 1955, the towns and cities were the seats of colonial administration, the places where commerce and industry were located, where the major and most influential educational institutions were established, all of which contributed to making them the focal point of migration from the rural areas.

Thirdly, to many observers, because urban life has some important negative characteristics, the towns of Africa harbour a wide range of social problems which merit the interest of researchers.

But there are also many theoretical reasons why social anthropologists are turning to the study of African urbanism. Like other researchers interested in the developing areas of the world, urban anthropologists believe that the growth of towns, and their social and cultural fabric, present a unique opportunity to test established urban sociological theory and to develop new hypotheses and propositions about the structure and the organisation of urban life. The basic assumption made is that in the developing nations, which contain a vast range of different types of societies, we can expose, observe and analyse how new institutions come into being and new rules of conduct are formed. Of course, we could as well stick to our modern mass-industrial society, but social science research rests heavily on a cross-cultural base. Generalisations about the "content" of culture and the organisation of society would be severely limited if we wholly restricted our observations to our own society. Because comparative scientific social research is still relatively new, we have only recently concentrated on research designed to find out how pre-industrial societies are changing. Although we are still very short of much basic data, we have already had to put aside a number of conceptual schemes for the interpretation of social change which used to dominate much of sociology and anthropology (Ryan 1969). Studies of the complex transformation of our own society over the last two hundred years from the early stages of the industrial revolution to the atomic age, might be significant to the understanding of modernisation in Africa, Asia or elsewhere, although it is important to recognise that social change today must be understood not only in terms of local conditions but also as part of a world-wide process. Nobody would deny that a diachronic perspective is important or that common conditions and stimulants are not involved.

Thus, whether our interest is in urbanism and urbanisation, in religion or family life, the developing areas provide the social scientist, who values cross-cultural research, with a unique opportunity to add fundamental information to our understanding of one of the oldest, and most constant, characteristics of the human group: the dynamic, the strategy and the ideology of change.

Contemporary social science is no longer bound by the intellectual straight-jacket of a Victorian ideology which set out explicitly that those societies which had not reached a comparative level had painfully to pass through numerous stages before they could aspire to the upper reaches of (white) civilisation. Modern social science has rejected the theory that social transformation follows as rigid an evolutionary sequence as biological evolution has done. Firstly, technological simplicity is just one measure to characterise societies. Secondly, as we have all witnessed, the people of Asia, Africa and Latin America have shown remarkable facility in adapting and incorporating, at very short notice, many features of modern industrial society. Indeed, we could present an argument to support the view that Africa has incorporated some modern industrial features, both technological and social, with such speed that the consequences are really much the same as for the West. And here we only need to add that the growth of towns is among the obvious manifestations of that great transformation from which there seems to be no escape.

The study of urbanism is to the behavioural sciences what the study of energy is to physics. Every branch of the science of society has a vested interest in urban studies. One reason for this is rather obvious: Western industrial society is now predominantly urban both ecologically and in its style of life. Social scientists are as concerned about urban government as they are about the psychological effects of congestion and overcrowding, building standards or recreational facilities. Exactly the same concerns and problems arise in African towns, while they suffer from the added disadvantage of lacking a national economic infrastructure of support services which can be instrumental in ameliorating urban conditions.

Successful multi-disciplinary or inter-disciplinary studies are few yet the rationale behind such an approach to research is particularly relevant to African urban studies. While cross-disciplinary studies are paved with many pitfalls, both in conceptual terms and on the level of personal cooperation, narrowly defined problems and the use of rigid definitions will contribute little to our understanding of how an urban system really works. We have long accepted the fact that there is a close connection between the political aspects of village life, the economic basis of subsistence, social organisation and ceremonial activity. To abstract from the totality the operation of one institution is an acknowledgement of practical need but lacks any other rationale.

The urban system is not only usually larger in scale but, probably, internally more differentiated and hence more complex. While we are faced with the same practical problem of limiting our field of observation, the consequences of abstracting one field of behaviour or organisation versus another are probably more serious. Not only will we fail to understand the exact working of the field of concentration, but we will know little about its relationship to other fields. Urban studies call for new perspectives and methods and as such they present the behavioural scientist with a major challenge. Ideally, urban studies should bring together the social anthropologist, the political scientist, the economist, the historian, the public administrator, the social service administrator and the psychologist. The core of their common interests is the problem: how are small-scale societies transformed into large-scale societies. Professor Lucy Mair (1963 : 13-14) has described the transformation in this manner:

When [people from a small-scale society] are drawn into the world political and economic system, their individual members form new relationships outside the village and the kin-group, which often entail their physical separation from their kith and kin as well as making it difficult for them to fulfil all the obligations appropriate to the small-scale society. This is the process sometimes described as the disintegration of village life and the word may often be appropriate when large numbers of the young men of a village leave it for work elsewhere. In contrast to the village, with its recognised physical form and established social order, the towns to which these young men go are new and strange and still largely inchoate. In the towns the necessary adaptation is gradually being made to the social relationships implicit in the large-scale society that modern techniques have created, and the disintegration of the old-style society of the villages is counter-balanced, for those who have successfully made the adjustment, by this integration into an urban society.

Explicitly, this shifts the common core of interest to a concern with social change and the various mechanisms which facilitate or constrain change. As we scan the literature in the behavioural sciences, be it in the Western or the non-Western world, the strategy and ideology of change seems to be the common thread. As we indicated before, African urban studies, and Third World urban studies generally, provide a most fruitful field of research for the social scientist. But the social sciences are deeply rooted in the rapid increase in the behavioural sciences, primarily in Western universities, which has taken place since the Second World War. Because of their Western orientation, they bear the cross of considerable ethnocentricity. While some models for the collection and analysis of data might have applicability beyond the Western world, others clearly do not. The social scientist, therefore, must be on his guard because the thoughtless application of Western models provides the most effective way whereby a barrier separates the researcher from his data. However, the social scientist also has it within his power to overcome this difficulty, penetrate the data and construct such models as spring from particular local situations. On a higher level this can contribute just as effectively to theory building, the testing of hypotheses cross-culturally and the objective of all social science: explanation and generalisation.

II *Some conceptual approaches to African urban studies*

1. *The Rural and the Urban Traditions*

People who live outside of cities are generally viewed as uncivilised and unsophisticated. Jokes about the habits and attitudes of the "country bumpkin" are legion in Western industrial society. The city is the cradle of human achievement, the countryside is intellectually sterile; the city is the consumer and the rural areas supply its needs. The dominating influence of the city is such that it can control those who live beyond its walls. The lure of the city is great and few rural people have been able to resist its seductive appeal. So great has this appeal become that large portions of the world are now more urban than rural in that fewer people, year by year, are engaged in agriculture. More significant yet, year by year more people fall under the influence of an urban culture. The "urban revolution" which started centuries ago is far from over. What is this urban culture?

The place of the city in history has evoked very different responses from those who have studied this unique form of settlement. To some people city life is an introduction to life in hell. "Hell", Shelley wrote, "is a city just like London." Yet Johnson observed, "When a man is tired of London, he is tired of life." Here are two different views of urban culture. In Lagos, Nigeria, a young African mother said: "Children should never be brought up in a city like Lagos because they learn bad ways and become thieves and vagabonds." Yet a senior Nigerian civil servant living in an exclusive residential area in Lagos had a very different view:

Our children must be brought up to be modern Nigerians. If they live in the village they will stagnate intellectually, economically and socially. Only the cities can stimulate their minds and give them opportunities (Gutkind 1966).

Thus to some people life in the city offers no more than poverty, misery, competition, violence and struggle; to live in the city is to suffer debasement, humiliation and the reduction of life to a cheap and worthless commodity; to others urban life is salvation and a release from stagnation. There is a city of God and a city of Babylon.

Most observers have only found it possible to describe urban life by way of contrast with rural life. It is true that this brings out some obviously startling differences but bears little relation to empirical reality. Not only do these strongly contrasting typologies make it very difficult to understand the relationship between rural and urban life, but what is more detrimental is the abstractions (grossly) oversimplify the exact nature of the entity they purport to characterise with precision. The city, its structure, and the way of life it generates, must be analysed in its own right; yet its organisational form reflects how and why it is linked to the rural areas, its central place in a regional context, and its place in the nation as a whole. Only when we get away from a neat typological ordering can we hope to understand the reasons for both the unique features of towns and why there are certain common institutions and certain shared ideas which are found in both city and village. Each town is unique, and every rural area has certain characteristics which it does not share with other rural areas. Yet we must not overstate the case for either the unique in urban culture or the allegedly common elements which put a stamp of uniformity on all cities and towns. What uniformity there is might not be related to urbanism and urbanisation but be better explained as illustrative of certain universals in the way in which the human group organises itself. What is suggested here is that there is a vital infrastructure which is designed to produce order, meet basic needs, and give some kind of cohesion to a *particular* style of life. But this style of life, this order and cohesion, assumes many different structural forms and is legitimised by a wide range of values.

We should not allow ourselves to explain these styles of life in terms of one exclusive set of variables. At times facts demand that we subordinate the unique to a more satisfactory general explanation which appears to be more appropriate, i.e. closer to reality, while at other times to dwell on the unique might offer greater insight. Historians have dwelt very strongly, but not always very wisely, on single factor explanations. Thus the life of the city and its functions have been explained in either economic, political or ideational terms. Others have suggested that environmental and resource factors offer the most penetrating explanations, while some have turned to social theories which helped them analyse different styles of life in terms of societal complexity, social organisation, and social theories. But the weakness of most of these approaches is that they trap the observer in an conceptual exclusiveness which does violence to the reality. This is the crux behind the difficulty of answering so deceptively simple a question as: What is a town? One of the opportunities we have in the study of African towns is we can begin from scratch. We need not adopt those conceptual schemes which have been applied to the study of the Western European, North American or Asiatic towns. To search for a suitable conceptual approach will be the task of students of urban Africa in the years ahead.

In our presentation we shall not always break new theoretical ground. Our approach will be essentially eclectic – a selection from different schools of thought and subsequently to arrive at a reconciliation of often rigidly held approaches, propositions and theoretical schemes. Above all, we shall steer clear from either too exclusive or too inclusive definitions which hamper the presentation of the actuality. Our effort will be to show what African urban systems are and how they appear to work. At times this will compel us to be descriptive and at other times more analytical. At many stages efforts at analysis and explanation will be restricted because of lack of precise information. Rather than engage in theoretical speculations, we shall frankly recognise that a descriptive presentation is all that we can hope to offer.

The main characteristics of urbanisation as a process, and urbanism as a style of life, can be described although little will be gained if we engage in a long semantic exercise to define what is a town. We all recognise that the physical lay-out and the environmental conditions of a town differ somewhat from those of a village. Whereas villages are generally small both in size and population, towns generally cover a larger area and most of them *get bigger all the time.* Of course both the size of a village and the number of people living within it are not static. But their rate of growth is at best slower, at least in Africa. Although new land is brought under cultivation, migration from and back to the village, and the rural areas generally, keeps this population in a constant state of movement. At best the population of contemporary villages in Africa maintains a balance between intake and outflow – but this needs documentation. Of course the population of rural areas as a whole is getting larger but this increase is widely dispersed whereas the migrant coming into a town adds to the total population concentrated in one area. Thus the particular patterns of population increase and movement contribute to different kinds of settlement patterns. Although some of the smaller African urban areas are not growing as fast as the larger towns, the fact is that towns take shape as a result of translocation of people and the natural increase of their settled populations.

Another approach is to show that there are differences in the siting of a rural settlement and of a town. Few people will deliberately settle in areas where conveniences are few and life is going to be difficult – although choices might be limited and a rational survey of alternatives might have led some people to live elsewhere. If people live in caves, in swamps, in deserts, and other harsh environments it is usually because they were driven there, deliberately sought protection there, and when they got there found ways and means to exploit their environment. Yet when people settle in large numbers in one spot they are compelled to look more closely at the suitability of their site. Many more services are required to meet the needs of many more people. The need for a water supply, while other environmental conditions might be reasonable, compels people to pay close attention to the site selection. Women and children of a village may not object to walking a mile or two for water, but the moment a large number of people comes together, having water conveniently nearby becomes very important.

Towns are generally sited where a large number of ecological conditions are favourable, or where they can be modified to make them favourable, to serve the economic, political and social needs of an expanding population. Towns are less moveable than villages and homesteads. Once people have settled in a town boundaries are constantly expanding and what technology is available is used to provide the people with their basic needs. To achieve this, the original site must have a good potential to cope with an expanding population and the greater and more diversified demands which come with this expansion. If no land is available to spread out, technology has made it possible to go upward (some people in the Hadhramaut achieved this a long time ago).

A glance at a map of Africa reveals that most towns, certainly most of the larger towns are sited at or near the coast. The explanation for this is, of course, simple. Most of these coastal towns grew up as a result of European contact from the earliest colonial days. The European penetration was restricted to the immediate coastal region and the coastal towns were really the anchorages from which this penetration took place. Of course they were also important as centers of commerce although as deep water harbours they did not become significant until the late nineteenth and early twentieth centuries unless they were natural harbours which allowed ocean going vessels to come close to the shore. Thus while most of the coastal towns were sited at places suitable for administrative and commercial purposes, the larger inland towns tended to be considerably older, particularly in West Africa, and to reflect different functions. The Yoruba towns grew up as protective enclaves and as centers of important kingdoms. Timbuktu, in the Southern Sahara, became an important commercial and cultural bridge between North and West Africa and a major center of Islamic learning and influence. The sites for some African towns were determined by suitable environmental conditions for non-African settlement as in the case of Salisbury and Nairobi, the latter also tracing its origin to a base camp when the railroad from the Indian Ocean to the interior was constructed. As elsewhere in the world, some African towns owe their origin to the presence of exploitable natural resources such as Jos in Northern Nigeria where large deposits of tin were located, or Enugu in Eastern Nigeria which developed around coal mining. The major towns of Zambia are located like pearls on a string as they grew up on the "line of rail" to the copper fields.

In these paragraphs we have shown, briefly, that physical and environmental factors should be taken into account when we try to give some definition to the distinctions between rural and urban settlements. Looking at a rural-anchored settlement and comparing it with a town we cannot fail to notice differences; there is a "townscape" and a "ruralscape". But what matters is the total environment. To recognise the physical characteristic of a townscape is not enough; after all a city is a place where people live and work. We must therefore turn to the sociological perspective to help us understand the differences between rural and urban life.

The first proposition which we must recognise is that whether a person lives in a rural or an urban area he lives with other people and this imposes on him certain restrictions as well as certain advantages. Because most people seek group life, they must order their relations in such a manner that as individuals and as members of a group they all meet their various objectives and satisfy their physical needs. From that point of view those who live in a rural area have clearly much in common with the city dweller. But certain distinctions arise due to size and complexity. As we indicated earlier, a mere counting of heads reveals that urban populations are substantially larger than those which are concentrated in one spot in the rural area. A larger population generates a more complex social organisation. But this is an argument which we must treat with caution. The social organisation of any people is complex as are the ideas and values which give meaning to their social life, to their actions and their habits. Social scientists have certainly learned that a little settlement in the very heart of the African bush is a portraiture of such organised complexity that students from many disciplines may have to spend years to unravel it.

Yet if we accept as our base line that all human groupings are inherently complex in their composition, their structure, their behaviour and the diversity of the ideas and habits of their members, there are nevertheless certain distinct characteristics which are a consequence of size and a particular kind of complexity. Indeed we might say that urbanism is illustrative of no more than such a particular kind of complexity.

Our understanding of, and our willingness to penetrate, this complexity has been badly constrained by the history and the orientation of social anthropology. Earlier we quoted Professor Gluckman who suggested that we had been "reared on the rural tradition of the tribe". As a result we have, or we think that we have, a clear idea of what that rural tradition is (or was) all about. The central concept for the study of tradition is culture and its use in the history of anthropology stems from E. B. Tylor's two volume work on *Primitive Culture* (1873) in which he introduced his definition of culture as "that complex whole which includes knowledge, belief, art, morals, customs and any other capabilities and habits acquired by man as a member of society". This is a rather inclusive definition which suggests that man is a social being but tells us very little about the organisation of society and specific social relationships between individuals and between groups. In more recent years, of course, social anthropologists have greatly refined concepts, definitions and models but have done so primarily by researching the institutions, the behaviour and organisation and the values of "tribal" people. When some anthropologists wanted to move away from tribal studies and follow the migrants into towns, they were at times censured for wishing to do so. Thus Professor Malinowski told one of his students, Audrey I. Richards, "not to meddle with these modern urban problems, but to stick to 'really scientific work' in an unspoilt tribe". (Gutkind, 1963 : ix). To be sure this was in 1931 and forty years of anthropology have greatly modified this narrow point of view.

In this monograph we will not devote time to a discussion of what constituted this rural tradition; literally hundreds of high quality monographs are available in any university library. The range of these studies is enormous; from the Arctic peoples to the dwellers in the Australian desert; from the most remote "tribal" peoples, living in small communities in New Guinea, to the large-scale, and settled kingdom states of West Africa. What we need to ask is: what is the relevance of these studies to modern urban studies in Africa or for urban research elsewhere?

On the level of basic sociological theory, the concepts of social system, social relationships, social structure and the like, there is clearly much relevance. Other concepts such as acculturation, adaptation, adjustment, integration and disintegration are probably of lesser relevance as they project on the analysis of African urban data not only unsuitable typologies but also presentations with moralistic and ethnocentric (Western) undertones. Furthermore, tribal studies are cast in a framework which assumes, to a considerable degree, the homogeneity of the unit under observation, the relative isolation of the group being studied, the connectedness of the parts which make-up the whole due to its small-scaleness, and the primacy of kinship as *the* organising principle. Without entering into the controversy of whether functionalism can adequately incorporate the concept, and the reality of, social change, or the issue of equilibrium versus conflict (Gluckman 1968), or the use of the concept of structure versus situational and network analysis, the fact is that the rural-oriented anthropologist is likely to experience considerable difficulties in defining his unit of observation in an urban context, in the definition of problems and, most significant perhaps, he may not recognise that urban populations constitute a "society". Thus a number of observers have used such terms as "unstructured fluidity" (Southall 1961 : 25), "unformed communities" (Gulliver 1965 : 98), "nondescript", "amorphous", "chimera", "aberrant", "formless" and "a formidable mass of confusion, a social chaos" (quoted in Epstein 1958 : 226), to describe urban life in Africa (and elsewhere). While we should not attach much significance to such labels, they do reveal a certain desperation and inability in recognising who are these groups of people living under these particular circumstances (Gulliver 1965 : 96-100).

To contrast urban with rural conditions utilises a measure which tells us as little about rural as it does about urban life. Neither does the typology either produce a theory of rural or urban social structure or social relationships. The substance of this argument is simple, as we suggested earlier: as the study of urban social systems, and systems they are, requires a theory of urban social relations (as has been attempted by Banton (1961), Gluckman (1961), Mitchell (1957, 1958, 1966, 1969), Schwab (1961), Southall (1956, 1957, 1961) and Mayer (1961, 1962, 1964), the anthropologist is called upon to begin with a new baseline which has no antecedents.

We are dealing with various conditions of incipient modernity which have broken with tradition and, some would suggest, with rurality. The rules which govern rurality are restricted to the rural areas, although the rules which govern urbanity are making ever deeper inroads into the countryside. What is implied here is not an uncompromising distinction between the rural and the urban "tradition", but rather that these distinctions have lost much of their alleged significance. Nevertheless, for the present we will operate on the premise that a theory of urban social organisation and urban social relations is possible, and desirable. At the same time we will not foreclose the argument that selective characteristics of rural life may play a part in the totality of the urban system. But when this is so our assessment must be precise and the analysis penetrating, as we must link these antecedents to the total life of the urbanite. It is clear from some of the more recent literature that this fact is being recognised and that the new links between urban and rural areas reflect a new symbiotic relationship, as each needs the other for individual and collective economic, political and social well-being. It is this development which might give urban anthropology a unique and creative role in social anthropology.

2. *Migrancy and Migrants*

What link there is between the rural and the urban areas is forged by the migrant both structurally and ideationally. It is the rural-based African who makes the trek into the town, joins his kin and friends, seeks work and establishes himself – and sometimes returns to visit his home. We use the word establish advisedly because however briefly a migrant lives in town, and however frequently he moves between the urban and the rural areas, he must at least *try* to establish himself in competitive and complex urban conditions. Every migrant does so quite independently of his adaptive qualities. The migrant has no choice; his survival, his ability to get work and the needed support from kin and friends, depends on his willingness to establish himself. That his initial experiences might make him feel alone, confused and depressed is more an ideosyncratic element than a general principle. Naturally, problems of adaptation do arise but these are generally not the central problem for the migrant. What matters is the availability of housing, work, and adequate wages. Furthermore, the argument about adaptation and adjustment faced by the migrants seems to rest rather heavily on at least two assumptions: that life in the rural areas is vastly different and that a move to the town invariably produces a wide range of problems which are difficult to overcome *simply because the migrant is a ruralite*. This places the migrant in the conventional Western image of a "country bumpkin". Also, the assumption is made that urban influences and a knowledge of urban life have not penetrated the rural areas; that no villager has ever left for the town, returned, and disseminated his ideas to others. Further, it seems to ignore the fact that there are selective factors involved in migration – about which we still know very little. The answer to the question – who migrates – is probably a lot more complex than we think. There is more involved than being "pushed" off the land and "pulled" into the town. Wealth, education, age, sex, family and marital circumstances, political dispensations, colonial policies (past and present), seasonal economic conditions, policies of national development, and the ups and downs of international trade, all play their part with the potential migrant.

Migration and migrants are a sensitive barometer of the totality of change taking place. Although migration to the towns, and inter-rural migration, has been a feature of African society for many generations it has clearly greatly accelerated during the last twenty-five years – particularly since the end of the Second World War. No African country has attempted to document the rates of migration so our only measure is in the increase of urban population. Census data is, therefore, our basic guide, but census returns are either serious underestimates (fears associated with being counted) or serious overestimates (primarily for political reasons).

It is likely that migration to the towns has accelerated still further since independent African governments took control of the new nations. Not infrequently, in the flush of independence excitement, African leaders made extravagant claims about the rapidity of economic development once the colonial powers had departed. This clearly acted as an inducement to the potential migrant to leave his home, trek to the town, and expect a good job. As we know, the hopes have turned into dreams and frustrations. Likewise, since independence has come to the continent, there has been a vast educational explosion, particularly in the rural areas. Whatever the objectives and content of that education, it has pried the ruralite still further from his natal ties and reinforced the desire to seek more fertile pastures elsewhere. The study of migration and migrants, therefore, is just one aspect of more complex changes taking place. Millions of Africans are now migrants in a more generalised sense. Thus, as a people, they are changing from subsistence farming to cooperative and cash-crop activities making for more flexibility in traditional economic activities. The kinship system is also changing in order to provide for new types of social relationships (which involve a great deal of mobility). In political terms, party membership, the civil service bureaucracy, trade unions, farmers' and teachers' associations and other groupings, all contribute to a massive movement of the population. To the migrant, the towns are merely the end of the road. Hence migrancy is gradually giving rise to translocation. Migrants not only move less frequently, but they stay longer in town each time they relocate and, finally, they put down their roots in the town, bring their families with them, and make the city their permanent home (Gutkind 1965).

An understanding of the causes of labour migration would take us rather too far afield in this monograph. But some aspects of these causes have a greater bearing on our understanding of town life and the composition of African towns than our understanding of migration as such.

As we indicated before, migrants are mostly young and unmarried males whose main desire is to obtain employment, to be established economically, and to learn and achieve a greater measure of skills than is possible in the rural areas. This they can only do, so it seems at the moment, by leaving their homes and trek to those areas which, in their view, offer them the possibility of this opportunity. The composition of the urban population is, therefore, a reflection of why men migrate; and for the same reason the kind of social organisation the migrant creates in the town is a reflection of major changes in African society. Having left his kin behind he must create new institutions and new social relationships which meet his particular needs. As migrants come from a large number of ethnic groups, the institutions and social relationships will reflect this diversity. Urban social structure anchored in ethnicity is thus a reflection of the diverse input into the town not merely from the nation as a whole but also from much further afield. Poor African nations encourage their people to seek work in the better-off countries. Thus until recently the Mossi from Upper Volta migrated in very large numbers to Ghana, while Malawians continue to move to South Africa. Mossi migration to the southern towns of West Africa was so well established over the last fifty years that it had been incorporated into the social norms of Mossi society. In the course of time this has had as profound an effect on the Mossi people as the impact of French colonial policy or the policies of the independent government of Upper Volta (Skinner 1960, 1965). Migration, therefore, should not be analysed in narrow cause and effect terms but rather should be seen as a complex process which transforms social systems be they urban or rural.

Clyde Mitchell (1959) has suggested that we ought to understand labour migration in terms of two basic processes which he calls centrifugal and centripetal, i.e. why does a man leave, and why does he return home? An answer to both questions springs from our understanding of the main characteristics of both the rural and the urban systems. The rural system will, of course, differ according to the main characteristics of particular ethnic groups, and the stake the migrant has in that group. Thus we need to ask, is it profitable and politically and socially important for him to keep one foot in the rural camp? Does he have rights and privileges which he must defend? Must he return "home" to plant and reap crops? Can he leave the urban area without losing his foothold in the town? How, precisely, does he weigh the gains and losses of leaving the urban or the rural area? Clearly a vast range of circumstances and perceptions determine such a complex decision. The limited evidence we have seems to suggest that an ever larger number of migrants view the rural areas as a kind of escape hatch, a sort of social and political insurance policy. Thus, while we need to know a lot more about migration as a particular process, migrants tell us a great deal about conditions in the nation as a whole.

Are economic conditions not only necessary but also a sufficient condition for migration? If economic conditions are satisfactory in the rural areas, does this mean that no migration takes place? But what if economic conditions are bad in the rural areas and people put up with them, what conclusions are we to suggest then? Millions of Africans scratch away at the land and live in great poverty.

The Ganda of Uganda are an example of a people whose economic conditions are far better than many African people – yet many of them migrate because they wish to add an additional source of income to their rural-based earnings, obtained from cotton and coffee growing. They migrate because they, like other people, consider urban life a mark of progress and sophistication although many of them maintain two homes partly because they do not seem to like to live permanently in a town but also because no Ganda is very far away from three or four fairly large towns. What then about people who ought to migrate because their land base simply cannot adequately sustain them, but don't do so? The explanation here might be that few towns have grown up in such areas, that the nation as a whole has not diversified greatly, that there are few natural resources that can be exploited or that communications are very poor. Or perhaps they are held in bondage by local chiefs or landowners, or they are encapsulated in a religious system which has kept modern education from their eyes and ears. Ethiopia, the Sudan, Niger or the Chad might all be examples which might help explain why less migration seems to take place from and within these countries.

Finally a word about the migrant. To label recent arrivals in the town as migrants, rather than as urbanites, hinders our understanding of how life is lived in the towns. We are not dealing with a (rural) migrant, we are dealing with an urbanite. The "raw" recruit who comes to a South African mine, the Luo from Kenya who becomes a dock or railway worker, the young lad from the country who becomes an office messenger, or the juvenile who makes a sixpence washing a bus in the buspark at Ibadan, are plunged at short notice into an urban style of life and nothing less. The criteria should be that they are urbanites in all respects, in outlook and habit, but neither should they be viewed as transients with one eye on the rural area, uncertain of themselves, lonely and alone and counting the days when they migrate back to their natal home. Of course there is conflict between urban practices and "customs"; of course strains and discontinuities appear and need to be resolved. But the fact is that they are now urban workers. They earn little and their jobs are not promising for the future, but they are urban workers and no longer migrants, though they may be more of an urbanite at some times than at others. On occasion they gravitate towards members of their ethnic group for help and comfort, but this does not make them once again migrants. When the Irish in New York get together, or the Poles in Milwaukee, are they suddenly more Irish or Polish than American, or more ethnic than cosmopolitan?

The problems faced by the migrant are not those of alternating between rural and urban, or between urbanity and ethnicity; rather they are how to make a decent living.

3. *The Urban System: The Macro Approach*

If the towns and cities of Africa are the social change pacesetters, then urban anthropological research must take place within a very large social field (Firth 1951 : 10-28; Fortes 1945 : Chapt. 13, pp. 103, 137, 233, 245; Lewin 1951) of which the town is merely the focal point. The reasons for this should now be obvious. The rural population makes use of the services unique to the town and in turn supplies the town with goods and services.

At the same time, it is very tempting to define the urban area as one major system which is sealed off from the surrounding countryside. The reasons again are fairly clear: everything about the town, its physical layout, and the composition of its population, the activities of its residents, indeed their total style of life is different, if not in kind certainly in degree. The institutions and behaviour of residents are geared to urban ends – the needs of the moment and the needs and objectives of the future. As towns grow in size and population so do services – albeit too slowly to meet pressing needs. As a total ecological and social system, certainly demographically and socially in their internal complexity, African urban areas are expanding.

Is there an urban system, as distinct from a rural system? Are we justified in using the concept of system? A system implies an arrangement (neither orderly nor disorganised) of related parts according to values, premises and rules which are operationalised in terms of structures, institutions and particular behaviour. As such the concept does not, nor should, imply harmony or disintegration between the parts which comprise the system, but suggests that a system is made up of various parts, often referred to as subsystems, which are interrelated rather than interdependent according to particular circumstances in time.

An urban system can be small-scale or large as the size and density of populations vary and the areas occupied by towns differ. Thus, are towns to be defined as that area within their legal boundary or are the "suburbs", the peri-urban areas, to be included? Scale of system is also related to degree of complexity according to the particular composition of the population, how heterogeneous is it, and to the occupational structure which, if diversified, will be reflected in complex social patterns. But what makes a system?

All human activity takes place in the context of communications designed to regulate, successfully or otherwise, exchange relations, arrangements to distribute goods and services, hierarchical political relations (however minimal) and kinship networks. While all these relationships and arrangements vary from one culture to another, and within each community, there is a certain degree of regularity and predictability of structure and behaviour which has continuity and coherence. It is these characteristics which justify the use of the concept of system. The reality of the concept is brought home to us even more when we discover that an analysis of urban (or rural) political life must be integrated with a study of the economics of distribution of goods and services. This is not to give emphasis to functionalism and interdependence, but to the view that various aspects of societal arrangements reinforce each other to produce a particular blend of structure, norms, institutions and behaviour. This blend may be productive of a considerable or lesser degree of reinforcement depending on the dialectic and the strategy of change whether it be radical and rapid or conservative and slow.

The study of an urban area presents us with a particular kind of system for analysis. Because it is a system, as defined above, we are committed to a "macro" approach. By this we mean that we must take account of the totality of the (urban) system.

In the anthropological investigation of "simple" societies, a small unit was customarily isolated within the larger (tribal) system; and assuming the homogeneity and identity of parts within the whole, the study of the operation of such a unit was considered sufficient to allow generalisations about the nature and structure of other parts and thus, of the whole of which the parts comprised. This was micro-analysis. Later, with the development of knowledge of and interest in the characteristics of peasant societies within complex societies, and recognition of the former as "part-societies" rather than independent entities, it was found that the established methods of investigation and analysis were inadequate to expose the complex of forces and relationships which made up these communities. It therefore became imperative that we took account of how small units were really part of far larger and more complex units and how individuals and groups operated in social fields which reached far beyond their kin and village boundaries.

There were, and still are, compelling reasons why anthropologists raised these conceptual and methodological questions. Whereas in the past anthropologists were studying so-called "simple" societies, they were gradually showing an interest in what they called "complex" societies, i.e. their own Western societies and those of India, China and Japan. These had been areas left almost entirely to the historians, the political scientists and archeologists. The study of these complex societies, defined as generally more literate, technologically more advanced, economically and politically more diversified, more urbanised and demographically large-scale, raised the question whether traditional anthropological techniques and conceptualisations were appropriate. Thus Professor S. N. Eisenstadt (1961 : 201) asked us to "analyse some of the problems arising out of the methods and approaches developed in (British) social anthropology to the study of more complex societies". Leo Despres (1968) some seven years later, again raised the same question and suggests that traditional anthropological methods, the holistic analyses of cultural systems, can be carried out in complex societies with only minor modifications. Indeed, he suggested that complex societies lend themselves particularly well to conventional anthropological study.

One important feature of complex societies, which many anthropologists either ignore or find too difficult to deal with, is the external determinants which play a particularly vital part in the evolution of urban structures and behaviour. Thus, A. L. Epstein (1964 : 98-99) whose creative contributions to urban anthropology are considerable, found it necessary to circumscribe his work on the African trade union movement in Zambia. He wrote:

A fuller understanding would have to take into account the policies and aims of the mining companies, and the ways in which these are affected, for example, by the question of foreign investment, as well as relations within and between various European and African organizations. But here we move into an area where the data required, as well as the technical means of handling them, are not normally available to the anthropologist.

True as this might be, it is exactly this wider context which is of prime relevance to urban anthropologists. The degree of magnitude of these external and allegedly extrinsic factors (indeed it is easy to show how in actual fact they are intrinsic) might turn out to be of greater significance than those aspects of the community study method on which anthropologists normally concentrate. The colonial history of Africa is one which makes these external determinants of vital importance; and the towns were the hub of the colonial economic and political system.

Having said this much it might be more readily understood why the macro analysis approach is the key to the study of urban areas. A city is not like a village which enjoys a certain, if overemphasised, degree of homogeneity. A town, particularly a new African town, is made up of a large number of different ethnic groups at different levels of skills, achievements and participation in the life of the town. While this is true of towns generally (and even of some communities), in the Third World towns there is little of what might be called a common institutional matrix which, as in Western and older non-Western towns, has crystallised to the point that we can readily expose its working. Thus not only are institutions constantly being made and unmade, but social relationships are not localised, i.e. they spread over a wider social field than is true in a village. Therefore, the particular conditions and structures which prevail in African towns can only be understood if we accept the fact that it is the urban totality (and we still lack the knowledge of the parameters of this totality), which gives order despite fluidity, stability despite the transitory population, integration despite alleged amorphousness, cohesion despite great diversity and a clear social ecology despite the alleged unplanned layout.

Because the towns themselves are so new, and the composition of the population so recent, it would be daring to abstract from a virtually unknown entity one or two single features, subject these to intensive study, and generalise about the totality – about the system as a whole. As long as we know as little as we do about Ibadan *as Ibadan*, or about Beira *as Beira*, particularly as we lack precise census data about virtually every town in Africa, we cannot assume that a study of one ethnic group, one neighbourhood or one occupational group gives us a comprehensive picture of the town as a whole. This is a matter we shall take up again in Chapter 4 when we expect to look at the methodology required to study a series of units, neighbourhoods, courtyards, streets or slum areas as a device to obtain the kind of comprehensive picture we need.

Because towns are so large, and getting larger, and because urban anthropologists have only just begun their research, we know very little about how the institutional matrix of towns has come into being. We have missed many opportunities to show how the complex of patterns has been transformed over time. We know virtually nothing about very important, if perhaps less so than in the past, urban-based groups such as the Europeans in African towns. This serious handicap also compels us to avoid abstracting narrowly defined problems for research. We are now dealing with an ongoing urban system and not one in the early stages of its birth. Time has established an urban system, although this system is clearly different from one town to the next. While new institutions are in the making, and new social, economic and political alignments are constantly being made, they appear to take place within a structured framework of action, i.e. within the system.

In short, we have very little choice. While the concepts of a system, and of macro analysis, are themselves sociological abstractions, we must base our research on the assumption, unless proven otherwise, that there is such a system which gives order, predictability and cohesion to urban life, and that it is by means of macro analysis that this system will reveal its many subdivisions. We must, therefore, turn to a brief discussion of these subdivisions.

4. *The Sub-Systems: The Micro Approach*

As every urban anthropologist knows, research work in an urban area is very frustrating simply because it is large and the population considerable, even though in some cases it might be possible to demarcate a nice little compact unit for observation. Anthony Leeds (1968 : 35), who has done research in Latin American cities, expresses this frustration when he writes:

... the anthropologist working in the city is logistically constrained to working at most in two or three sites given any standard amount of time that he is likely to have. This constraint is the more severe, the larger the city and the fewer the co-workers he has, and especially if he is alone.

This is a dilemma which, for the moment, we must accept but need to overcome.

We need to operate at two basic levels. First, for the reasons given, we must conduct our research at the macro level. This implies that we seek out oral and documentary evidence to illustrate the historical evolution of the town. Secondly, still operating at the macro level, we must ask ourselves what were, and are, the major economic and political determinants which have shaped the structure and the institutions of the town as a whole. How have these structures and institutions changed over time and what are the circumstances which have produced the changes? Thirdly, we must gather as detailed demographic data, whatever its quality and precision, as we can find. If absolutely no information is available, which is a little unlikely especially since 1950, we have little alternative but to conduct random demographic surveys in various areas of the town. Unskilled as anthropologists are in this specialised field the risk of serious error is clearly great, but some method must be found to establish the most basic demographic characteristics of the urban population. Impressions, intuition, and guesswork as to the size, composition, and vital statistics of the urban population will not establish the kind of basic information which is needed and from which more specialised micro studies are defined. Finally, a macro-analytical approach must be applied to the more recent history of the town, in relation to colonial policies and practices, the working of its contemporary economic and political institutions, its resource base, its linkages (via economic and political activities) to its rural hinterland, to the national region of which it is part, to a larger cross-national region, its place in the nation as a whole, and its ties with world political blocks and world trade (Green and Fair 1962 : 96-102; Beckman 1970). It is these procedures which establish the major parameters from which micro studies spring. It is on this basis that a clear definition of problems becomes possible, i.e. that the magnitude of specific forces and characteristics are revealed.

Macro studies reveal that African towns, as towns everywhere, are the composite of both discrete and overlapping units and sub-systems. Furthermore, these sub-systems enjoy an independent existence and at the same time a blending of groups in specific aggregates of the population takes place. The exact nature of these discrete or overlapping groups will, of course, vary from town to town and over time. It is this variation which introduces the element of organised complexity, and integration despite diversity. It is up to the urban anthropologist, using new and more appropriate models than those applied in the past, to unravel this organised complexity. However, because of the size of towns, and the complexity of their populations, some degree of arbitrariness in the selection of smaller units is virtually unavoidable, though there are safeguards.

Professor Gluckman, in his *Analysis of a Social Situation in Modern Zululand* (1958), has clearly demonstrated that it is possible to take a specific event (in this case the opening of a small bridge in a rural area) and construct from this not only the basic features of Zulu society, both in historical and contemporary terms, but also the dynamics of social change, both internally and externally generated, which have moved this society along over the past few generations. Thus a micro study, to take a single "event" as a starting point, has great potential in revealing not merely the features set out above but also in identifying the extrinsic determinants of the colonial dispensation under which the Zulu people still live. Although this kind of reconstruction was applied under rural conditions, it is an example of how micro analysis can reach to the macro level. This is the reverse of what has been stated above.

When we turn to the recent urban studies conducted by Professor Clyde Mitchell (1969), and those associated with him, we find the same kind of emphasis on micro units, i.e., the structure of social networks, a concentration on specific occupational categories and elite groups, on particular ethnic groups, and associations of many kinds. The concentration on these micro social, economic and political studies (Swartz *et al* 1966, Swartz 1968) are based on the assumption, which still needs further testing, that entry into the urban system, at most any point, can be the starting point in documenting the structure and the organisation of the macro system. The theory behind this view is that even specific events, of seemingly low level of significance, reflect aspects of the urban totality: that the study of a particular ethnic or occupational group reveals how these groups overlap with others, or are in conflict with one another, and in process of documentation and analysis, the most vital features of the macro system are revealed. A. L. Epstein (1961) has demonstrated how the "social network" of a single individual is spread widely over the town, and in the process of tracing the linkages, and their purpose, it is possible to piece together how social relations are established and how they are made and unmade. What emerges is a large "map" show-ing how personal and group contacts are spread out, the constituent groups which make up these networks (and from which further networks flow), the focal points of these networks (which reflect special points of anchorage for the individual), the cluster around specific groupings, i.e. ethnic, occupa-tional and political groups, and the mobility of individuals as they move back and forth and in the process "shut down" some lines of contact and open others. Methodologically and logistically some very complicated prob-lems are involved, but as an approach to the study of the urban system this method should be applied more extensively. One major merit is that the level of analysis is not too abstract as the documentation of how the urban system really works is rooted in the reality of daily activity.

While we spoke about safeguards, there are also risks involved in the building up of the macro system from below. The danger is that those features of urban life which we set out in the previous section at the macro level, are not clearly brought out by the building up of the total system by means of a series of micro studies. We should, therefore, follow, if not a different at least a complementary procedure using the macro approach as our baseline to be followed by micro analysis.

We indicated earlier that the urban system is really a series of sub-systems which at various times are discrete and localised entities and at other times widely distributed and overlapping. In as much as these sub-systems are of-ten made up of ethnic units (or parts thereof), occupational, class or political groupings they will, also at various times, be in conflict or join in common cause. In this fortuitous circumstances, historically rooted animosities, con-temporary social, economic and political circumstances and the momentary situations are the major determinants. The following conditions can be in-strumental in the formation of sub-systems: the size of the town (the larger the town the more numerous the sub-systems is a proposition which might be tested); the policies allowing for growth and the lay-out imposed on the town by the colonial administration (i.e. racial divisions, housing estates oc-cupied by one ethnic group, "stranger" quarters, the city core population versus the suburbs, elite residential areas versus slum locations, trading areas or recreation areas); the nature of the migration into the towns (leading to bachelor quarters or family housing units); whether the town is the capital city or regional headquarters (we would expect to find a larger number of sub-systems in the former); the degree of economic specialisation (resulting in more occupational specialisation); the age of the town (sub-systems will form around the recent arrivals versus "old" inhabitants); and its political culture (resulting in sub-systems anchored in political parties and various types of associations).

Thus sub-systems will develop through a variety of circumstances. They may be culturally explicit and easily identifiable (such as ethnic groups whose members bear clear symbols of identity, or the well dressed versus the poor), or loosely knit and ephemeral (a large number of associations might fit this description). Likewise, some sub-systems are internally highly structured (some ethnic groups and some political parties) while others bring people together on an egalitarian basis. Some sub-systems have continuity through time (socio-economic classes), while others are of short duration passing from a phase of rapid growth to one of sudden decline (socio-economic pressure groups). Some sub-systems are restricted in their membership and composition (ethnic associations and associations of traders, male or female organisations, youth groups versus the elders) while others are open (religious sub-systems).

This concept of sub-systems is, therefore, closely identified with membership in various groupings. But this alone is not a sufficiently precise use of the concept. Each sub-system has a wide variety of symbols, norms and mechanisms for their enforcement. Each sub-system is internally complex to the point that it can become the basis of a detailed and prolonged study documenting its evolution and changes over time. Membership in a sub-system serves a multiplicity of purposes geared toward the needs and aspirations of the urbanite. While some sub-systems are distinctly urban in character and function, others involve the individual in maintaining links with his ethnic and rural background.

Individuals and groups are simultaneously involved in the structures, activities, and objectives of many different kinds of groupings which, on the surface, may appear contradictory. It is in this kind of situation, which is extremely common, that the true nature of the macro system is revealed. Thus ethnicity may conflict with class and occupational groupings, political sub-systems may clash, trade union membership may accommodate itself to government demands to the disadvantage of the rank and file, or the unemployed may challenge the bureaucratic sub-systems. Each of these sub-systems, therefore, overlap; nor are they necessarily integrated with each other. Each has its own institutional and normative complex serving specific individuals and groups at particular times, or constantly, and for particular, or recurring, ends. We must now ask ourselves, what kind of organised complexity is this, and how does this total urban system hang together?

5. *An Approach to Organised Complexity: Integration Despite Diversity*

It would be good to know what the answer might be to the question with which we concluded the last section. One is tempted to turn to "game theory" which attempts to explain complex systems in terms of such models as dyadic or triadic models, conflict or alliance theory. The theory behind game theory is to develop models designed to explicate the complexity of basic interaction processes such as integration and conflict. Because game theory is really a branch of mathematics, its relevance to societal analysis has only recently been tested in some depth (Buchler and Nutini, 1969). Anatol Rapoport (1965) argued that game theory abstracts the structure of events and particular conditions entirely from their context and etiology in order to reduce these events to mathematical form. Thus defined, game theory is coldly mathematical and shorn of any aspects of behavioural content. But even with this limitation, and the fact that we are at a very early stage in the application of game theory to societal structure, its relevance to the study of complex societies might be considerable. If we assume that the structure of complex (urban) society is strongly influenced by various "strategies" adopted by the players (the urban population, i.e. members of ethnic groups, occupational categories, socio-economic classes, associations and political parties) in order to achieve given ends, and resolve conflict, we might then say that the particular structure and organisation of urban life was determined by "games of strategy" played according to certain "ground rules". The need for rules of the game, for individuals or groups to achieve given ends, becomes particularly important in complex societies which are made up of opposing interests (Bailey 1969). Strategies, therefore, call for coalitions and alliances and a rational basis for the determination of alternative choices of action. The study of complex society should in large part concern itself with the identification of those related variables involved in the strategy of competition, and the strategy of decision making. What are the options within which players operate; what are the core structures which produce cohesion (of urban life); and what are the rules and the strategies of interaction processes? Game theory models, therefore, might uncover the basic assumptions which motivate actions, the basic structure and etiology of conflict situations, the rationale underlying networks and "systems" of communications, and the rules of selection among alternatives of strategies of action, i.e. the question of values and cultural influences.

The concentration on rules and strategies of action, which determine the particular kind of structure and organisation of the urban system and its subsystems, reveals simultaneously sources of conflict, attempts at resolution or otherwise, and forms and patterns of interaction and integration. Game theory models applied to urban society, particularly the "incipient" urbanism of Third World towns, might expose the *interdependence* of opposing groups, the dialectic of opposing groups, the dialectic of decisions, choice of actions and the complex blend of common and conflicting interests in interpersonal and group relations. Whether we need models which clearly discriminate between conflicting and common interests and strategies is a matter for further debate.

There is no reason to believe that African towns exhibit a greater measure of anomie than more developed towns elsewhere. But measures of integration, or anomie, have been distilled primarily in the course of research in Western towns and cities. As a result of our work in the African, and other non-Western towns, we have not yet refined alternative measures and models. This is clearly one of the main tasks for the urban anthropologist. But as a preliminary suggestion we might accept the statement that integration and coherence is achieved around variables which, in the past, we have not associated with that potential. Variables which we have assumed to have a basically negative effect on the urban social structure might in fact produce rather different results, i.e. ethnicity and conflict. Ethnicity in particular has frequently been viewed not merely as a deterrent to integration but also as the source of political instability. While no doubt some features of ethnicity have these consequences, the alternative view is to treat this characteristic as part of the overall dynamic of political and economic behaviour and expose its integrative functions. Both Professor Gluckman (1955, 1965) and Coser (1956) have shown what the integrative potential of conflict might be, although Gluckman's illustrative examples have been drawn from rural "tribal" society and Coser's from modern urban-industrial society. We have yet to apply these conceptualisations to African urbanism. We might even ask ourselves whether it is not explicitly because of discreteness and the diversity of urban-based groups that cohesion, a particular kind of cohesion, has emerged over time.

The various sub-systems which we described in an earlier section do not exist in isolation. While they may be discrete culturally, politically and economically, they not only adapt to each other (even if negatively), but they are also collectively part of subordinate or superordinate relationships. Every town in this regard exhibits its particular hierarchical structure and competition as well as its built-in blend of cooperation. How these opposing forces mesh to produce an organised complexity can only be documented if we apply macro and micro analysis.

If African towns are the catalyst in the transformation of African society, we must expect that the particular complexity we attribute to the urban system is a reflection of the changes taking place in the nation as a whole, and researchers have clearly had some difficulty in characterising these changes. Thus, there are aspects of this complexity which have given the urban anthropologists a good deal of difficulty such as the exact relevance of the rural-urban (or urban-rural) equation; the "part" society aspects of town life; the amorphous versus circumferential characterisation of urban structure and system analysis; the rationality of interaction processes versus their eclectic and unstructured nature and the mechanism of decision making, i.e. the force behind individual perception and action versus collective action according to accepted norms.

Thus it is just as difficult for us to extrapolate, analyse, and explain how this organised complexity works as it is to find the key which unlocks the system. But it is very likely that it is the urban situation which most explicitly demonstrates the concept of organised complexity. To extrapolate this complexity, research will have to be conducted on several levels, i.e. on individual and group communicative interaction, on the organisational and institutional matrix, and on the historical-processural versus the situational change level (Mitchell 1966), the latter being essentially concerned with the dynamics of social change, and finally on the macro level to analyse the inter-relationships between various sub-systems. Much of this work still needs to be done, the concepts still need to be refined and new analytical models need to be brought into use.

Perhaps we can now conclude that organised urban complexity implies that structural and organising principles produce a working system which functions because there is considerable overlap between sub-systems, mechanisms to regulate interaction, norms to guide reciprocity and exchange in the face of considerable heterogeneity, and stability despite rapid changes. In short, the ingredients of community life are found not only within each sector of the urban community but also in the town, as a town.

6. *The City, Town, Suburb and Hinterland: A Symbiotic Relationship?*

Years ago the few towns there were in Africa were small, unique, and isolated. While this was generally not true of most of the West African towns because they were linked like beads of a chain along trade routes, and their residents went to work in the rural hinterland, the Eastern and Central African towns, because they were primarily non-African in composition and character, were isolated (racial) enclaves. They were the centers for European trade activities and headquarters of the colonial administration. Their links to the rural areas were limited.

The growth of the towns, and the proliferation of their functions, the steady migration into the towns, the circulatory nature of this migration (Elkan 1967), the recruitment of labour in the rural areas, the introduction of cash crops and the gradual development of more efficient communication, all these developments resulted in the progressive breakdown of urban isolation.

In the process the influence of the towns, as towns, was not merely enhanced but their influence over the immediate and regional area in which they were located was likewise increased. Although all along Africa has remained predominantly a continent of agriculturalists, the political and economic influence of the towns was spreading, like a spider's web, over regions far larger than their immediate hinterland. Recent studies by Abiodun (1968) Soja (1968), Ominde (1968), McNulty (1969), and Mabogunje (1965, 1968) on the spatial characteristics of urbanisation, and the characteristics of population movements, all attest to the importance of rural-urban interrelation.

As the towns became internally more differentiated, and the occupational structure became more specialised, the urban population depended more directly on food and labour supplies from rural areas. Few urban Africans are able or willing to grow their food needs. Hence in the surrounding rural areas an extensive market garden economy has grown up which has become an integral part of the urban economy as markets for fresh products have grown rapidly over the last few years. The evidence in support of this becomes very clear if one bothers to rise early in the morning to watch the streams of produce sellers from the rural areas enter the town along the main roads.

In addition to such activities, the rural-urban-rural links are forged by the circulatory migration of the lower strata of the urban population, and the constant stream of shoppers and visitors who form a significant percentage of the urban population at any given moment. The rural-urban links are also a reflection of the perceptions and the desire of a large number of Africans, mostly those whose agricultural earnings are inadequate, to seek an alternative way of making a living. In the process they become the carriers of an urban style of life which they take back to the rural areas. In the course of time they establish close social, economic and political ties with relatives and friends in both rural and urban areas. For it must not be ignored that political and economic ties work in both directions. The African politician who represents a rural constituency forms an effective bridge not only between the rural and the urban population but also between local and national political institutions. The same can be said of certain urban-based traders, particularly those in the food retail field, who to a large extent depend on the effective operation of a network of relatives and business acquaintances to supply them with produce. In addition there have come into being "brokers" who operate at crucial points of economic and political articulation between the local (rural) and the national (urban) levels. Such persons, chiefs, local government officials, entrepreneurs, local and traditional leaders, carry the demands of the rural population to the national government and in turn interpret policies to the people in the rural areas. While these links are often tenuous and irregular, and exploitative of the rural population, they nevertheless serve to emphasise the functional interrelationship of the town and its hinterland.

Some observers have suggested that, as a result, many Africans live in a "dual" system (Gugler 1965, 1966, 1968) using urban wages as a supplement to their agricultural activities. Others state that large sections of the population are in a "transitional" stage (a concept to which objections were expressed earlier), a twilight existence in a sort of no-man's-land, because of the inability or unwillingness of the migrant to put down firm roots in the town while expressing great dissatisfaction with rural life. Rather than weaken rural-urban links, these circumstances add strength simply because they appear to increase the circulation and the symbiotic relationship between town and country.

On the other hand, rather than being a relationship of symbiosis, tensions have developed between town and country. There are several reasons for this. In the first case, national governments seem to be more urban than rural oriented in as much as the political leaders seem to show some reluctance to spend prolonged periods in the rural areas. This clearly makes the government, and its leaders, remote from the rural population. The politicians enjoy the sophisticated urban life, the diplomatic cocktail circuit, the recreational facilities, the commercial life, the international atmosphere and the jockeying for power and prestige. This is all in strong contrast to the seeming drabness of rural life, its lack of social and intellectual sophistication and the general absence of progress and modernity. Rural people are generally very mindful of this in their behaviour towards the "city boys" whom they treat with a certain sense of awe and considerable deference.

Secondly, in economic terms, the towns receive a disproportionate share of the national revenue to meet the heavy recurring expenditures which are swallowed up by a wide range of services from which the ruralite gains but scant benefit. Thirdly, in political terms national development policies, at least until rather recent times, seem to reflect a strong elitist and class bias, i.e. the limited resources of the nation are appropriated by the few at the expense of the masses. Thus rural people will often express anger and frustration at the corruption and nepotism practiced by the urban politicians. While no doubt this might be a case of "I-too-want-to-put-my-hand-in-the-cash-box", rural people not infrequently suggest that urban life is bound to corrupt because the temptations are so great. For these and related reasons, mothers often express the view that they do not wish their children to live in the town even though educational and health facilities might be better.

As the gap between the rural and the urban areas increases, we can likewise expect increased tension between the respective populations. But this will not detract from the fact that town and country are linked in an economic and political embrace which is not likely to loosen in the near future.

Finally we need to say a brief word about the development of suburban life in Africa. Historically, the expatriate colonial elite lived separate from the African population. As a group they quartered themselves some distance away from the city center. They occupied spacious homes and tended to their lavish gardens. Today most of these homes have been taken over by the African civil service elite who like to have it both ways: to live close to where the "action is" while never being far away from the countryside. As the suburbs expand they eat up more of the surrounding countryside with the effect that urban influences are pushed ever further afield. Villages and rural homesteads thus suddenly find themselves incorporated into the urban areas. Municipalities take up land in anticipation of future expansion. There is no reason to believe that this will not continue. In addition more African housing estates are being constructed and invariably they are located on the outer fringes of the town.

We will close this chapter with part of an interview (Gutkind 1966) with an Ewe speaker living in Accra:

The town is like strong drink because if you start living here you can't get away. You always want more and more. At times you get drunk, very badly, and then you want to run away to the village and sleep for a whole week. But then you wake up and you talk to your old friends and you find out that they have done nothing all the time you have been away. They have done nothing but sit and talk and do a little in their gardens. So you are ready to run away again and you say to yourself: Do not get drunk on the city again. But you do get drunk and the drink is very strong but it also tastes good until you wake up the next morning and you feel bad and sad. But you don't have to drink in the city every day. You can also do better things. But you must have money.

And so said Shamu, the truck driver, who has a wife and seven children and has lived in Accra for eleven years.

III

Some basic organisational and institutional characteristics of urban complexity

The first distinction to come to our attention is the greater social diversity of residents of an urban area. They come in all shapes, sizes and colours. Of course, there is some physical and social diversity in a village settlement. Not everyone looks the same and not everyone acts the same. But we are not immediately impressed by the variation and diversity as we are when we walk along any street in a large metropolitan area. In an African rural area people more or less dress alike and they speak a common language. In New York, down 42nd Street, the diversity of dress and the babel of tongues is almost unlimited. The houses people live in tend to conform to a common pattern in an African village; not so in an urban area. While they all might have a door and a roof, they come in a bewildering assortment of shapes and styles. But these are measures of diversity which are obvious and, perhaps, insignificant.

More important, and more subtle, are distinctions in institutional structure and social organisation in terms of personal and group relations, in ways of work, in occupations, in family life, political culture, in religious and ideational views, in economic and social mobility, in the "tempo" of life, and, perhaps, in the motivations of the people. Let us take some of these and find out whether it is possible to delineate some clear and realistic distinctions between rural and urban life.

1. Personal and Group Relations

It is often argued that life in the city is impersonal, that residents of the 27th floor of a skyscraper do not know each other; that the stranger who asks for directions on a street in Detroit is told: Sorry buddy. I can't help, I only live here. If this is correct, and recent research in urban Africa indicates that at best this proposition is a half truth (Marris, 1961), what might be the reason? We should ask ourselves the question: what contributes to, and what prevents, the impersonalisation of personal and group relations in an urban setting?

We can throw light on this question if we consider the variables of size, diversity and complexity. As we have already indicated, the ruralite generally lives in a smaller community in which it is not only possible but also necessary to know one another. In such a community, the individual is woven into a fabric of kinship and reciprocity – at least ideally this is said to be so – which provides him with rewards, but also imposes upon him certain important responsibilities. However, this alone would not clearly distinguish differences between rural and urban social organisation simply because persons and groups in any type of settlement are dependent on each other not only socially but also economically. Each and everyone makes some kind of contribution to the total well-being of the society. But one important distinction is that in a small community each person is within social *range* of everyone else. It is not the case that each person is watching everyone else but rather that the individual finds it is much more difficult to contract out, so to speak, from that complex and wide ranging set of relations of which he is a part. Because the community is small, there is greater *frequency* of contact with one another. But this alone does not make for greater intimacy. Impersonal social interaction and conflict are not avoided in this manner. Indeed, as we well realise, the closer the ties are between people, the greater the potential for conflict – however hard people try to avoid this!

But let us set aside the question of either intimacy or conflict. In a small-scale African rural-based community contact is not only frequent, but it is almost always face to face. This kind of primary relationship often does stand in strong contrast to the less frequent and often less close contacts which are the hallmark of urban life. Of course, even in an urban setting, individuals rub shoulders constantly, but they are usually strangers to one another. They may not speak to each other because they have no reason to do so – after all, they are not related, not even distantly. Even if they wanted to speak, there might be significant barriers, such as language, racial and residential segregation, and different occupational, economic, and educational strata of the society. The quality of inter-personal and intergroup relations does bear some relationship to the size and composition of the community.

But we must also consider another view. In an African village social institutions are meshed together so intimately that it is very difficult to isolate that which is exclusively political, economic or familial. In a rather more abstract sense, this is also true of modern industrial society, i.e., the family could not function without goods and services and the link between economic affairs and political power is, as we well know, very close. But in a small rural setting, the family is part of a network which, rather like the web of a spider, proliferates throughout the total social system. The point we must make here is that with size of community comes a greater exclusiveness of various activities and an institutional matrix which is more segmented, because social, economic, political and educational objectives and activities have become more specialised. As we indicated before, specialisation of activities and a measure of differentiation of social life is certainly very much part of the social organisation of any group of people. In the city these characteristics are not only more clearly visible, but also have an important functional basis.

The question of complexity is more difficult to define. It would not be very difficult to show that social anthropologists have always studied societal complexity, if by this we mean that there are really no "simple" societies. We are primarily talking about differences of degrees of complexity which, do however, lead to radically different styles of life. Nor should we assume that it is easier to study a rural community because we can observe a wide range of activities taking place in a limited area. Yet up to a point, this is true because the social anthropologist who stakes his tent in or near a village has the opportunity, at least theoretically, to see all that people do. But we can just as easily select a small urban neighbourhood, a street or a backyard, and devote twenty years of study to the varied and changing life of its inhabitants. The generally vastly greater scale of an urban agglomeration is reflected in a particular kind of complexity which can only be comprehended if we study the total entity. But this is clearly impossible. It is a more complex entity we are looking at, both in layout and composition of population. A city, and even a small town, is most often made up of people who, because they come from different cultures, live in different areas; because they have different customs, ideas, education and values do not mingle together as freely as the inhabitants of a small African village. It is this more diverse social and cultural infrastructure which makes the city a more complex place. This is a view which is strongly opposed by those who insist that urban life forces everyone into the same mould, keeps everyone in the same economic and social straight jacket and thus eliminates individual diversity. There are those who conform, those who cannot compete, and whose very individuality is lost in the sea of (urban) diversity. The expression of individuality has a much freer reign in the city because its potential divisiveness can be more effectively incorporated, although at times not without violence. Of course we can add to this that people of the city also possess a more complex technology to aid them in their work, their home life and their play. It is the impact of technology which is yet another way to highlight what we mean by complexity. If we were to spell out the consequences of this impact we would see, quite clearly, that it produces quite different styles of life. The subsistence farmer and the cash crop peasant live, if we may use a cliché, close to the soil. Their very livelihood springs from their ability to produce crops. Thus, much of their social, economic and political activity rests on this base. This is clearly not so in a city where, at least in the Western world, the inhabitants earn their living by means of non-agricultural activities. To be sure, the wealthy country squire leads a dual kind of life, spending some of his time on his land and some in the city, but this is rather rare.

We could also suggest that "world view" has something to do with complexity. But here we need to be more cautious than ever. Most of us readily accept the premise that urban man is a member of the "literati", the sophisticated, literate, cosmopolitan world of learning. The city is the citadel of civilisation, it is the habitat of innovation and discovery and of the application of rationality to the human condition. In contrast we often suggest that the people in the rural "wilderness" are illiterate, suspicious, intellectually backward, fatalistic and fearful of the unknown; they reject innovation because they are satisfied with what they know and with what they have; they do not think rationally as evidenced in their belief in magic, witchcraft, and the healing skills of the "native" doctor; perhaps they believe in many gods and in the fact that stones and trees are really alive; when men die their spirit lurks everywhere so that much energy has to be devoted to keeping on good terms with the ancestors; when things go wrong, when children die, when a flood sweeps away the village, when triplets are born, or the crops fail, the men of the wilderness can only seek a supernatural explanation. Of course, if all these were really true attributes of the rural people today, we might have to conclude that their future was indeed an unhappy one. But today, there are few, if any, rural communities which are so encapsulated that change and modernisation has not made considerable impact, has not changed attitudes. Missions, for good or ill, have worked for many years among the people of Africa. Education has made deep inroads in the lives of Africans – and not only among those who have attended school. Roads have been pushed inland, so that mobility has greatly increased, and all the people of Africa now find themselves under administrative and political systems which are transforming the perception a people have of their place in the world. The perceptual and cognitive world of the ruralite is no less complex than that of the urbanite, it is merely different. Whether the latter is the more civilised, the more liberated individual, is another matter.

2. *Ways of Work*

Work, hard work, is almost invariably seen as an attribute of an industrial, urban-based society, in contrast to the work done by the "carefree" and "lazy natives." Many an expatriate manager of a factory or office, be it in Lagos or Salisbury, complains that Africans do not know the meaning of work, of regular hours and regular attendance. They complain that they appear inexplicably prepared to give up employment which has considerable potential in terms of earning, training and promotion. The African worker, some critics have said, does not feel comfortable in an urban-industrial climate (Davis 1933, Elkan 1956, Gussman 1953, Gutkind 1968a, University of Natal 1950.) The rural rhythm of work is dysfunctional in an urban context. Seasonal work on the land, mixed with periods of relaxation and social and ceremonial activities, does not prepare a man for the demands of factory or office. Because managers have not been trained as social anthropologists, they have considerable difficulty in understanding the work performance, the commitment and the attitudes of the African worker (Gutkind 1968). Work is work, but the ways of work differ greatly.

If the real distinction between different kinds of work is the use or non-use of machines, then the differences in the Western world between the agricultural worker and the factory worker are no longer very significant. The modern machinery used by many farmers today approaches the complexity of the most automated factory. In the non-Western world, however, the contrast between the use made of machinery by the factory worker and the very primitive tools used previously on the land is very considerable. Yet no people are without some measure of technology even if this is restricted to the digging stick or the knowledge required to make a house from the branches of a bush or tree. But clearly, limited technology limits potential production and output. A subsistence economy requires consistent effort and frequently very hard physical labour, but once certain major agricultural tasks have been completed the African farmer devotes his time and energy to other activities. As a worker he is not wedded to an eight hour day. The regularity of his work is dictated by seasonal factors rather than by the demands of heavy capital investment to obtain a return on goods, services and profits. Of course, the desire for profit is not alien to the rural worker who finds this return in terms of a surplus of crops and the time which he may devote to other activities of equal importance to him. In a sense there is very little separation between work time and non-work time. Leisure is not an exclusive urban trait, although the need to relax does not appear to be of great significance for the industrial urban worker.

Work in a rural African setting is immersed in the total matrix of a rural-based society. Hunting, gathering, and/or farming are not distinctly separated from other activities. Work is an expression of collective needs and objectives rather than an individual effort. The work unit is more often than not the family or larger social grouping. The emphasis on effort is seen largely in collective terms rather than in individual satisfaction. Thus, when a farmer cannot till his crops, or the hunter cannot join his friends, his place will in all likelihood be taken by somebody else. Not so in the factory. When a skilled machinist is away his bench will be unattended. With other words, work in a rural African society places the worker under less pressure to be there, to carry out his duties. A factory worker who does not show up for work, unless the reasons for his absence are accepted by his employer, loses his pay. The rural worker is rarely punished in this manner as he continues to be rewarded through the efforts of his kin and friends.

In a modern industrial urban society, work is wholly geared to the exploitation of local, regional, and national resources, to the production for a "market" which can utilise goods produced on a mass scale, and to the distribution and marketing of such products both locally and internationally. Both the use of manpower and the kind of work men do is intimately linked to a refined technology applied to production and, consequently, the reduction of labour costs as machines become highly competitive with manpower. The African rural migrant who leaves his original anchorage, in a subsistence or cash-crop economy, to enter in the wage market of an urban area is thrown into a highly competitive system with new types of entrepreneurship and economic structures with which he is unacquainted. The migrant is generally a young, unskilled man who has had little education, if any, and who is suddenly faced with a situation which places a premium on all those attributes which he either does not possess or possesses only to a limited degree. These attributes are not only economic, but also social and political. He has to adapt to a new style of life which is thrust upon him in large measure by the compulsion to participate in economic arrangements which he does not understand and over which he has very little control.

We must be careful not to leave the impression that the moment an African crosses into the urban world he is lost and wholly dependent on a relative and friend for aid and support because the very idea of work, particularly regular work, is completely alien. This is clearly not so. Nor need the transition to urban habits and ideas be a very drastic one. The local craftsman who practices his trade in a village might also make and sell his products in the city – perhaps even more successfully. This might well apply to carpenters, tinsmiths, leather workers, basket makers, pot makers, tailors, medicine sellers, caterers, and others. Many of these occupations are not based on major technological innovations nor do they require regularity of performance. Most of these craftsmen are self-employed and set their own pace, hours and output. Having such skills to sell, they can explore opportunities and settle where they believe they can best trade. They can take time to develop their entrepreneurial activities and learn management skills. If their skills are rewarded they will gradually hire others to help them and slowly begin to use machinery such as electric saws or machinery for the stitching of shoes. As their skills increase, the rhythm of their work becomes more regular. Indeed, as they become part of the new industrial and commercial complex, they have to cope with the far superior competitive output of the mass production industries. Thus, the shoemaker is put out of business as huge quantities of plastic shoes are stamped out daily, and the carpenter finds that it is impossible for him to produce as cheap a product as the local furniture factory. The result is that some are forced to give up their trade, try something else, or join the long lines of the unemployed at the employment exchanges. Their efforts have not been rewarded and their experiences have made them cynical about the future. Some will hang on and reap some rewards. They try to perfect their production techniques, cut back on overheads, learn to keep careful accounts and generally respond to the competitive pressures from modern industries.

The adaption for the totally unskilled is rather different. While a small percentage of such workers may find the opportunity to become self-employed, for example as petty traders, the majority seek employment as unskilled workers in the construction industry, in the public works department, as night watchmen, messengers, factory hands, cleaners, load carriers or odd job men. To hold down such work, the worker must be prepared to attend regularly and to put effort into his work. In the work situation he must learn to understand and to obey orders, to work with strangers – perhaps in particular those from other ethnic groups. He must learn the new rhythm of the job, shift work for example, and to apportion his free time between the need for relaxation and social obligations to his family whether they are with him or not. He must learn to adapt himself to the total urban environment. Above all, he must learn to budget his earnings. Because his pay as an unskilled person will be very small, the greater part of his wages will have to be devoted to food. A large number of rural migrants find it very difficult to adapt to this. In Kampala, Uganda, for example, newly arrived migrants usually complained that the most difficult adjustment they had to make was that they had to "eat the wages", meaning, clearly, cash earnings should be devoted to other needs. The unskilled workers, therefore, have far less latitude in making a gradual adjustment to urban conditions compared to the self-employed entrepreneur and craftsman. As the years go by the balance swings steadily in favour of the skilled and toward those African workers who have made a commitment to the urban-industrial way of life. The specialisation of work will squeeze out even the semi-skilled as new processes and technology make deep inroads everywhere in Africa. Even outside the town the farmer has to learn a new style of agricultural productivity, the use of machinery, fertilisers, the use of better seeds, adapt to more regular hours, how to use farm records to cut costs, and increase productivity and profits. So the urban man is not alone in learning how to handle the myriad of new demands, the skills of new jobs and greater specialisation. Yet the way of work, the attitudes to and the demands set by new forms of labour are perhaps more extreme in the towns than in the rural areas. To marry the ways of the agriculturalist with the ways of an urban-industrial order is not easy, although in some parts of Africa (for example in Buganda, Uganda) some Africans have managed to combine agricultural activities with urban wage work. (Elkan 1960). To some observers this is the best of both worlds.

But it is in the wider social context where the African worker finds himself which is of far-reaching significance. Work in an urban area is the most direct introduction to new social relationships and institutions. The desire for regular work, and its rewards, links the worker intimately to urban life. The work situation increases his social contacts, and as he improves his occupation the previous social contacts and friendships may lapse. As an urbanite, membership in a trade union or other less formal occupational association may rank of greater importance (utility) than close relations with members of his kin group and ethnic community. This is certainly one of the lessons pointed out in the work by A. L. Epstein (1958). A great deal of work, particularly heavy industrial work, i.e. mining, medium and heavy industry, dockwork, railway work and skilled artisans, produces its specific industrial and commercial climate and structure. What conflict there is likely to be between a rural and urban style of life, will surface as men are asked to perform tasks which have no antecedents whatever in rural work activities.

Perhaps more important yet, steady urban work with its potential for upward social and economic mobility, produces new problems related to aspirations and motivation, response to incentive, achievement and success and various political demands. The latter, as they grow out of the commitment to urban life, are translated into new structural and organisational patterns such as class sentiments and class structures. From these flow demands for particular political representation, better working conditions, security of employment, fringe benefits, better housing, and of course, spiralling wage demands. In short: the established urban worker fathers much of what we understand as true urbanism.

Thus, those urban areas which contain a true industrial labour force are structurally more complex. Their political and economic impact on the countryside is likely to be greater. Migration to these towns is probably more persistent, as is the problem of unemployment. Here we could cite, as examples, the mining towns of Northern Zambia and Southern Zaire, or such harbour towns as Lagos and Mombasa with their large number of militant dockworkers. Among these workers, who will not readily give up the foothold they have created for themselves, the trade unions and the strike weapon are firmly established. The impact on the town is clearly very different than what we might expect from a small labour force in the lesser urban centers in Africa.

The study of the urban worker, therefore, reveals aspects of major political, economic and social transformations at the national level. As a worker he is the creator of what has come to be known as modernisation. No other Africans, not even the "progressive" farmers, are as directly involved in modern technology, and, like the "elites," such as the professionals, the upper ranges of the civil service and the large-scale entrepreneurs, the established urban worker is consciously shaping his urban-anchored future. A recent study by David Smock (1969) of mine workers in Enugu, Nigeria, indicates how militant they are and how important it is for those who might wish to study the town of Enugu to understand their activities.

3. *Occupations*

Sociologists say that one of the major characteristics of urban life is the "greater specialisation of functions." This is true: in simple terms it means that people have many different kinds of new jobs. In a small-scale village economy in Africa, based primarily on subsistence, the division of labour and the specialisation of function is limited – it is different both in kind and degree.

In a rural area most of the residents obtain their living from the land as farmers, as pastoralists, or as hunters and gatherers. Women often do most of the agricultural work while men look after their herds training young boys in the skills of the herdsman. Young girls assist their mothers in the home and watch her prepare the fields, plant and harvest the crops. The specialisation of jobs is simple, while their performance is very skilled. The careful eye of the Masai herdsmen tending their cattle has no equal. In agricultural, permanently settled, societies we can expect a greater variety of jobs carried out by men and women. There are political leaders, religious leaders and craftsmen – that is often the extent of specialisation. Of course today, even in the rural area, in the course of social transformation, there is much more specialisation, many more jobs and many more entrepreneurs with a wide variety of businesses, mostly very small scale and often involving a number of family members· In a number of West African societies, particularly those in Nigeria, skilled crafts have been established for centuries and, no doubt, skills within each craft. Young men serve long apprenticeships with a master craftsman, a tradition which has taken on new significance in Nigeria and Ghana (Callaway 1964, Peil 1966) as a large number of young men, with very little education, are drifting into the cities. Today, the apprenticeship system is an important safety valve which absorbs quite a large number of the rural and urban unemployed.

The jobs men do are now not only more diverse, but different occupations have greater social, economic and political significance. The more important

one's job, as a political leader, a major businessman, a highly skilled techni-
cian, an artisan (such as a plumber, a painter, or an electrician) or a professional (such as a doctor or a university teacher) the more important one's
position in the body politic. Jobs confer, as never before, status and rank;
and in African society the higher one's education, the greater one's wealth,
the more important one ranks in the social order. New occupations help
us to understand how men have created new positions of power and
prestige. The hierarchy of the social order flows directly from the proliferation of new occupations. But so do other arrangements such as where people
live. Today over much of Africa the senior civil servants live in exclusive
homes once occupied by the expatriate colonial administrators, and most
of these homes were established in well planned urban enclaves. On the
other hand, the unskilled live in slums which literally burst with humanity
existing under the most congested conditions. The semi-skilled live in housing
estates and the skilled build their own homes in areas far removed from
those of the unskilled. New York, London or Rome are hardly different.
Occupational diversity is a major index of social change and modernisation.

This occupational and social stratification is seen more clearly in urban
areas than elsewhere (Mitchell and Epstein 1959). Perhaps no other setting
brings home more dramatically the changes which are occurring in Africa,
and which Africans actively seek and encourage, that is new status, prestige
and power rating. Education and technology have provided African society
with a new base for future development which is directly related to the new
occupations for which Africans are being trained. Each occupation creates its
own particular milieu, its own cadres, its particular response to economic and
social change, its own training schemes, its own political outlook and its own
development ideology. Also, each of the new occupations is assuming a more
formal structure with its special internal hierarchy, its officers and spokes-
men, all of which bring the African miner closer to miners elsewhere, the
African doctor closer to others in the same profession and the African businessmen invariably closer to the world community of commerce. Once again
these developments are seen more clearly in the towns of Africa where the
range of modern occupational diversity is highly concentrated. Thus, Mitchell and Epstein (1959 : 22) write:

A significant aspect of the newly developed towns of Central and Southern Africa is the degree to which social relationships in certain situations are being organized in terms of social strata. One method of approach (to the study of stratification) which promises to be fruitful, is through the ranking of occupations by their social prestige.

What their research revealed was that there was both a scattering and a clustering of prestige and status linked to occupational groupings ranging from high (professionals) to low (unskilled). Furthermore, occupational ratings were often assessed against widely different value scales. Thus the question is raised: who is ranking whom, for what purpose and in what context? Ranking, although internally consistent for the individual respondent, will vary from person to person. This led the authors to conclude that "There are no objective criteria by means of which prestige rankings may be assessed." But this scatter, rather than introducing confusion, is a clear reflection of the fact that African urban workers are still in the process of defining concepts of power and prestige, and that we ought to be careful before we assume, *a priori*, that occupation is invariably linked with social status. While we have some indications that this is so, i.e. that white-collar jobs are more desirable than manual occupations, and that different occupations are measured against European models, we cannot yet conclude that the ratings "provide a basis for the recruitment of corporately acting groups." What we can perhaps suggest is that those who have acquired certain positions of political influence, in the context of the urban system, and as that influence is relevant to specific segments of the urban population, also enjoy high prestige. Such a conceptualisation can then be applied both to particular groups and individuals. The point to be understood here is that social ranking, prestige and power (as these are invariably linked) are ways to order and categorise the urban population. The responses by individuals asked to scale occupational groups *as groups* give us an idea how the urban hierarchy is organised. What is "up" today is "down" tomorrow. As specific situations arise, particular individuals and groups will rise or fall in the eyes of others. When the unskilled construction workers go on strike, there is an economic spin-off affecting other workers and, for the time being, the militant unskilled workers are the heroes of the hour. Governments can make trade union leaders appear like traitors to others and force down their high prestige, while at different times they can be used by governments as powerful weapons against the elites. Until political, economic and social patterns are more crystallised, not only in the urban areas, but also in the nation as a whole, to link occupation with prestige can be a hazardous matter. A good example of this can be found in Mafeje's (1963) article on "A Chief Visits Town" where he described (in the South African urban context) how urban workers responded, mostly negatively, to the authority and respect accorded a chief. The message conveyed to the chief was simple: *vis-à-vis* the urban workers, his authority and prestige had little meaning.

What we need to recognise is that the scenario of political and economic life in urban Africa is played out on a stage whose setting changes from day to day – although the broad outlines are gradually being formed. In some African countries, i.e. parts of Southern Africa, the setting changes little, as racial segregation has introduced a caste-like system whereby all Africans are inferior (whatever their occupation) to all Whites. In most other African countries, however, all attempts at assessing rank, prestige and power must take into account a multitude of forces which determines who is "down," for how long and for what reason, and who is "up."

4. *Economic and Social Mobility*

In the study of social and occupational mobility, it has been conventional to draw a distinction between ascription and achievement. In the former, individual and collective status and rank is "fixed" at birth by virtue of colour, ethnicity, creed, hereditary principles, elitism, education and wealth, while in the latter upward or downward social and occupational mobility is determined on merit, through ability and achievement.

In a social system anchored on ascription, the individual, whatever his ability and efforts, is in a fixed position socially, occupationally and politically. It is impossible for him to rise in status and rank, although it is possible to be pushed down to a lower rank. This arrangement tends to be characteristic of pre-industrial (particularly tribal) groups, peasant societies with a feudal economic base, and theocratic and oligarchic societies. The relative, if not absolute, fixed position of individuals and groups can also be traced to the structural principles of social organisation of small-scale societies. In such societies the rules of kinship play a far greater role than in technologically advanced societies (the example of present day Japan is illustrative here). While a tightly knit kinship system by itself does not inevitably restrict mobility, it might greatly reduce or impede it. Because in such societies there is limited occupational specialisation largely due to the absence of an advanced technology, the pressure for vertical mobility, while by no means absent, is limited. This is true prior to the arrival of major external influences which are transforming small-scale and economically undifferentiated societies. As soon as education, commerce and industrialisation make even limited inroads in these societies, conventions and a restricted mobility are gradually replaced by varied responses to new opportunities and ideologies. While under conditions of incipient urbanism and industrialism upward mobility is generally restricted to a select few, and frequently elitism replaces ascription, many individuals find themselves with a new freedom of movement (rural-urban movement or total translocation), new opportunities, new alternatives and choices (Mair 1963), new friendships and associations, and such fundamental questions as whether or not they should reject the past or keep a foothold in the socio-economic system which reared them.

In a modernising society the need to create opportunities for upward mobility is very considerable. Fixed and enduring economic and social groups are not, generally, characteristic of urban-industrial life. Many aspects of urban social structure, particularly in the newly developing countries, are in an almost constant state of change which is fanned by a dialectic on the strategy and objectives of modernisation and national development.

Occupational mobility, based on acquisition of skills and achievement, is a major feature of modern industrial society. However, to achieve this mobility in an African context we must recognise the existence of certain obstacles which impede mobility. First, sociocultural conventions often clash with the demands made by modern commerce and industry so new economic opportunities which are available do not always lead to increased mobility. Second, African urban populations are not merely extremely heterogeneous in composition but are mostly unskilled and unschooled making it difficult for the individual to participate effectively in a modern commercial-industrial economy.

Other impediments are the basic shortage of development capital, which retards the creation of new employment opportunities, and the pressures of a modern technology which relies less and less on labour for various productive processes. Under such conditions real social and occupational mobility are greatly restricted and African leaders, whatever development policies they might adopt, are faced with a serious situation in rapidly increasing unemployment. As we know, Africans migrate to the towns in search of new opportunities, hoping to increase their upward mobility, an objective they are unable to achieve in the rural areas. Only a very small percentage of Africans have been able to better their status as a result of increased economic specialisation in agricultural activity. But even when they have been able to do so, they prefer to try their luck in the towns because they identify change and progress with non-agricultural activities.

The main thrust behind occupational mobility is education and the acquisition of technical skills. In a non-Western agricultural society occupational specialisation is more limited and newly acquired educational standards cannot easily be translated into remunerative jobs in rural areas. African economies allow for little room to manoeuvre, i.e. to move the labour force from one productive process to another. There is a limit to which the economies of rural areas in Africa can be diversified. Not only is the cost of rural development enormous, but we also need to ask whether it is sound policy to anchor more and more people to the land. At best this is a stop gap measure until agricultural efficiency has been increased. Then fewer farmers will be required because the few will produce more. Unless economic development schemes can create annually a vast number of new jobs, mobility will be severely restricted. What then? There are those observers who have suggested that the real "Pains of Birth" are not yet over. For example, Stanley Diamond (1963 : 178) has written:

Millions of Africans, radically disengaged from their traditions, are being rapidly proletarianized in both rural and urban areas, and are being forced to substitute a mere strategy of poverty and survival for authentic cultural expression. Put another way, they are being rapidly converted into marginal producers and marginal consumers on the remotest fringes of contemporary industrial society.

It is in the context of these characteristics and contemporary features of Africa that we must assess the potential for economic and social mobility. The growth of urban areas has increased only minimally this mobility for the vast majority of Africans. However, this observation needs to be modified. In the first case it must be seen against the background of increased migration which restricts mobility to the few who find employment in the few existing job opportunities. Second, it is possible that the mobility potential for the urbanite was greater between 1939 and 1960 than it is today because when the colonial administrations were gradually moving the African countries to independence, the result was rapid urban growth and many development projects (particularly in the construction and public service sectors) requiring a good deal of labour. Third, in economic and occupational terms, urban life is highly competitive making upward mobility very selective. Hence the true extent of mobility is difficult to detect.

It is probably incorrect to measure mobility solely in terms of upward job movement. We need to ask ourselves again, why do Africans move to the towns? Of course they expect to get a job, and try very hard to get one, but more fundamentally the actual move itself from rurality to the urban area is viewed by many as a move up the ladder. To be an urbanite and to face the toils and tribulations of the city, shows initiative and motivation and a determination to get on; it shows a desire to be "where the action is" for where else is there the possibility of making something better of oneself? Life in the town at least presents the migrant with the illusion, on which he feeds, that better times are round the corner. To hang on to this illusion is, perhaps, a very important aspect of the "Will to be Modern." It may just generate that aggressiveness and political militancy which prys open a rather stagnant economic and political order and thus creates true mobility. The urbanite may not be far removed from such militancy. Despite many failures, one of the achievements by Dr. Kwame Nkrumah was his attempt to open the channels of mobility for a large section of the Ghanian population.

Mobility in the urban areas is further restricted by the negative consequences of tribalism and the nepotism and corruption which go along with it. Thus what little mobility potential there is, is restricted to the "string pullers" and those able to offer monetary rewards to those who can offer jobs. Sometimes the situation has deteriorated so badly that a government has had to issue a proclamation warning civil servants of the penalties which they might incur if they just give jobs to their friends or sell them to others (Gutkind 1967 and 1968). In addition, job opportunities and upward mobility may also be restricted by such new organisations as the trade unions which, being very conscious of the few jobs available, will demand that their members get first choice. Likewise, other groups will restrict their membership so as not to weaken their political, and economic, position. Mobility, therefore, must run the gamut of endless pressure groups.

In this regard, it would be a mistake to study social and economic mobility in urban Africa without taking into account the political and economic policies allowed by the national government, and these policies as they are applied to the nation as a whole. Here we need to ask a whole set of questions concerning ideology, economic doctrine, foreign trade and aid and who controls what economic and political power. What jobs and mobility exist for the urbanite is, after all, merely a reflection of what is taking place in the nation as a whole.

5. *The Political Order*

The larger the number of people who live together, the greater the need for mechanisms to regulate their relations. This generalisation does not exclude, of course, the importance of such mechanisms in small-scale societies. The only distinction is that in the former these mechanisms are highly formalised whereas in the latter they are often diffuse and, hence, harder to detect. We shall call these regulatory mechanisms the political order.

The political order concerns itself not merely with the allocation of authority and the exercise of power; in a more abstract sense, political mechanisms are basic to the organisation of the total society. The political order, as embodied in the kinship system, regulates not only personal and group relations but also attempts to resolve conflicts which arise in interpersonal and inter-group contact. Virtually every aspect of personal and group life generates a conflict potential which in turn calls for mediation or, perhaps, punishment if the breach of norms is too severe. In small-scale rural-based societies such as "band" societies, it is frequently very difficult to abstract that which is clearly "political." In such societies, the exercise of authority is submerged in the total fabric of the society, particularly in the segmentary kinship order. There are generally no office holders who may give orders although the position of older people is respected. Key individuals in the kinship system, or religious leaders, may be privileged to exercise authority. But then again there are large-scale settled agricultural societies among whom the exercise of power is just as diffuse. Yet a segmented and egalitarian society is not an anarchistic society. There is order, there is conflict, and there are means to restore order.

Anthropologists have devoted a great deal of time to the documentation of various types of political systems in non-Western societies, concentrating on the formal mechanisms designed for the legitimate exercise of power. In the past we have been satisfied with a simple, and highly abstract, typological classification of political systems, now less frequently applied. We used to analyse these systems as mutually exclusive structures. On the one hand there were the kingdom states which were highly centralised, i.e. power was exercised by a hierarchy of officials, assisted by a bureaucracy, and formally constituted political institutions such as a king's council or a chief's court. Even in such centralised political systems certain key individuals in the kinship order sometimes exercised competitive authority which a king or a chief had to take into account. Those who failed to do so frequently found themselves in conflict with those who represented the power of various clans or specially important lineages. These centralised systems had many of the attributes of a state. They had administrative machinery, judicial institutions and the power to defend the territorial base of their society. In short, they had a government. But because the systems were centralised there was unequal access to power, privilege, status and wealth. The centralisation of power may have been exercised autocratically or benevolently.

All this was in contrast to those societies, both large and small, which the anthropologist has labelled as decentralised, i.e. without a formally constituted government. They lacked formally consituted administrative machinery, clearly identifiable judicial organs, and the capability to defend, particularly at short notice, their boundaries. Also wealth, status and rank were generally not as important. The anthropologist has defined the first type of political order as a "primitive state" and the second as "stateless societies." However, we ought to recognise that these are typological abstractions which help us simply to order our documentation and highlight certain basic differences. The important distinction to be made is that in centralised political systems the political order, as well as the economic and social order, is enforced by an administrative organisation which is partially independent of the general kinship system, while in a decentralised system the corporate nature of the segmentary unilateral descent groups, which comprise the kinship order and have continuity through time, regulate political relations between the segments. Whereas in the former system the political unit is administratively anchored, in the latter the territorial unit is rooted in the lineage (kinship) system (Mair 1962.)

Political organisation regulates and maintains the societal order, of a particular group of people living in a clearly defined area it considers its own. Thus one of the factors which might disturb the effective functioning of the political order is migration: people move out of the area and greater dispersal takes place. The moment this happens the individual is no longer under the control of those regulatory mechanisms which tied him to the group of his birthplace. This applies to both the micro and the macro level, i.e. the control exercised by the kin group and control by the "tribe" as a political community. Not only does this outward migration weaken the force of political controls, but immigration introduces into the body politic new expectations and demands acquired during the sojourn away from home. To this we must add the most direct force which has transformed the political order in Africa, namely the domination by colonial powers. Although this is a dimension of major significance, we shall not be concerned with it here.

As we have indicated before, the particular "political culture" (defined by G. Almond as the basic framework in which political activity takes place) of a people whose base is that of a rural economy is operative and meaningful only in that particular context. The moment individuals and groups enter the urban system they are subject to a new political culture, i.e. to a new normative belief system, and hence to new regulatory controls born out of circumstances which prevail in an urban area. There are two distinct, but often also overlapping cultures: one rural and one urban.

Urban political culture is a civic culture. It is designed to meet the needs of a very diverse population, of a new scale of social organisation and a new complexity. Neither the regulatory mechanisms of the primitive state nor those of the stateless society can operate effectively in the urban context. To be sure, as we shall see later when discussing urban political organisation, individuals and groups try to recreate in modified form that political culture in which they were socialised in their youth and to give it expression in those situations in urban life which make this desirable and perhaps possible. The clearest indication we have of this is from the insightful work of A. L. Epstein, *Politics in an African Urban Community*.

Epstein, writing about the history of the trade union movement in Zambia, shows how in the early years of development of the copper industry, African miners turned to headmen and chiefs to mediate with the companies on behalf of the workers. For some years, this use of "traditional" leaders worked reasonably well. However, over time an industrial climate developed among the African miners, a social, economic and political climate which the chiefs did not understand, with the result that the workers began to turn to trade union leaders to represent their interests *vis-à-vis* management. Eventually the "traditional" authorities lost their influence, and the legitimacy of their authority, rooted, as it was, in a different kind of political culture. Their authority, their outlook and attitudes were, in sociological jargon, dysfunctional in an urban context. While it is dangerous to generalise, it might be possible to show that African chiefs have moved from a sacred to a political role and, today, to a mainly ceremonial one. In most cases, however, they have been incorporated into the network of a new bureaucracy. At times, particularly during elections, political parties will mobilise the chiefs to gather in the votes and they are subsequently rewarded for this. But these functions seem to give them little more than a temporary lease in exercising a fading authority.

The urban situation, though, might indeed produce just the opposite result. Once again the work of Epstein (1953) in Zambia is instructive, as is the work by M. Banton (1957.) Epstein showed that the use of (traditional) chiefs and headmen in the urban judicial system worked quite well as long as problems which were brought to the urban courts could be dealt with in the context of "native law and custom". The smooth operation of these courts illustrated clearly the proposition made earlier that particular aspects of a rural political order can be transferred to the town and be made applicable in those situations which can be resolved meaningfully in terms of the normative system which has evolved under urban conditions. Epstein (1958) also formulated a theory of tribalism in town which can serve to illustrate the same arguments. This is discussed more fully at the end of this chapter.

By ethnicity, a rather less emotive concept than tribalism, is meant a particular kind of political culture, particular political activities and roles, particular values and meaning and objectives. Ethnicity can also be treated as an attempt at social organisation; a mechanism to categorise a heterogeneous urban population. Viewed politically, ethnicity can be analysed as collective political culture and power an activated "Primordial Consciousness" (Geertz 1963). As various ethnic groups in an African urban area jostle for positions of prestige and power, they may become organised along ethnic lines. This is, to a large extent, the etiology of the voluntary urban-based association which Kenneth Little (1965) has described in such detail. Of course these associations also have the micro (individual) function of helping the newly arrived and rather lonely migrant to find friends, support, lodging and work. On the macro level, the voluntary associations frequently are the urban arm of major national ethnic groups such as the Ibo State Union whose branches, under various names, are found in virtually every Nigerian (and many West African) town, or the Luo Union in East Africa. Such associations, particularly if they represent large national ethnic units, can and do exercise considerable influence on urban political life.

The study of political cultures in urban Africa is still in its infancy. Thus far, political scientists have devoted most of their time to the study of formal political organisations and structures which are clearly identifiable, such as political parties, the civil service and the machinery of government, the composition and functions of parliament, the use or misuse of the constitution in many areas of national life, the role of the military, and the political role of trade unions and cooperatives. Only recently has attention been paid to urban local government (Jenkins 1967) and such topics as the particular political role, which might turn out to be significant in the years ahead, of such quasi political groups as the urban-resident unemployed. Although until recently few political scientists have worked outside the towns, they have treated the urban context in which so much national political activity takes place as peripheral to the definition of the problems in their inquiry. Thus, few political scientists have recognised that the urban areas are, probably, the pace setters of change and modernisation, that they have generated a wholly new political culture, new institutions, new attitudes and new demands all of which radiate outward from them. Nor have anthropologists tried to clarify the concept and operation of urban political culture – although one might have assumed that the "cultural" component of political structure and behaviour might be of interest to them. Some anthropologists have asked themselves the question: what might be the relationship between various types of rural-based political systems and their suitability and operation in an urban context? Thus Aidan Southall (1956) suggested that, in East Africa at least, segmentary political systems seem to produce urban ethnic associations more readily than centralised and hierarchically organised systems. This proposition has not yet been tested very widely although when applied to Nigeria it is true that the Ibo are far more effectively organised outside their homeland than the Yoruba who are a more centralised group. We also know that each urban ethnic association is differently organised and seeks different political and socio-economic objectives. The Efik in Calabar use their association to help members obtain high status jobs, while the Ibo urban associations encourage their members to aggressively compete at all levels of the job market (Henderson 1966; Morrill 1963.) Because they have been extremely successful competitors, they command considerable political influence in many areas of urban life.

Yet another approach to the study of political life in towns might be to ask whether a political culture emerges around these ethnic associations or whether migrancy *qua* migrancy, and migrants *qua* migrants, are not the important variables for analysis so as to learn how, in extremely heterogeneous urban situations, a political culture comes into being. Here we are asking an extremely important question which is central to all institutional arrangements; how significant are cultural antecedents in the restructuring of institutions, behaviour and ideology induced by change and modernisation? The answer to this question is vital for anthropology and its future relation to other social sciences. It is therefore important that the urban anthropologist finds out why there appear to be differences between the political culture of the migrant and those indigenous to the town. There are many modes of migrant adaptation to and participation in urban life versus the modes adopted by the indigenes which appear to be more closely related to their numerical size, the economic positions which they occupy and the political dominance they have achieved. While the cultural background of either group might break through in certain contexts, how events and situations are handled might be more closely determined by individual characteristics, group relations and the fortuitous in urban situations. While different styles of life, social, economic or political, might initially be related more closely to ethnicity, continued urban residence results in a progressive incorporation of the urbanite into a non-ethnic urban system which is uniquely different from the ethnic background of either migrant or indigene.

This change from migrant to urbanite is in part facilitated by economic opportunity and political action. Factionalism and discontent give rise to a competitive political situation which generates new leadership and further political action. The situation discussed by Epstein illustrates this point.

While these are conceptual and theoretical considerations, we must not overlook those aspects of the urban political order which are more clearly distinct from political life and institutions in the rural area. First, it is in the cities that the national government is most active. Legislation is written and debated in the city, the political parties have their headquarters there as do the newspapers and the other modern media of communication which play a vital part in the new political culture. Second, the towns are probably the most influential centers in the political socialisation of the population. Those who have not lived in the towns are usually not considered to be politically sophisticated, they are observers of the new political scene rather than participants who use the new order for their personal advantage. Third, the cities and town link, politically, the district, the region and the nation state to the international community of nations. Visitors from foreign countries visit African capitals and African leaders actively participate in world diplomacy. Fourth, most African urbanites are now very much aware of the manifestations and instruments of political power as one military coup follows another; and invariably this means that armoured cars and tanks rumble through the streets of the towns rather than the countryside. Thus Africans are beginning to understand that the exercise of power is not only restricted to the party politician. How power is obtained, maintained and enforced, springs from intense competition between various groups. As modernisation makes deeper inroads into African society, this competition will become more severe, and hence, the political order will become more complex. The rural areas are only gradually being drawn into this new complexity; for example, when the rural population is called upon to vote.

In an earlier section we spoke of new "ascending interest groups" coming into being and cited the urban poor and the unemployed as examples. Whether these interest groups, which reflect the growing segmentation of African urban society, will be formally organised and assume a militant political posture remains to be seen. Joan Nelson (1970) who studied the urban poor in (primarily) Latin America and asks the question: The Urban Poor: Disruption or Political Integration in Third World Cities?, suggests that:

. . . contrary to widespread speculation by both foreign observers and elites in the countries concerned, neither new migrants nor the urban poor are likely to play a direct destabilizing role. Indeed, historical experience in industrialized nations suggests that the urban poor are not likely to play a significant political role at all. However, there are major demographic, economic, and political contrasts between today's developing nations and Europe and North America in the late nineteenth and early twentieth centuries. The differences in context make it possible that the urban poor of Latin America, North Africa, and Asia may come to take a more active part in municipal and national politics than did their historical counterparts. (p. 394)

It is, we believe, too early to tell what the exact scenario will be in the years ahead. There can be little political activism by the urban poor while their political socialisation is still in its infancy. But there is also much evidence that their activism is increasing. The evidence comes from both Lagos and Nairobi (Gutkind 1967) where the urban poor have made frequent attempts to politically organise themselves in associations of unemployed. Having done so, they have marched to the offices of various ministers and demanded to see them. It is true that many of these associations have limited staying power, but the reasons for this are themselves an indication that their potential political power is respected and feared. The policy seems to be to request the police to watch the activities of the leaders of the unemployed, to watch politicians who establish contacts with these leaders (as Oginga Odinga in Kenya attempted to do) and to break up their meetings because their "message" might fall on "unsophisticated" ears. At times, however, their political activism is clearly highly militant as Dorothy Nelkin (1967) notes in her article on "The Economic and Social Setting of Military Take-overs in Africa," in which she reports that the overthrow of President Fulbert Youlou of Congo, Brazzaville, in August 1963, seems to have been actively supported by a coalition of unemployed, urban youth generally and the trade unions. However, Joan Nelson has the support of Myron Weiner (1967) who, writing about the migrants (of whom a large number are unemployed) in Calcutta concluded that:

... there is neither a logical nor empirical reason to assume that migrants to cities are more prone to support extremist political groups or to oppose the government than are settled residents and many reasons to expect just the reverse. *To be discontent with the city, one often has to be integrated into it.* [Emphasis added] Moreover, the agency which socializes the rural migrant to city life – the local political party, for example, or some other political or social welfare organization – may reduce the disorganization which we associate with political violence and political extremism. Perhaps the only sure conclusion that our data allow is that urban life does not automatically breed discontent among rural migrants. (p. 49-50)

However, Weiner also adds an important caveat:

It would be misleading to conclude from these findings that nothing in the rapid influx of rural migrants to an urban area need make the urban area more violent or more a centre of extremist political behaviour. For one thing, as the flow of migrants increases, typically there is a deterioration of services and a decrease in job opportunities for the residents, thereby increasing the dissatisfaction of the residents. And for another, as migration increases, the absolute number of residents similarly increasing as migrants settle into the city, bring their families, or marry local residents. (p. 50)

Whether the distinction which Weiner makes between residents and migrants can be as clearly applied to African towns is open to question. For it is pointless to make this sharp distinction and at the same time conclude that "cities in developing areas with a high urbanisation are characterised by violence and extremist political movements." Surely our observations have told us that when violence does break out it involves many different segments of the urban population, each participating for their own specific ends, or collectively as a coalition of the oppressed and dissatisfied.

However, in a previous quotation from Weiner, we gave emphasis to the following sentence: "To be discontent with the city, one often has to be integrated into it." It has been our view in this monograph that when a migrant comes to the town he cannot fail but to be integrated into the urban system. We suggested a number of reasons for this. To be sure, there is great variation as some migrants (as well as residents) will have achieved a greater degree of integration than others. Furthermore, the migrant (as the resident) will be more integrated in some structures than others and will respond more effectively (as an urbanite) to some situations than to others. But this raises topics for future research by students of urban Africa.

The political dimensions of African urban life must, we believe, be documented and analysed at two levels, i.e., at the macro and the micro level. At the macro level the major urban area is the seat of the national government, the political party (or parties) and the politicians, alongside the municipal government and its politicians. All this brings the urbanite close, if not close enough, to the new political forces which compete for his support and loyalty while determining his place in the political, economic and social order. While the ruralite is further removed from contemporary political activity, the urbanite, even though he might not be an active participant in the political process, receives his political socialisation by watching and listening. While the majority of the new migrants may not be able to express clearly their political orientation, they usually know what they dislike and what stands in their way of getting employment. The skill with which they manipulate their kin and their political friends gives the lie to their alleged political naivety. In short, active or inactive politically, being an urbanite in Africa, or for that matter elsewhere, is probably the best political socialisation arena in the low income countries.

Of course much of our analysis of what constitutes political behaviour is related to our own ideological postures. If we take a particular Marxist view we ought to come to the conclusion that the towns in Africa are seething and heaving with economic and political discontent. While we might wish this to be so, the conditions do not support, thus far, such a conclusion. To apply Marxist analysis would lead us to assume that the masses of the urban population, workers and unemployed, in cooperation with the exploited farmers, are not only politically sophisticated but also politically active. This is clearly not so – at least not yet. What we can say is this. Many of the consequences associated with "overurbanisation" are rapidly developing in African towns, a condition which Philip M. Hauser (1963 : 203) has defined as whereby "larger proportions of . . . (a country's) population live in urban places than their degree of economic development justifies." When this condition arises, as it has in many Third World nations (Sovani 1964), social and economic circumstances create extremely difficult and frustrating conditions for the urbanite. Not only do a vast number of people compete, aggressively, for a very limited number of jobs, but what is equally serious is that basic services for the population are so overtaxed that they may break down completely.

What we are suggesting here is simple. As economic and environmental conditions in the urban areas deteriorate, the masses of the disadvantaged population become more susceptible to political socialisation and, in time, take up militant postures and actions. But, as we have learned from isolated incidents in Africa, a high degree of political sophistication is not a pre-requisite to an awareness that "the system" is not serving the most fundamental needs (Nelkin 1967). From that perspective, a Marxist analysis has relevance to the African urban situation because there is no reason to believe that environmental and economic conditions will substantially improve or that political awareness will decline.

What information we have at the moment on the political culture of the towns, and the events we have been able to observe, does not allow us to conclude that the towns are on the verge of a political explosion. But we must not draw our data from too restricted a field. The towns constitute only a very small segment, albeit an important one, of the African population as a whole. It is just as possible that considerable political agitation will flow from the rural areas and spill over to the towns where, no doubt, demands would fall on open ears. The experience of Algeria, while particular in certain respects, is a case in point. Economic conditions are no better, indeed they are often worse in the rural areas, as farmers scratch the feeble soil and toil to make a living. Indeed the fact that Africa's economy is deeply embedded in agriculture makes the continent uniquely susceptible to economic fluctuations – at least the cash crop sector is highly exposed. It is not unreasonable to suggest that the subsistence farmer too will one day translate his struggles into those actions which he feels will achieve for him a more viable existence. Under such circumstances the urban population might well make common cause with the farmers.

Thus the political dimensions of African urbanism ought to be studied in a much broader context.

6. *Family Life*

A good many students of Africa have suggested that the family is the core institution of African society. If this is so, it is likely to be a sensitive barometer of whatever changes have occurred in Africa. There, as elsewhere, it is the most basic unit of social organisation although, unlike its counterpart in industrial Western society, its membership is not restricted to husband, wife and children· It is characteristic of this basic unit to be part of a larger extended family which was central to the social organisation and social structure of African society in the past – today its composition and functions are changing. This does not suggest that it is of lesser significance, but it is important for us to recognise what the changes are and why they have taken place.

The normative structure of marriage and family life spills over into many other organisational and institutional features. Thus marriage involves far more directly the families of the bride and the groom than in our own culture. While the two individuals are central to the marriage, a large number of kin on either side become involved in the rearrangement of social relationships which follow. Complex rules of exogamy determine who may marry whom. The marriage of two people encompasses new social contacts and economic and political relations between such groups as segments, lineages and clans. This "intrusion" of one group into the affairs of another and being strangers to each other, calls for a careful regulation of the new ties being established. It is, therefore, not unusual for conflict to arise between different lineages and subgroups. However, such conduct is handled by means of a wide variety of ceremonial and ritual activities designed to give symbolic expression to the new relationship.

In a patrilineal and patrilocal system the bride moves to the home of her husband and becomes a member of her father-in-law's household. She is a "stranger" in their midst, a situation which has to be regularised. Furthermore, to make the break even more complete at the time, the children born to this marriage "belong" to the husband's group. In a symbolic manner, the kin group of the bride continues to view with some hostility members of the lineage and the clan which has "adopted" the bride.

In a matrilineal and matrilocal system the arrangements are, of course, rather different. Here the groom moves to the home of his bride's kin group. The children born of the marriage belong to this group while the groom's brother-in-law may exercise considerable authority over his sister's children. Frequently little, perhaps no, bridewealth is passed. The stability of marriage, as a consequence, is sometimes rather brittle and high divorce rates are not unusual.

In Africa the family is the basic unit of production and consumption. Its activities, in the rural area, are closely linked to the agricultural cycle. All its basic needs are met through its own productive efforts. The land the family farms is its major anchorage. Its younger members receive their education and training primarily within the family. In patrilineal societies in particular, the authority of the older man was respected but each member of the extended family occupied a clearly defined rank in the socio-economic and political order. The bond which held members of the extended family together were their strictly allocated duties, reciprocity of mutual aid and support, responsibilities and rewards which gave each individual the satisfaction he sought and the knowledge that should dependency overtake him he would not be cast out. However, family life was no more perfect then as now. There were tensions and joys, those who conformed to the norms of the good family and communal life and those who were the "exceptions." As families everywhere, they suffered disturbance through death, misfortune, disease, breaches of morality and the like. No doubt conceptions of what constituted good family relationships varied. The great gap between the ideal and the real is not unique to secular urban existence. Indeed, it has recently been suggested that the system of (traditional) family relations is far more flexible in regard to social change and modernisation than we had thought possible. Rather than the extended family being an impediment to social transformation, it seems to adapt itself readily enough to changing economic circumstances. This is an approach which still needs much further testing in the field. Some (traditional) family systems may not adapt as effectively as others. A new emphasis on individual achievement may play havoc with the role of mutual aid and reciprocity. This may depend on how individuals perceive their opportunities and whether their newly adopted, or sought after, style of life is compatible with the norms, the objectives and activities of the past. David McClelland (1961 : 403-404) has argued forcefully that:

The family is the social nucleus of the society, the main carrier of the basic motives and values of the culture. And it may be as hard to alter it intentionally as it was to crack the nucleus of the atom.

Individual achievement, by virtue of this argument, is invariably frustrated by the "iron" bonds of family and kinship. A good deal of contemporary development policy is based on this premise and hence governments try to break down those traditions they consider an impediment to progress. For progress is seen as basically motivated by individual initiative and desire.

These assumptions interpret family and kinship systems as non-dynamic and stagnant institutions characteristic of the isolated, custom bound rural society which is fearful of change, conformist in character and emphasises a style of life which crushes individual self-expression. While the non-perceptive observer sees these as the major attributes, more penetrating research often reveals very different circumstances. Peter Marris (1968 : 20) who is a most perceptive observer, seems to have given the lie to these assumptions. He writes:

I believe that the most widely accepted answer is probably mistaken. Where patterns of family life in contemporary Africa seem to inhibit the exploitation of economic opportunities, it may not be because of attachment to an outworn tradition, but because these patterns offer the greater security. Family structure seems more typically to reflect a realistic calculation of economic advantage, than to sustain irrational inhibitions; and essentially the same structure can sometimes accommodate very divergent attitudes towards individualistic ambition.

This introduces the essential dynamic in the discussion. Where the extended family has contracted, and where we see the gradual development of a nuclear conjugal unit based on the Western model, the reason is that a smaller unit is more within the context of the present economic order which currently prevails. But where this has not taken place, the explanation will be just as simple: there is opportunity and security in adapting the structures of the past to suit contemporary conditions. Where individuals place ability, merit and enterprise before ties of blood and marriage, they do so without totally rejecting those reciprocal responsibilities which were so important in the past. We could sum up the argument by going just one step further. Traditional modes of conduct, in family and kin relations, are suitable in a traditional context (although we must state once again that societies are never static), but in the context of modernisation new patterns of thought and behaviour arise in response to change. This response may take many different forms, it might even mean that a people willing but unable to compete will draw in upon itself, reject the "modern" world and return to the ways of the past. In other cases a new strategy is developed, a new style of life emerges, and people learn to handle contemporary situations in a contemporary manner. From that point of view the family in social change is probably one of the most sensitive indicators of the great transformation from rural to urban life.

Having given a very brief sketch of some major characteristics of African family organisation and marriage, we must now take a look at family and marriage in the urban context.

Perhaps no other aspect of African urban studies has been as subject to moralising as the study of the urban family. This is frequently revealed in discussions on the wide range of "unions" which can be detected, the patterns of courtship, the negative consequences resulting from the introduction of the idea of "romantic love" and, generally, when the matter of family and marriage "stability" is being analysed. It would be most rewarding if the same "concern" were being shown for the other complex problems which African people face at the moment. The fact is that the African family, and the institution of marriage, is "alive, healthy, and in good order" as a high ranking Canon of the Church in Nigeria informed the writer just two years ago. Of course the family is changing, of this there is no doubt. Yet it is far too early to say what the consequences will be. Nor is there any doubt that some of these changes are for the good and some for the worse. While it is now possible to detect the gradual emergence of certain directions of change, they have not yet crystallised into clear patterns which allow us to generalise and predict. Like so many other aspects of urban life in Africa, family organisation and marriage must not be abstracted from the totality of changes which are taking place in Africa as a whole, in particular nations, in particular regions, and particular towns. If indeed the family is central to all societal organisation then changes taking place in economic, political and religious institutions will be clearly reflected in family life. While this raises rather complex theoretical issues, for the time being it should guide our discussion.

Changes in family and marriage must be studied against the background of who migrates and why; who stays in the town and who circulates back and forth between rural and urban areas; what are the employment opportunities in the town; what are the demands made by agricultural activities on women left behind in the rural areas; what is the ratio between men and women in the town; what were, or are, the colonial policies which had a bearing on whether or not families could or would settle in the town; what kind of services are available in the town, i.e. housing, and what is, or was, the wage structure? No doubt many other criteria should be added, but each one mentioned above will have some bearing on the structure of marriage and family life and on the perceptions held by individuals about an aspect of life which is personal and private. Space simply does not allow us to deal with each one of these influences.

Despite the variations which exist, the impact of certain changes have produced some common characteristics. Perhaps one of the most fundamental changes is that the African family, as the family in Western society, has lost some of its "traditional" functions while it has taken on new ones, i.e. it may have dropped some ritual and ceremonial functions and taken on new economic ones. Also, it is possible that the individual is not as closely affiliated to his family, both nuclear and extended, as in the past. The size of the extended family, in particular, has probably somewhat contracted. But here we ought to say that while this might well be so, many occasions remain when the members of an extended family are brought together to celebrate a birth, a marriage, or mourn a death. The aid and support that members of the family give each other in the rural area has to some extent been replaced by relationships with, and associations based on, non-kin. This is, of course, particularly true in the urban area where ethnic, political, social and cultural associations take on some of the functions that the individual at one time received from his family. Clearly, this is more significant when a migrant comes alone rather than when he brings his family. Finally the role of particular members of the family is probably changing to allow for greater individualism, cooperation and equality between the sexes and between age groups. Most of these changes are structural and hence they are easier to document; more subtle changes are in individual perceptions, in identity, in role performance, in achievements and motivation, in conflict and cooperation, in the rationale of a personal style of life as this affects the other members of the family, in the rejection of certain norms and the adoption of new ones, and in the degree of aggressiveness with which new values are sought and new ways of behaviour adopted.

All these criteria noted in the last two paragraphs need to be taken into account. Perhaps nothing shapes African urban marriage and family life more directly than the demographic features of the town and the composition of the population. Thus, as we indicated earlier, the towns attract primarily young and unmarried males, with the result that the ratio between men and women is often very unbalanced (although this is changing rather rapidly now). It requires very little imagination to suggest two consequences. First, there is little opportunity for young men to find a spouse in the town. This alone sends many migrants back to the rural areas to find a wife. Second, if few women are resident in the town it is not unreasonable to suggest that they might be rather particular women, themselves young and unattached, who have recognised the unique position they occupy. They capitalise on this in two ways: either they circulate rather freely among men or they make unions of short duration. What we must not forget is that much of the great transformation which is taking place is seen clearly in the gradual emancipation of women. Many of the men who come to work in the town have no intention of marrying a "town woman", a designation frequently heard and offered with some opprobrium. But it is not merely the often acute shortage of women which drives men to seek a spouse in the rural areas. Many of the migrants are under twenty-five years of age and are not yet prepared nor financially able to settle down.

Second, we must look to the composition of the population to understand the nature of marriage and family life. We have indicated that the population is ethnically, and hence culturally and linguistically, extremely heterogeneous although one dominant ethnic group may comprise 40% to 60% of an African urban population. Although some ethnic groups may have a more balanced ratio between men and women, this does not necessarily attract men of other ethnic groups to any "surplus" of women who might exist. With other words, urban Africans are as ethnocentric in their choice of marriage partners as we are. If you are a Jew the chances are better than fifty-fifty that you will marry a Jew and if you are a Kikuyu the chances are even better that you will look for a Kikuyu spouse· Thus from this point of view, too, the town is not the most suitable and attractive place to conceive a marriage.

Having set out what we need to take into account, and why, and some of the negative features which act as a deterrent to urban marriage, the fact remains that not only do some Africans find their marriage partners in the town, but they settle there and raise a family. We need therefore to ask what kinds of unions are contracted, and why, and what kinds of families are established.

In regard to the first question we need to distinguish between unions made according to "native law and custom", unions based on Western models (church weddings or a civil marriage) and extra-legal unions. Those who are married according to "tradition" may either do so on returning to their natal community or attempt to do, as well as possible, in the town. The use of the word attempt is deliberate because close analysis of how the courtship was conducted, and how carefully the traditional marriage procedures were followed, is likely to reveal considerable departure from the norm. This is due either to a matter of choice, and as such becomes a measure of change, or to genuine difficulties which are difficult to overcome in a town having in mind that the partners did as much as possible to follow the prescribed rules. Distance might keep some kin away, or the lack of privacy in the town might prevent extensive festivities which often go on for a day or two. It is perhaps for these reasons that many young couples, who prefer to be married according to native law and custom, will return to the rural areas and show their respect for tradition and for the members of the two kin groups who are temporarily brought into close contact. The choice of this kind of marriage may also be determined by a reluctance to follow a monogamous relationship as, in some cases, a marriage in customary terms will allow a man to have more than one wife. In this way one wife can look after his rural home and land and another can cook for him and look after his urban home. Such an arrangement, which is not uncommon, points to the importance of considering various economic determinants to help explain various arrangements. New economic opportunities may either reduce or increase dependence on kin and as such will determine the nature of household organisation.

Those urban Africans who do not elect to marry according to customary rules do so for a wide variety of reasons such as that such marriages are "difficult", "not suitable", "too costly", or "not possible in town." Others cite new economic demands made by women, or "educated" people have "modern" marriages and customary unions "involve too many people and hence you are not free to make your own decisions." Whatever the reasons, fewer people contract such marriages in the town and many of those who find their spouse in the rural areas, but return to the town, seem to modify customary marriage procedures quite considerably. Relatively little is known about the stability of customary unions versus marriages based on civil law. While statistical measurements might hide more than they reveal, observations may be made which apply to all types of unions.

In the first case, the stability of a union in an African town depends on as many circumstances and conditions as in any society. Second, the rural-urban variable may have very little bearing on this stability. Customary unions do not assure greater or lesser stability. However, when further data has been collected it might reveal that the normative system which supports such unions is difficult to fit into changing conditions. Here we need to know a lot more about how matrilineal and patrilineal structures can be, and are, modified under changing and in particular urban conditions (Mitchell 1969). While the literature on marriage and life in urban Africa is now quite considerable, information on this topic is still scanty and inconclusive. It has been suggested that people with a matrilineal background have less stable urban unions than those urbanites with a patrilineal background. Much of course depends on the structural position occupied by the children of the union and on the education received by, and the expectations of, both partners to the union. While there might be certain common characteristics which determine these expectations, they tend to be ideosyncratic in nature. Prediction, therefore, is extremely difficult. In view of this, measures which are designed to analyse and predict stability tend to be superficial as they simply cannot take into account the large number of variables which must be considered. Customary unions are, perhaps, more attractive to those who have maintained a rural anchorage, who have economic interests in these areas, and those who are first generation urbanites deeming customary procedures still important. Much too depends on the history of the urban area itself. Thus, in Ibadan, which is a long established urban community, customary marriages and procedures are still fairly common and considered important (Lloyd 1967), presumably because much of the normative system of Yoruba life is still meaningful in this rather unusual town. Thus Ibadanites find marriage partners largely within the town community and as such cannot as effectively "escape" (as one young man explained) from the watchful influence of kin. In newer towns, with lesser roots, the individual is in a better situation to determine for himself what type of marriage is most suitable and most desirable. It is, perhaps, this element of freedom of choice which leads us naturally to some comments about the remaining types of unions.

First we must treat those unions based on Western, imported models. Today, church weddings are socially important to a large number of urbanites. To many people they are a mark of progress, of education and achievement. Indeed, it is not unusual for those who have had a customary union for many years with one woman to have a second church marriage with their children and perhaps their grandchildren actively participating. These solemn church marriages may incorporate a large number of traditional elements, particularly in the festivities which follow the actual wedding ceremony. While the rich will follow procedures based almost wholly on Western models, the poor may join with others so that three or four couples can be married together and share the costs and fees paid to the minister who officiates. Church marriages involve such matters as best men, bridesmaids, flower and ring girls, trainbearers and photographers, confetti, and perhaps a rented car to take the couples to a reception and festivities. Particular importance might be attached to inviting members of the press so that a picture of the event will appear in the local paper. Clearly, as church rules differ so does the nature of the ceremonies, some churches being more willing to make concessions to special wishes, perhaps reflecting a traditional element, than others.

Modern wedding ceremonies and marriages are treated as one aspect, indeed an important one, of the person's education, occupation and social position in the community. To the male such a wedding is an acknowledgement that he has married a woman according to his status. While his wife may not be as educated, she is worthy of a "showy" wedding not being an illiterate country girl or an "urban woman." But perhaps more important, monogamous weddings are treated as more suitable in the total context of upward social and economic mobility.

Western models of marriage are merely one aspect of the mosaic of a modern man who reflects all the changes taking place in the society of which he is a member. Such marriages are, therefore, the base of the new nuclear family and the desire and obligation by the couple to create a "modern" family and do the best they can for their children. This type of union is considered to be particularly suitable in the context of change and modernisation, particularly as these changes are so clear and so compelling in town life. Without hindrance, and perhaps with welcome support at times, husband and wife can construct for themselves the kind of life they wish to lead. However, in the process they must not cut themselves off completely or too successfully from the vast number of kin who are usually determined to press demands of aid and hospitality. There is, therefore, a clear tendency for the couple to withdraw from their obligations to the larger kin group. How each couple responds to these demands, what demands they accept and what they reject, ought to become an important aspect of research into African urban family life. Yet, we must not give the impression that when a couple settles down to shape its own life the break with kin is radical or final. Family life must be seen in the context of the urban totality. Much depends on the background of the partners to the marriage, and yet more depends on the situational context be it personal, ethnic, financial, occupational, educational or the unpredictable circumstance which invariably arises.

Should the situation demand it, the couple will fall back on support from kin members; should the interference by them be too demanding, the couple may move to another town or find other ways to stop the interference. The social field of relations and contacts will, therefore, vary considerably. Much too will depend on whether the couple live in their own home and enjoy some privacy or whether they share their residence with others in the same house – perhaps the most common pattern. Still further, we need to take into account the ethnic background of the couple (particularly if it is an inter-ethnic marriage) and the distance they are away from home, as well as such other matters as the educational background of the wife and whether she is working or not.

Clearly the factors of wealth and social class will be manifested strongly in the kind of partner selected, the investment in the wedding and related arrangements, and in the way the new couple sets up housekeeping. Among the elites lavish weddings are important events involving much showiness – such affairs are more a reflection of the status and wealth of the families involved rather than the couple. Indeed, it is for this reason, as in some Western circles, that some African couples, usually those highly Westernised and with professional training, prefer to have a non-church civil ceremony. But this is restricted to a very small number of couples. Lavish weddings, particularly those of public personalities, are extensively reported and commented upon. Thus recently, the marriage of a Senior Commander in the Federal Military Government of Nigeria, during the Biafran-Nigerian conflict, drew much comment as the wedding took place in lavish style (with food-laden tables at the reception) in a newly liberated town while a few miles away starvation was rife. (*West Africa* 1970 : 122). The marriage of the present Head of State,

General Y. Gowon, in Lagos, however, drew much favourable public comment.

Poorer people aspire to church weddings and will make financial sacrifices to achieve them. To many it is the first display of their achievements and status, and to many, the last. The festivities are deadly earnest, often somewhat Victorian in character, but more relaxed and jovial after the formal ceremony. Parents who have been married in a church ceremony will almost certainly encourage their children to do the same, although their wedding will be even more Westernised than their own. The immediate urban community, the neighbourhood in which the parents or the couple live, old and new friends, and a not inconsequential number of onlookers, become involved in the festivities.

Whether or not the man is married in the town, or whether he brings his wife to live in the town, the effect seems to be that he puts down his roots more deeply in the urban community. To have regular employment is now more important than ever, and the need for good medical services and schooling for children, tend to make more of an urbanite of the man. Much of his effort is now devoted to establishing a more stable, and perhaps more attractive, home which he might find at a local housing estate. Young married men who reside in the town are, it seems, rather conscious of their responsibilities as the following comment, made by Oloyo a skilled Yoruba master carpenter who had always had regular employment in Lagos and had lived in the town for seven years, indicates:

When I was married, last year (1965), I was not sure that I could support my wife but I wanted to get married. But now I find that we are quite happy because my wife is trading in the market selling rice and salt. She and I are working very hard and I know that when she will have a child my responsibilities will be greater. But I am very lucky to work, good work. I have never been without work because I have had good training.

... I am now glad that I am living in Lagos because a married man has a lot of responsibilities. My wife is making her own money but I must help her to buy food and pay the rent. ... She also wants a lot of dresses and that is very expensive.

... I am also living here because we need to be near a good hospital and later I am thinking about a school for the children. You know, our schools in the villages are not very good. But in Lagos the schools are large and many nice teachers from England and America teach there. I was once working in a school doing some building and made friends with Mr. S. from England. ...He was a nice person and perhaps my children can go to that school when I have some children.

But Oloyo also indicated on many occasions that married life in the town was not all roses and honey. He thought:

When you are married and live in the village you know that your wife has friends and that people are kind to her. ...But in the town there are so many troubles (he explained that he meant "temptations") and that gives me no sleep. I trust my wife but there are so many bad people in Lagos and all they look for is money, drink and women.

My neighbour he was married but his wife went off with another man who gave her a baby so now his first children are living with her mother. I do not think that this is good and the way it should be.

...Oh yea, I know that some married men play with other women and I think that is not right. ...I do not do that because I have just married. (Gutkind 1966)

As we have said before, what information we have at the moment does not allow us to conclude that church marriages are better, more stable, than either customary or other unions. It is, of course, a little more difficult for a church marriage to be dissolved. The cost of obtaining a divorce is great, and knowledge about the ins and outs of the law is not well known. Like anywhere else, the stability of African urban church marriages depends on a vast variety of personal and institutional variables. To detect the relevant ones, isolate them and then see their relationship one with another is far more important than a mere headcount, a comparison of one kind of marriage with another. Perhaps a church marriage is more difficult to maintain for more or less the same reasons as in other societies. The state of monogamy is not an easy one to follow; the fluid nature of much of life in the urban area, the wish to explore new patterns of life and the ever nagging financial worries all contribute to normal tensions which are associated with marriage anywhere. On the other hand, it is possible that church marriages do lead to more lasting relationships simply because they are church marriages. It is too hard to tell because so much of our research is narrowly quantitative. We are still badly in need of a wide range of family case studies. At present we barely know what are the parameters of marital patterns or premarital relations.

Anecdotal accounts, as presented by Southall and Gutkind (1957 : 66-91, 153-182) make exciting reading but lack analytical depth – a charge which can be laid to much writing. The most substantial publication, which pays relatively little attention to urban life, is the lengthy contribution by L. P. Mair in a *Survey of African Marriage and Family Life* (1953) and is, inevitably, dated. Since then there has been a considerable outpouring of generalisations, but few case studies of marriage and the family in towns, and a considerable amount of statistical material which has been (crudely) abstracted from the much broader context in which these major events in life take place. Thus we have studies by Aldous (1962), Barnes (1951), Caldwell (1966), Clignet (1966), Colson (1962), one of the more perceptive studies, Gutkind (1962 and 1966), Gamble (1963), Harries-Jones (1964), Izzett (1961), Jahoda (1958 and 1959), Marris (1961), Parkin (1966), Pauw (1963), Du Sacre-Coeur (1962), Sofoluwe (1965), Powdermaker (1962), Okediji and Okediji (1966). This list is by no means exhaustive; additional material will be found in virtually every study on African urban life.

Finally, we must turn to extra-legal unions. It is these rather than either the customary or the church unions which impress the observer as being the dominant pattern in towns. The range of possible arrangements is enormous and vary from one individual to another. It is, therefore, exceedingly difficult to detect many common characteristics which would allow us to generalise about them.

The actual nature of the union, the exact structure it takes, is perhaps less significant for us than the reasons why individuals engage in such unions – although the structure itself might tell us something about attitudes to marriage and family life and more generally about many features of urban life. But a mere structural analysis will lead to some of the shortcomings pointed out earlier.

Because so many urban Africans are young and unskilled males, they express an unwillingness to meet the demands of marriage and family. At the same time they frequently express a need for a partner who will cook for them, wash their clothes and offer a special kind of companionship – a feminine, sexual relationship. To this we must add that many migrants are in the very early stages of establishing themselves in the urban area and this introduces a considerable measure of uncertainty. This uncertainty seems to be translated into a kind of exploration to find out what urban life has to offer. Thus, in Kampala, Uganda, it was not uncommon for young Africans to say that they "were trying out" a wife. And in Nairobi a young Luo, who had been resident in the city for two years and had finally decided to live with a girl, commented in a similar vein:

I am now living with a woman who cooks for me and watches my place. ... For a long time I was living alone and then I was living with four other Luo men who were also working in Nairobi. But we often had fights when one of them got drunk, so I moved away.

I then met a girl in the market whom I liked. She agreed to live with me and cook my food. So I managed to find another place which is big enough for both of us.

No, I have not married her in the best way. I am too young and do not have the money to pay for a proper wife. I will not be married for a long time and I will never marry a woman from Nairobi. I will go back to find a wife and then perhaps bring her to Nairobi.

Many young men do what I do. It is the only good thing to do because you must have somebody to cook and wash and to be your friend. (Gutkind, 1966)

These sentiments, which are not uncommon, do indicate a reluctance to settle into an urban marriage. Urban circumstances are such that few men give very high priority to finding a permanent spouse. Besides, there is generally a shortage of women so that the few who are available gain more from frequently "circulating" among men than making any kind of final commitment. Not only is housing very scarce, but privacy is even more so. The whole social and inter-personal climate of the town is such that men and women alike value the freedom which allows them to construct their lives as they wish. Relationships are such that conflict and suspicions are easily generated much of the time. Some young men feel strongly that urban marriages are destined to fail because "when the cat is away, the mice will play," which reflects nicely the distrust which seems to govern male/female relations in the urban context. In addition, men and women alike feel that the urban environment is inimical both to the rearing of children and to strong family ties. The agony involved making ends meet, the demands from relatives and friends, the insecurity of employment and the strong desire for further achievement all contribute to the view that short-run relations might have

more to offer, at the time, than more permanent responsibilities. As a system,
despite its raw edges, it works quite well because such temporary unions meet
both personal needs and the particular circumstances which all migrants find
themselves in.

These "free" unions range from very short duration to reasonably stable
and long-term relations, the latter often becoming a normal family life. Indeed, in the Kampala study, conducted between 1953 and 1955, it was found
that many of these "free" unions enjoyed a remarkable stability and duration and were often indistinguishable from customary or church-contracted
unions (Southall and Gutkind 1957). Those of short duration, usually contracted in beer bars, bus parks, markets, or various kinds of clubs, clearly
shade into commercial relations, although these too may last a fair length of
time, such as a month or two, depending on what the woman, rather than
what the man, can get out of them, i.e. a temporary home, clothing and
spending money. While men, rather than women, will discuss these affairs in
anger and generalise their experiences to include all town women, in the end
they accept these temporary and rather exploitative relations.

Yakubo and Mukasa were sitting in a beer bar in Mulago, a peri-urban
area of Kampala, and they were chatting about the favourite subject of
those who frequent these bars: women and drink.

Mary is a bad woman, said Mukasa, because she took all my money last week and then run
away. I gave her dresses and good food but when I came home from my work I found that
she had stolen all my property. . . . I went to complain to the police and asked them to help
me find her. But they told me to go away.

Why do you trust women, asked Yakubo, when you know that all the women here are all
the same? I have lived here a long time, in that house over there, and I know that a woman
will play with you and like your money but then run away when she goes to another man.

Yes, said Erifaso, who had been listening to the conversation, we are all fools. We never
learn. Women should not be allowed to rest in the town because they are just like a wild
animal.

But you know my friend that we cannot do without women. Can you and you and you? I
know I can't. So our life is just like the railway because we are all pushing and moving
about. (Gutkind 1953)

It should not be assumed, however, that temporary unions are an indication of the general state of affairs of marriage and family life – that a progression is involved from stability to instability or vice versa. The nature of these unions reflect far more than a response to urban conditions. Particular urban patterns merely reflect changes in these institutions which commenced years before in the rural areas, and which now find new and free expression in the towns. Nor must it be assumed that these unions are restricted to the masses of the urban poor. Non-customary and non-church contracted unions will be found at all levels of urban society. Indeed, it is not unusual for the urban poor to discuss the pre-marital and the extra-marital activities of the elites. This is clear from the following conversation which was recorded in a bus park in Freetown, Sierra Leone:

I know more about all the playing about that Chief M. is doing than anybody else ... I will tell you what he is doing. He goes to bed every night with a different woman. Sometimes she will stay with him for two days or three but then he is hunting again over the top of the hill where all the rich people live. Last week I saw Mrs. A. come out of his house late in the evening and I know that she went home to her real lover Mr. S. who comes from **Botown.**

Yes I know. If you have money you can run for women as much as you like. But we do not have money so we must find what we can ... I know that sometimes the important people take the woman to a doctor who can get rid of the baby with medicine. (Gutkind 1966)

In a broader context these sentiments feed into the particular nature and structure of urban unions of all types. Temporary unions reflect more so than others, perhaps, the tensions between the sexes which seem to be a concomitant of change generally. Thus Southall and Gutkind (1957 : 72) wrote:

The relations between the sexes show every indication of tension. Neither men nor women are consistent in maintaining the attitudes appropriate to their usual behaviour. When it suits them to do so, they tend to invoke the values of the past, or of more traditional and stable rural conditions, in opposition to conditions which at other times they accept and exploit. Thus, many men and women live in irregular unions which leave both parties free to break off the relationship at will. Though men give women no permanent security in such unions they are none the less possessive towards their concubines and resentful of their contacts with other men. Though they often obtain their mates by persuading them to infidelity, they are annoyed that the habit, once formed, persists. Living in town, they retain the rural marriage of the idealised past as their standard. Despising town women for roaming from man to man, they give them little encouragement to form more lasting attachments. On the other hand, those women who develop insatiable appetites for sexual pleasure make harder the task of others who look for husbands to give them companionship, children and the security of some recognised marital status.

Urban unions of all kinds, therefore, appear to involve as a primary element a redefinition of roles. This is a process which brings together many aspects of change and modernisation – not least important of which is the example set by European ways, Western education and Western ideas of romantic love (Jahoda 1958, 1959), new economic opportunities and the less compelling nature of certain rules of kinship. It is, of course, almost impossible to say whether the patterns set by these free unions will become far more widespread than at present. So much will depend on the direction and the form which change will take in the years to come. What is perhaps more certain is that a system of rigid control over marriage and sexual behaviour would not by itself have much positive effect. Urban pass laws or the expulsion of all single women who are not attached to parents or guardian will not alter the situation.

At present the urban system is one which generates its own particular kind of orderly social world based on a set of norms which, while they may be understood, are frequently rejected because it also is recognised that mechanisms for their enforcement are not effective. We are not saying that urban life spells death to the stable family and ushers in a hedonistic style of life which knows no limits. Nor should we conclude that there is no order and stability, no cohesion or integration in the urban areas. If this were so we could not easily identify common patterns of social organisation and values. Rather, the urban system is one of considerable group and personal diversity, and hence of immense complexity. It is a complexity which is not just a conclusion born of research but, more realistically, it is recognised by each and every urbanite. His preferred style of life, his efforts to satisfy his sexual needs, the unions he makes and the family relations he establishes, all reflect quite consciously the recognition of this complexity, its scale and the freedom and the restrictions it imposes.

If this is an acceptable point of view, then marriage and the family are not in as unhealthy a state as some observers would have us believe (favouring such phrases as "The Erosion of the Family" – Caldwell, 1966). Change is multi-dimensional; it is rarely downhill all the way as it is rarely on and upward to better things.

7. *The Ideational World*

It is often asserted that religious beliefs, cosmology and "world view" and the institutions designed to meet the religious needs of individuals and groups change more slowly than other institutions. This might well be true in small-scale pre-industrial societies which are subjected to a rather rigid enforcement of the moral code in personal and group relations. The strong influence of a pre-secular world view produces a "scared" or "little tradition." It is an outlook on life which threads itself like a spider's web throughout society; religious leaders hold political and economic power, and political leaders may be viewed as sacred or divine. Natural calamities are explained in supernatural terms; the will of the ancestors is imposed on social organisation. The little community is the religious community. Order prevails as long as men are prepared to submit to the organising principles which determine and guide human actions and ideas. There are those who insist that the religious dimension meets a vital and primordial human need, that this need exists quite independent of complexity, culture, socio-economic and political base or the location of society. While this is clearly not a question we can treat now, the importance of religious beliefs as part of the total fabric of all societies must be taken into account.

It is also often asserted that when pre-industrial societies are drawn into the technological and modern commercial world, when machines depersonalise human relations, secular pressures invariably make deep inroads into society. It is the appearance of secularism, it is argued, which more than any other influence plays havoc with those norms which guide personal conduct, motivation and objectives. Secularism gives rise to social diversity, non-conformity and individualism. In fact, it gives rise to all that is allegedly wrong in the modern world! The subverters of a stable, integrated, and sacred moral order in society are industrialisation and urbanisation.

If there was a pre-determined relationship between urbanisation and a decaying social order, the future of mankind would indeed be very bleak. By the year 2000, it is estimated, probably ninety per cent of the population of North America will live in cities and towns, while in Ghana, where thirty per cent live in cities at present, it is estimated that some forty-eight per cent will do so in 1985, and sixty-three per cent by the year 2000.

While we cannot be seers who divine the human condition from one day to the next, it is likely that our understanding of the complexity of ideational changes is greatly increased if we take a non-moralistic position.

The ideational moral-religious order changes slowly. Why it does so is open to various interpretations. While new ideas, the product of a specialised and exclusive group – the *literati* – diffuse only slowly through all levels, segments and groupings of society, the ideational order of a small-scale society gives its members a sense of security, a sense of belonging and a feeling for the cycle of daily life. Ritual and ceremonial, the outward expression of the ideational order, regulate and give stability to daily life. New ideas and new ways of dealing with everyday affairs, particularly if these are externally imposed and if the speed of their intrusion is very rapid, tend to be looked upon with suspicion as their thrust penetrates to the furthest recesses of society. Innovation challenges convention, it is not by itself destructive of an idealised state of order and cohesion.

Most ideational changes result from a progressive complexity – population increase and social diversity, migration, contact with other cultures, conquest, conversion, education and a wide range of innovations which slowly and sometimes selectively, gradually encroach upon a society making it more diverse both structurally and ideationally. Its "world view" gradually changes, is reinterpreted, becomes perhaps more flexible or, in some cases, more rigid. When innovations can be incorporated into the ideational system of the past all is well, but where this cannot be done, only two significant alternatives exist: total rejection, which may take many forms, or a very gradual and perhaps reluctant adaptation.

Certain ideational perspectives and patterns are not suitably geared to modernisation (Bendix 1967, Eisenstadt 1969, Gusfield 1967, Rudolph and Rudolph 1967, Singer 1966). In smaller scale rural-based communities which are pre-industrial, there is great pressure for acceptance of a single belief which attaches great significance to supernaturalism, superstition, and fatalism. The view might be held that the past was stable, ordered and clear, that the future springs logically from this past and that to replace this with another can only result in uncertainty. Where the past becomes the sole guide to the future, innovation is generally rejected.

Industrialisation and urbanisation cause considerable pressures on a small scale rural-based society, both from outside and within, applied in a new or modified rationale in the ordering of its affairs, objectives, productivity, organisation and outlook. However, whatever this new outlook might be, for the time being it will combine the ideas and attitudes of the past with those of the present. The urban environment, rather than making certain ideational perspectives impossible, allows for a large measure of self-expression.

Of course we must take into consideration the profound impact of education and technology on a future-oriented outlook. While not rejecting the past, this outlook questions certain of its basic premises. This should not be seen as destructive of the past, but rather as an attempt to see the past in a more analytical manner, and to let the past be brought forward into the present when the situation might call for this.

Urban life places major emphasis on initiative and the ability of the urbanite to create for himself a social and political niche. His view of the urban world (Bascom 1963) is determined in large measure by his access to opportunity and education, by his background and adaptability. The newly arrived migrant is suddenly faced with a much larger range of alternatives and choices than was the case in the rural area. To be successful, nay to survive, he must be pragmatic in exploring opportunities and the potential of various types of entrepreneurship, friendships, membership in both formal and informal associations and groups; he must sort out competing political ideologies which seek his loyalty (each one promising him the "good life") and, above all, he must decide the degree to which, as a migrant, it is important for him to maintain ties with a way of life which he has left behind. All this is on top of finding a place to live and obtaining work. These demands are not easily handled in the context of those ideas and attitudes which were suitable for a rural style of life.

It is these decisions which place a particular ideational stamp on the African urbanite – both the migrant and urban indigene. Perhaps we can say that African urbanites, whatever their length of residence, pass through a sequence of ideational changes, from attempts to modernise tradition to a rejection of it; from a state of encapsulation to an active participation in urban life and its modernistic ideology; from a state of dominance of the past as a point of personal and collective reference to a selective borrowing from the past, each "stage" being related to a change in economic and social position.

The problems of ideational change in the context of urbanisation can perhaps best be analysed as a measure of urban involvement when we attempt to find out why the past has meaning, or why the past is rejected. We should, therefore, attempt to tackle problems of ideational change in the context of situational analysis rather than posing false dichotomies.

At least two students of urban Africa (Mayer 1969, Powdermaker 1962) have suggested that there are two basic types of urbanites – those who are willing to put down roots and treat the town as their permanent home, and those who live in the city but are not of the city. Mayer has called the former the "School People" and the latter the "Red" or "Incapsulated" while Powdermaker has referred to the non-participants as the "Intransigents." There are several other labels we might use to describe these two major groupings – which are not as mutually exclusive as it might appear. Thus we could call those who try to participate in urban life in all its totality, as the modernisers and the others as the conservatives; or we could say that the modernisers are true urbanites and the conservatives have brought the life of the peasant into the town; or we might draw a very broad distinction and say that the modernisers are the "residents" and the conservatives are the migrants, and in this way we would follow somewhat the same distinction made by Nelson (1970) and Weiner (1967.) But these distinctions are not wholly satisfactory because anyone who lives and works in an African town, whether it be of short or long duration, is clearly, in some measure, a participant. But perhaps the degree of participation varies and the *attitudes* to urban life might vary in both groups. Thus one group really wants to get involved, because they see their future as urban residents, while the other stays aloof because, *at that moment*, they are ideationally and emotionally more tied to their natal, rural, community. While the active urban participant uses every opportunity to become more deeply part of the town, his job, his friends, his political activities, his recreation, his social life and his intellectual activities, the conservatives are more cautious; they seem to reject being tied too intimately to what life in the town has to offer. Their preferred style of life has a different point of reference – a different moral order. Powdermaker (1962 : 292) makes following comment:

There are a number of hypotheses to account for the difference between the two groups: Individuals committed to the new *moral order* [emphasis added] have faith in the eventual reward from it and an ego sufficiently strong to accept the risks and anxieties which always accompany change; they have the desire for the more personal autonomy inherent in the new order and do not always think in terms of opposing polarities. Conversely, the intransigents do not have these characteristics or possess them to a much smaller degree ... My hypotheses are concerned with unconscious internationalization of values, as well as overt learning, and with some theories underlying the concept of ego strength.

The problems raised by these hypotheses are more complex than is evident at first sight. Psychological, psycho-analytical and social-psychological explanations raise a vast number of speculative variables which, in the African urban context at least, we are still not equipped to handle very well. No doubt the selective factors in migration bring more than one type of migrant into the town. There is a range of personalities involved, each with a particular constellation, each with a different social, political, economic, cultural and moral background. These do have some bearing on how the migrant views the town and the manner in which he eases himself into that complex fabric we have tried to describe. But there are also other factors which play their part and are, perhaps, a little more easily analysed in an objective way such as composition of the population, economic opportunities which exist and environmental conditions which prevail. A counter hypothesis might, therefore, be offered suggesting that when demographic factors are more in balance, when ethnic composition is less heterogeneous, when employment and entrepreneurial opportunities are reasonably good (facilitating a steady income and perhaps, also, upward social mobility and when environmental conditions such as housing, services and privacy) are satisfactory, then change and a new moral order are not only accepted but also facilitated by both long term residents and newly arrived migrants resulting in a minimal distinction between so-called "modernisers", who accept the new moral order, and so-called "conservatives" who are hesitant or antagonistic to it. The Powdermaker hypothesis leads us into a consideration of the relation of variables over which we have only limited control, and in which many concepts lack in precise definition, while the hypothesis just advanced allows analysis of more objective data. Both hypotheses need to be used together although it is better to start with more basic data.

It is, we believe, false to suggest that the "conservatives" resist becoming involved in the life of the town because they reject its moral basis. While both Mayer and Powdermaker suggest that this group is unwilling to give up "traditional" values and goals, and that their urban sojourns involve them in a social and cultural network designed to perpetuate these values and goals, they have in the process ignored many aspects of the diversity of urban life which make "conservative" choices not incompatible with being a true urbanite. Choices change, of course, and it would be instructive to find out whether those who were the "conservatives" yesterday are still encapsulated today or will be in the future. Although the towns are constantly being occupied by migrants at the lower socio-economic levels, whose conception of the moral order is (still) coloured by their recent (rural) experiences, research in Lagos, Accra, Kampala, and Nairobi (Gutkind 1953-1966) suggests that there is a rapid progression into the ranks of the modernisers. Perhaps more fundamentally, however, the use of the category "conservative" assumes that the rural moral order has not changed significantly in the last few years, and is unchanging. As this is certainly not so, one would assume that the conservative urbanite will also lose his point of moral reference. We really need to take a far closer look at this allegedly more conservative and non-participating individual. Rather than put him into a convenient and rather watertight compartment, a social and moral world isolated from the rest of the urban community, we need to take a far closer look at how his more "traditional" behaviour, and the network in which he moves, is a measure of socio-economic circumstances, and hence of a particular style of urban life. Such a style of life does have, of course, particular ideational and moral components which can be contrasted with other styles of urban life. But it is a superficial comparison which does not take into account the significance of those common patterns of urban life which touch every member of an urban community. Thus Mayer's description of the cultural differences between the "School" and the "Red" people is strongly accentuated at the expense of the institutional and structural overlap between the two groups. What does, however, come through very clearly in his otherwise very perceptive study, and that by Powdermaker too, is the simple fact that the conservatives are generally at the lowest level of the economic order. While they are workers, like others, they seem to fill the most menial jobs and, above all, have the least education. Both the Mayer and Powdermaker studies were conducted in highly racially segregated societies where Europeans held very tightly to the reins of economic and political power and where mobility for Africans was (and is) very restricted (in South Africa and in pre-independence Zambia). At numerous points in the Mayer study, he points to these facts, but fails to see their significance in his overall analysis. Powdermaker, on the other hand, offers the following hypothesis (1962 : 304-5):

Another hypothesis is that those who resisted change (on any but material values) had more conscious and unconscious resentment toward Europeans than did the modern African... Overt resentments were primarily over wages and attitudes of supervisors. Unskilled and uneducated workers, among whom were many of the intransigents, tended to have more uneducated and intolerant supervisors than did educated Africans. Nor were unconscious hostilities channeled in the formal etiquette of the past, customary in relations with the first Europeans. Neither did the intransigents enjoy a catharsis through identification with the victorious cowboy hero of the movies. There may likewise have been unconscious hostility toward the Africans who were becoming part of the modern world. *The intransigents knew their world was moving* [emphasis added], but they did not have the ego strength to risk the ambiguities of change. Not in the past or today did they have the kind of experiences with Europeans which would make identification possible. They saw the two races as polarities, which must remain forever differentiated.

Whether it is racial differentiation or extreme ethnic and cultural diversity, the same hypothesis might be usefully applied to other African urban areas.

At times it has been suggested that the conservative style of life includes many traditional rural-oriented customs and behavioural traits. Central as a measure seems to be the practice of magic and witchcraft, and such entrepreneurial activities as basket making, bead making and the like. In addition conservatives are often pagans, or share a belief in some syncretistic belief system, which contrasts strongly with membership in a Christian church or the more secular views of the educated and Westernised elite. The belief in a non-secular moral order is said to reinforce many aspects of the life of the conservatives. Not only does it pre-determine their ideas of change and progress, but it also structurally restricts their social field of associations and contacts with the urban community as a whole – the true meaning of encapsulation. The influence of particular urban sects and cults which cater to the needs of the economically depressed groups is probably far greater in impact than the influence of the Christian churches (Parrinder 1953, Taylor and Lehmann 1961, Sundkler 1961).

But this is not the place for a discussion of either magic and witchcraft or the particular nature of religious belief systems in urban Africa. Just two observations are perhaps relevant. In the first case non-secular ideas and activities seem to cut right across all sections of the urban community and, secondly, the continuation of certain customary beliefs and practices might actually increase as the individual "becomes enmeshed in the modern social system" (Marwick 1958 : 107). This suggestion is rather contrary to the view that such belief systems are basically altered as a result of contact with Western culture because "the civilisation into which the African is drawn is founded in a scientific technology and inspired by a monotheistic religion long since freed from the superstitions underlying a belief in witchcraft." (Marwick 1958 : 106, Jahoda 1963).

Anthropologists working in Africa have for long held the view that witchcraft and magic basically reflect the stresses and strains in the social structure, and within the social relationships, which link individuals and groups (Krige 1947, Marwick 1963, Nadel 1952, Wilson 1951). Thus the theory holds that as economic, political and social competition increases, so does stress and conflict. As matters go wrong for individuals, a politician does not get elected, an unemployed man cannot find work, a business enterprise fails or a student fails an examination, customary beliefs seem to offer satisfactory explanations for a large number of people. It is perhaps this which explains the large trade in herbal products and the vast variety of other "medicines" which are obtainable in West African markets. Herbalists, diviners, prophets and folk doctors all do rather a flourishing trade in the towns. Whether or not these practices are on the increase is extremely difficult to tell, but casual observation seems to suggest that business is good. On the second observation made above, Jahoda (1963), Marwick (1958) and Weinberg (1970) report that members of the educated elite continue to believe in a supernatural orientation. Thus Weinberg (p. 23-4) writes:

In general, urbanization – by its rapid changes in family structure, its impersonality, the secularization of ethnic values and practices, the occupational uncertainty, the shifting status of women, the increasing inter-generational discontinuity between parents and children, the rising individualism and anomie amidst political strife – has generated conditions of stress and conflict among urban residents more intense than those in the relative static and familiar village. But despite this acquisition of mechanical, clerical, and intellectual skills, many Africans in the city have retained their animistic and supernatural orientation towards their interpersonal experiences and their personal conflicts. Forty African college students were asked to estimate the percentage of their associates who viewed their psychological experiences supernaturally. They reported that from 65 to 99 percent, an average of 85 percent of their associates, had such supernatural orientation. In fact, the majority of African people in all social strata approach their experiences supernaturally. For example, Lambo, in his study of Nigerian students, reported that ninety percent of the students who broke down while studying in universities in Great Britain believed that witchcraft and the machinations of enemies contributed to their conditions.

This ideological system, persisting even in an urban environment, regards well-being and illbeing as polar resultants of spiritual forces. Ideally, this spiritual harmony, which is more social-psychological than biological, involves cooperative and harmonious attitudes in relationships with family, friends, and neighbours. But the changing urban community disrupts... traditional unity. Moral behaviour becomes difficult to gauge and social control, difficult to enforce. Since moral norms are in flux, the person's moral behaviour as a means to health is less easily sustained under urban conditions.

Although it must be clear that we do not share all the ideas set out above, we cannot reject the conclusion that customary belief systems are a powerful influence on the behaviour, style of life and manner in which the urbanite constructs a moral order. To label this moral order as traditional, syncretistic or modern may be convenient, but it does not tell us how this moral order operates and, above all, how individuals can move from one order to another depending on the particular situation which calls forth this or that response and attitude. It is this situational context as it determines the ideational perspectives of urban Africans which has, thus far, received very little attention. However, some information will be found in the literature which deals with the "Independent" churches in Africa, the messianic and prophetic movements, and the vast number of sects and cults which have come into being from virtually the earliest days of colonialism, but which seem to have increased both numerically and in general importance during the last forty to fifty years. A great many of these movements (as many operate also in the political and economic field) are almost exclusively urban-anchored, and it is generally assumed that the urban poor, including occasionally the unemployed (Chambers 1964) are particularly attracted to these groupings. While some sects and cults have a small membership, and are subject to repeated fission, the message they preach, and the aid and fellowship they offer, speak to the condition of a large number of the urban poor for whom the particular brand of moral and ideational order provided is an important stabilising force. The "Independent" churches have, usually, a large membership and draw their followers from urban and rural areas – such as the Aladura movement in West Africa (Turner 1966, Mitchell 1970).

The theological doctrines of these movements tend to be of the "fire and brimstone" variety. Great emphasis is laid on communalism, love, righteousness, cleanliness, hard work, personal discipline, honesty, the rejection of "false gods" and considerable scepticism of many aspects of modernisation. A number of these movements may make a special effort to attract the urban unemployed, such as the Black Jesus of Oyingbo (Chambers 1964), and provide work and residential quarters for the down and out urbanite. The smaller scale urban-anchored movements are usually led by men or women who have had visions, who have been "reborn" or who have heard voices commanding them to serve God. A recent example of this, although primarily rural-based, is the Alice Lenshina movement in Zambia and Southern Zaire which has been described by Rotberg (1961), Howard (1964) and Roberts (1970). This movement, in particular, commands its members to reject any participation in political activities and to withdraw to rural villages away from active participation in the temptations which urban life offers.

Whether the reasons for the relative success of these urban-based movements spring entirely from the negative circumstances of town life or whether a selective factor is involved (which attracts individuals with a particular constellation of personal, cultural and social backgrounds), is still largely guesswork and a good deal more research should be done in this direction. Certainly as hard as the new migrant tries to gain a foothold in the town, the competitive conditions which he faces and must overcome are such as to lead to discouragement and frustration for him. But how individuals respond to difficult conditions is as varied as there are migrants in the town. Prediction is near to impossible. Whether membership in the urban independent churches and other movements can be interpreted as a commitment to the moral order advocated by them, or whether there is a large element of deceit and gullibility involved, is yet another question worth asking. Thus Jahoda (1963 : 17) writes:

While it would be a mistake to overemphasize the consequences of widespread supernatural beliefs, it would be equally wrong to underrate their importance. Perhaps the first and obvious danger is that gullible people are open to exploitation on the part of those who are able to take advantage of their beliefs ... One of the more amusing examples of this is a confidence game known as "money-doubling." The trickster approaches a likely mark, usually a well-to-do trader or lorry owner with limited education, claiming that he is able to multiply currency notes by magical means. With astonishing readiness the unhappy victim parts with his hard earned wealth in the hope of seeing it vastly increased. Less spectacular, but far more frequent, are cases where magical devices are used in the employment relationship. This may be in order to gain promotion, prevent one from being sacked, or as a protection against similar machinations by others who are trying to usurp one's job.

This alone does not adequately explain the willingness and the need of many urban Africans to accept the supernatural, or quasi-supernatural, belief system with all its customary or syncretistic features. The more likely explanation lies not in the absence of education and enlightenment but in the economically depressed conditions which are a feature of an otherwise rapidly changing continent. Urban life involves risk and uncertainty for all which the individual must attempt to overcome. For the majority of urbanites this makes demands upon them which only the politically and economically strongest can handle, although often only after repeated failures (Plotnicov 1967), but which the economically weak, and socially uprooted, find far more difficult. Under such circumstances adherence to a belief system uniquely styled and presented to meet particular dilemmas is likely to be warmly received. However, as circumstances change, the same individuals will move to membership in other, perhaps more secular, groupings until a final break is achieved and loyalty is given to occupational, class and political groups with an ideational perspective rather different from the fundamentalist view beamed at the masses of the poor. This would suggest that these non-secular movements will continue to gather in a large number of people, as there is no indication that economic stability and social mobility is just around the corner.

The points made and the questions raised in this section point essentially to the urgency of designing intelligent research propositions in an attempt to test the relevance of those variables which are thought to bear on the relationship of economic factors and the moral order. The urgency of this kind of research is all the greater as there is a clear temptation to moralise about the African's inability to adopt a secular philosophy of life. Not only is this quite untrue, but if it were true it might well be cited as an indictment of colonialism worse than its economic exploitation and its political hegemony. We will close this section with a further comment by Jahoda (1963 : 15):

In countries lacking the shelter of the modern welfare state, where disease is more prevalent and infant mortality remains extremely high by our standards, one would expect a greater readiness to have recourse to supernatural protection. Whether the extent of such beliefs is less, the same, or even greater than it was in the past constitutes a somewhat moot point. Some anthropologists hold that the unquestionable improvement in material conditions of life has reduced the incidence of supernatural beliefs; others, and they are in the majority, argue that it would be a mistake to consider only physical well being: rapid social changes produce their own problems and anxieties, which may be met by a rise in magical beliefs and practices. The issue is difficult to resolve, as there is insufficiently detailed information available about the past, with which the present level might be compared. Furthermore, there is also very little reliable knowledge, and much guesswork, regarding the extent to which magical ideas are prevalent.

It is time that we substituted scientific enquiry for guesswork.

8. *Summary and Synthesis*

In this chapter we have ranged from a discussion of the relevance of certain structural and processual characteristics of the African urban system to some comments on the ideational and moral aspects of urbanism as they are translated by the urbanite into particular responses. Rather than engage in a detailed documentation and analysis of the major institutional features of the urban system, we have concentrated on a rather limited number of critical aspects of urbanism, such as personal and groups relations, the world of work, the relevance of the occupational structure, economic and social mobility, the political order, family life and the ideational world. These critical aspects of urbanism were selected because each of them solicits a good deal of controversial interpretation which allows us to add our own rather than merely synthesise the views of others.

We preceded each section with a brief discussion of the structure and operation of these critical features in the rural context. We did this not in order to engage in a discussion of rural-urban contrasts, but rather to point to contrasting degrees of complexity, and also to indicate that towns should be studied *as towns* to bring out, as it were, the essence of urban life. "African towns", Leo Kuper writes (1967 : 127), "should be studied as structures in their own right", and he goes on to say that we should not encourage the

analyst to perceive the townsmen as creatures of antecedent custom, and thus to underestimate the flexibility of the relationship to custom, the capacity of persons to use different cultural idioms in different social contexts and the role of human creativity. (p. 128)

And in a footnote to this chapter he points out:

It is usually Africans who are thought to be ruled by custom, while Whites are perceived as innovators. This invidious contrast seems to be present also in discussions of modernisation. There may be a projection of sentiments of racial superiority in a conception of Africans as creatures, and Whites as creators of custom. (p. 149)

In this chapter, as in Chapter Two, we have suggested that the African urbanite, because he is an urbanite, is not just a creature who is tossed and manipulated by forces over which he has little or no control. The reason why these critical points of the social fabric have been selected is to indicate that the urbanite is creator and innovator of organisational forms which clearly take into account the conditions of, and the demands made by, the urban environment. Not only have we tried to lay to rest some myths, such as the alleged impersonal nature of urbanism and the decline of family life, but we have repeatedly put forward the view that the basic institutional and organisational patterns of urban life can only be analysed in a situational context. To discuss social organisation *qua* social organisation of urban life is impossible; it is an abstraction which we would be chasing. What is more relevant is to ask what do people do, why do they do this or that, and how do they, if they can, explain their behaviour and ideas. It is questions of this sort which lead us to more complex matters such as the relationship of economic variables to, let us say, political culture; it is such simple questions which help us to document and analyse the relationship between economic factors and family life, or between the legacy of colonialism and political culture. And at the more abstract level, it is the situational context which helps us to understand the forces of ethnicity, customary behaviour and ideas, and the why and how the past might be brought forward into the present. The situational approach prevents our analysis from being set into the rigidity of polar types. It is not a matter of tradition versus modernity, but rather the focus is entirely on the urban system – and in particular on the critical points which we have selected for special treatment. Neither is the focus for analysis either *the* individual or *the* group; rather it is the urban situation – that multitude of conditions, events, and circumstances which calls forth certain responses and behaviour.

Thus, each of these critical features of African urban life cannot be treated in isolation. The world of work cannot be treated as just economic activity; political culture is more than bureaucracy; family life is more than sexual relations and marriage; and occupations and upward and downward mobility are more than a mere ordering of the urban population into categories and strata. Collectively these aspects of the urban world are operationalised in terms of events, activities and responses. They assume their particular structure and meaning both because they are at the heart of the urban system and because they exhibit their own internal complexity which allows us to treat them as critical points in the social order.

These basic characteristics of African urban society are neither pre-industrial nor modern. They add up to a particular kind of urbanism which can only be understood if we accept the relevance of a number of variables which have helped to shape the particular entity under observation. These variables are to a large extent historical although, at the same time, more contemporary conditions, which are worldwide, are also very influential. African urban areas bear the imprint of colonial policies which have seriously constrained not only their growth (until recently), but also the modernising influences which are normally associated with urbanism. The control of migration into the towns, as in South Africa, racial zoning, as in most of the towns of Eastern, Central and Southern Africa, and serious economic and political barriers prevented Africans from permanent settlement and advancement in the towns. All this has left the towns with serious problems and major disadvantages. At the same time the towns are exposed to virtually all the forces of modernisation and change. Much of the life of the urbanite, therefore, is concerned with the building up of an urban culture. To attach a label to the current characteristics of this culture would seriously bias the analysis and interpretation of contemporary African urban life. Those who label this urban culture as pre-industrial might then be tempted to interpret African urban marriage and family life as indicative of the unstructured and amorphous conditions of urbanism, while those who use the label of modern are likely to view the same structure as an indication of hedonistic depravity. Only in one sense are the towns of Africa, and elsewhere, modern, and that is when the residents and the municipal administrations have to deal with problems for which there seems to be no easy solution. Rather than apply typologies, we ought to look at events, at processes and structures. In combination they give rise to the kind of urbanism which will vary from town to town depending upon its history, its size, the diversity of its functions and the composition of its population.

Some readers of this chapter will, no doubt, register their objection that under its title we should have referred to many other features of urban life, such as a discussion of ethnicity and the role it plays in urban social organisation. After all, almost every study of urban Africa makes a major issue of this – treating it invariably as a negative feature. Although not in depth, we dealt with this matter in Chapter Two. In defence, all that we wish to say here is that ethnicity is merely one aspect of urbanism and that its significance can only be understood in the total context of urban life. It comes to life under certain conditions, and it declines when certain conditions are removed. As such it is not, as has generally been indicated, a constant and

major determinant of urban social organisation. If this appears as an un-
supported generalisation, we would merely plead that anthropologists have
devoted so much time to the study of "tribes" that they have become the
most basic unit of their observation. The view put forward in this monograph is that this should not be so. The "Sociology of Tribalism" is, at best,
just one aspect not only of African urban life, but of African society as a
whole. Furthermore, ethnic groupings in African towns do not operate independently of the totality of urban life. Such collectivities, as much as any
other, are strongly affected by the diversification of behaviour and social relationships; as collectivities they are as much caught up in changes as non-
ethnically constituted groups. The "Sociology of Tribalism" appears to concentrate on what might be the easiest identifiable unit in the urban system
(although that is questionable), one which is viewed as the main reference
group and, hence, determines the social organisation of the town and the values of the urbanite. This precludes a more holistic, and perhaps more dynamic, analysis which can take into account the possibility that structure, process,
behaviour and values are determined by a wide variety of conditions and
non-ethnic rooted collectivities. The influence of ethnic factors, important as
these are under specific conditions, should not be elevated to that level of
magnitude whereby they become the base for all analysis. The limitations
which flow from such an approach have been perceptively and critically analysed by Magubane (1968, 1969). Although Magubane is primarily concerned with the study of conflict situations, and not directly with (conflict
in) urban areas, he points out (1969 : 535) that the concentration on tribalism
"represents . . . the triumph of stereotypes over reality." The concept "is
false", he writes (1969 : 537), "and pays attention to mere symptoms of a
much deeper problem."[1] By concentrating on tribalism and pluralism, as the

---

[1] Davidson (1969 : 214) in a rather similar vein makes the following comment:
Europeans unhesitatingly called them 'tribes' in a sense that was explicitly pejorative and
meant everything opposed to any development of the means of material progress or even,
with more extreme interpretations, opposed to any form of juridical and moral order. This
term 'tribe' has stayed with us because it is convenient; yet even without its subjective over-
tones it may at best be misleading.

main focus of analysis, there is a clear "danger of trivializing some of the very important questions which . . . have (been) raised." (p. 546)

We must also recognise that concentration on ethnicity as the main focus places the analysis of social change in a special context on the ground that "tribalism" is generally thought to make a conservative and non-dynamic input into the urban system. Thus the emergence of new associations, new personalities, new authorities and the re-structuring of social relations are all measured, as it were, against a single determinant. Conflict and inconsistency are likewise seen as rooted in the tensions between ethnic groups while in fact they arise more directly from the difficulties of distilling common norms from extreme social and cultural diversity and the basic inequities in economic opportunity. We must, therefore, reject the view that "tribalism" is at the core of the social organisation of African towns. We must instead concentrate on those features of the urban social system which cut across ethnicity, while at the same time our model must allow for an analysis of its importance when the evidence demands this. Thus Banton (1958 : 232) has summed up this argument as follows:

In its common connotation 'tribalism' tends to become a unitary concept, and carries the implicit assumption that, because the evidence points to the persistence in the towns of strong tribal loyalties, those loyalties will operate with the same strength over the total field of social relations in which the urban African is involved. This difficulty is avoided if we approach the town as a field of social relations which is made up of sets of social relations of different kinds, each of which covers a distinct sphere of social interaction, and forms a sub-system. Although it is the interrelations of these various sets which make up the total system, each set may have a certain measure of autonomy so that the tempo and character of change are not evenly distributed over the whole field.

In this chapter what we have attempted to do is to concentrate on those critical aspects of the African urban system which reveal most sharply the interrelations. How these interrelations are put together, and for what purpose, determines the particular character of the town. It also determines the particular nature of urban man. We cannot yet say, with any precision, what kind of urban man this is, but we can say that there is a Townsman in the Making.

IV

Problems of methodology in African urban research: The search for new dimensions

1. *Introduction*

Until recently anthropologists have kept their research methods secret. Why they have done so is a bit of a puzzle. Perhaps they have never had a method. However, in the last few years a number of them have tried to rectify this deficiency by giving us both introspective (Bowen 1964, Malinowski 1967, MacGaffey 1966, Powdermaker 1966) and scientific (Beattie 1965, Berreman 1962, Golde 1970, Henry and Saberwal 1969, Jongmans and Gutkind 1967, Middleton 1970, Spindler 1970 and Williams 1967) accounts. But even before this recent outpouring, many fieldworkers added an appendix to their mongraphs to say: This is how I did it. With some exceptions (Evans Pritchard 1940 : 7-15) their accounts were not very penetrating, precise and insightful.

Although urban anthropologists are a more recent addition, they have not done much better. Standard African urban studies have likewise restricted themselves to an odd paragraph or a brief appendix. A recent survey by the author of perhaps the ten best known African urban studies, published over the last few years, revealed a minimal concern with matters of methodology. Marris (1961), Mayer (1961), Fraenkel (1964) and Southall and Gutkind (1957) devote three or four pages each, while Plotnicov (1967), Leslie (1963), Powdermaker (1967), Epstein (1958), and Banton (1957) make virtually no mention of their fieldwork methods. What comments they do make are usually about statistical procedures, sampling methods and definitions of the basic unit in their observation, i.e. family and households.

More significant than the absence of information appears to be the common agreement among these writers that they used "classical methods" which had been worked out over the years by anthropologists working in a rural context; or that they used "standard procedures" of intensive interviewing such as participant observation and modified survey techniques. Thus Plotnicov (1967 : 9) writes: "Some anthropologists have carried out research in urban areas just as they had in tribal communities." However he questions this approach because he goes on to say:

Other anthropologists doubted the utility of employing conventional techniques of investigation and instead borrowed the methods developed by sociologists studying Euro-American urban areas. But this approach also had its disadvantages.

Gulliver (1967 : 97) makes this point about these disadvantages:

By necessity, recourse was had to extensive questionnaire techniques and statistical treatment with their obviously impersonal flavour, to the employment of numbers of field assistants who, despite their real worth, intruded between anthropologist and people in a way to which he was unaccustomed. Facts and figures which could be collected and quantified began to take precedence over attempts to assess phenomena: the number of people per house and their formal links, if any, rather than the actual state of relations between co-residents of a house, and the norms of behaviour they followed; the number of times a man shifts his residence, rather than the nature of relations between neighbours or the possible persistence of friendly relations with former neighbours; what a man says he does, or did, or would do (in reply to a questionnaire) rather than what he actually does or did in respect of, say, his kinship obligations or the trade union.

He goes on (p. 98) to express some of the discomfort felt by anthropologists working in urban areas:

These modifications in research techniques [see above] and the kinds of data obtained have brought complementary modifications in the kinds of accounts written by anthropologists and in the interests they sustain. Many anthropologists continue to be chary of involvement in urban studies because they are disinclined either to embrace these new interests or to accept the diminution of contact and rapport between themselves and the people they study. It is not at all certain in which direction anthropological research and interest will eventually move in this field. It cannot be denied that fact-finding, the rather impersonal and extensive data collecting and measuring, and the examination of the social skeleton of these unformed communities, is essential. Both anthropologist and sociologist are faced with research into a novel situation in Africa. But anthropologists especially seem to be uncomfortably aware of what appears to be a lapse, as it were, back to a kind of old-fashioned ethnography, and they are dissatisfied with the state of their urban studies to date. They are seeking new theoretical ideas, hypotheses, kinds of approach and methodologies, which will help to take them beyond description and statistical correlation to the means of deeper understanding and interpretation. As a result, social anthropologists have attempted a number of experimental approaches, which, although not necessarily proved, have begun to lead to significant contributions to this whole field.

The views expressed by Gulliver set out clearly a number of fairly standard misconceptions and responses. They are conditioned very largely by his view that the study of African urban life is the "examination of the social skeleton of these unformed communities". If this is the conceptual baseline then clearly methodological problems are of great magnitude. In the previous three chapters we have tried to make it clear that African towns exhibit as clear a picture of coherent social structure and social organisation as any other community but that the key to the unlocking of their complexity has still to be found. In our search we have concentrated on appropriate conceptual models rather than on the methodology of problem definition and data collection. Now that we have a fair number of alternative theoretical models, be they useful or not, we must devote an increasing amount of time to the nitty-gritty of methodology. Of course, the link between concepts and method is close – certain methodologies solicit particular data relating to the particular problem.

As indicated earlier, few anthropologists working in African towns (and still fewer sociologists and political scientists) have written about the research techniques they employed. A notable exception was Ellen Hellmann who, as early as 1935, published an article in *Bantu Studies* on "Methods of Urban Field Work". It is, as far as we know, the earliest article out of Africa on this topic. It tells us little as such about method because the author is more concerned with getting across some new perspectives (on culture contact, absorption, assimilation, the tribal environment, heterogeneity and slum life) which resulted from her pioneering work in an African slum in Johannesburg. However, she also makes some comments about what were then rather novel ideas such as the need for a "rudimentary knowledge of statistics", and the use of questionnaires and survey techniques of one kind or another. She was also faced with such questions as, what is the most suitable unit for observation? She also recognised the problems raised from the fact that "the urban field worker is inevitably confronted with a heterogeneous conglomeration of Natives representing a great variety of tribes . . . " She set out particular problems associated with the use of informants in an urban environment saying that she "endeavoured to keep the range of my informants, in respect to tribal origin and degree of assimilation to European culture and urban conditions, as wide as possible." Wisely, she insists that the urban anthropologist must watch out for "fortuitous circumstances" as these are so important in urban life. In the course of her work she learned to collect data in which anthropologists had shown little interest such as "attendance at and membership of different political groups and the embryonic formations of workers' unions [as] . . . indications of the growth of political consciousness." Not many anthropologists would have thought these matters important some thirty years ago. About four years later, Dr. Ray E. Phillips (c. 1939) published *The Bantu in the City*, a study of urban Africans on the Witwatersrand, which made only a minimal contribution to the methodology of African urban research. .

It seems that almost twenty years elapsed before the subject of methodology was raised again. Leo Silberman (1954) published an article on "The Urban Social Survey in the Colonies" in a rather obscure journal, which no doubt prompted the Editor of *The Colonial Review* to reproduce an abridged version in the same year. Silberman's article, which showed how he obtained his material for his "Social Survey of the Old Town of Mombasa" (1950), is probably the first real guide to urban research in Africa. Retrospectively, as we now know, his methodological suggestions had severe limitations. Although he strongly advocated the use of social survey techniques, as an all-purpose tool, he concluded that "qualitative surveys will always be superior to questionnaires", although the latter had the advantage that "it is broadly based and directed at the people themselves."

Five years later, a new kind of literature appeared stimulated by urban demographic and medical research conducted by Flegg and Lutz (1959) in the city of Lourenço Marques. The purpose of their survey was to "estimate accurately the numbers and the age and sex structure of the population as a basis for a Cancer Rate Survey . . ." The authors offered some suggestions on the need for specially trained field personnel, team work as "the keynote of success" and the need for expert statistical advice. The reason why this study is noted here is because it is illustrative of what subsequently became an important problem for the urban anthropologist, as we shall discuss later, namely the collection of basic demographic data. As such data rarely exists for the communities the anthropologist wishes to study, he has to turn himself into an amateur demographer and census taker.

As we come a little closer to contemporary times, what literature there is becomes a little more problem-centered and analytical such as publications by Gamble (1963) about a small town in Sierra Leone, Gutkind (1967) who analyses micro and macro research techniques, Peil (1966) who suggests that urban survey methods provide a "wealth of data on which hypotheses for further research can be based," Hanna (1966) who is interested in the reliability of interview data, and Schwab (1954, 1965) who in his 1965 paper skillfully contrasts the "advantages and limitations of a particular combination of methods as they were applied in studies of two African towns." In particular he seeks an answer to the question "how variables in the field determined both the kinds of problems that could be investigated and the effectiveness of the methods used" (p. 374).

We should not ignore three further publications, also recently published, although they do not directly deal with African urban research. There is much that is relevant in the publication edited by Jack P. Gibbs (1961), particularly in Part 1 which deals with "Urban Units, Their Nature and Boundaries' and in Part 3 which is devoted to "The Spatial Structure of Urban Units." Hauser and Schnore (1965) edited a detailed survey of urbanisation which contains chapters by Hauser, Sjoberg, Keyfitz, Ginsburg and Lewis all of which deal extensively, if not exclusively, with non-Western towns and touch on questions of methodology – particularly the contribution by Sjoberg. Finally Hauser edited (1965) a particularly useful little *Handbook for Social Research in Urban Areas* which covers an enormous number of topics. It, too, spans the field from conceptual schemes to methodology. The reader is strongly advised not to ignore this little known publication.

In the section to follow we shall not be able to deal with all the research techniques which have been used in the past and which might be tried in the future. Nor shall we put forward a specific research model which can be used in whatever town one happens to carry out research. Rather we shall try to concentrate on the relationship between certain characteristics of African towns and the research problems they present. But we shall not leave it at that for we shall also make certain methodological suggestions, most of them untried and therefore experimental in nature.

2. *Initial Problems of Contact*

To settle in a town, for the purpose of research, is rather different from the slightly romantic image which is associated with the anthropologist pitching his tent among the people of some remote village. While the overall objectives of the anthropologist are the same, to learn as much as possible about a particular people, the setting for the urban anthropologist is so different that the first reaction is most often one of confusion and bewilderment. While it may not always be so, village life has many of the attributes of a small-scale community. Unlike an African urban neighbourhood which is likely to be crowded and highly congested, a village setting usually has a more generous physical layout of houses and a slower tempo of life. In both cases, of course, the anthropologist enters as a stranger, a fact perhaps more acceptable to urban people than to the villager. Common to either research area is the feeling that one has come to a strange and unfamiliar place. All the conventional habits and services which one has taken for granted are suddenly problems ranging from "How do I say hello?" to "Is the water safe to drink?" Trite as these matters are, they tend to make the period of initial contact one of slight apprehensiveness. This is quite clear when one turns the pages of the case studies prepared by Spindler (1970). Alan R. Beals, who settled with his wife in Gopalpur, Central India, describes their initial efforts to settle down and get some domestic chores out of the way as a matter of "survival", yet Jeremy Boissevain describes in graphic detail his early efforts to get his house fixed up and the children settled, all of which was "painless and pleasant." Others talk about "getting adjusted to village life", or "establishing rapport", selecting a site, getting a feel of the lay-out of the place, making friends, getting one's credentials approved, and sorting out a vast number of "impressions." In this regard, research in an African urban area is no different than anywhere unfamiliar. Perhaps those who have worked previously in a rural area know how to cope with the myriad of problems a little better than those starting on their first field experience.

The initial problems of urban contact spring from the size of the town, its social ecology and the diversity of its population. Even when a particular research problem has been carefully researched, on arrival in the town modifications might have to be made because the reality of conditions is so often different from the information obtained from a text. The first problem which is likely to arise is: Where should I settle? Of course, if one wishes to do a study of a particular ethnic group in the town the answer seems obvious enough: live among them. While this is usually possible, this is not the end of a quest for a place to live. The next question arises: But where in that community? Should one settle down next to a chief or a headman? Would that be acceptable to other members of the community? Or would it be better to be a little further away, at some other equally strategic place, which allows for a little greater freedom for observation away from the watchful authority of a chief or headman? While the answer to such questions is determined by a large number of factors, most of which are unknown to the researchers, they might subsequently turn out either to facilitate or to impede the research. Like a village, an urban neighbourhood is internally a complex entity with particular focal points and a specific structure which reflects internal sub-divisions based on a wide range of differences.

Perhaps a more fundamental problem faces the researcher who comes to the field with a more generalised problem, i.e. a comparative study of family life in three different urban communities, or the role of middle-range entrepreneurs in the town. These problems raise far more directly the question: Where should I live? To live in the midst of one community might be misunderstood among members of another from whom information is to be obtained. Yet one cannot live in two places at once, nor is it very convenient to be always on the move from one area to another. There is no easy answer to these considerations being matters of physical, social and political logistics. There are, perhaps, some factors which ought to be taken into account; contact ought to be established with members of all the groups among whom research is to be carried out. On this basis a good deal of information will be obtained which will help in making the right decisions about where to live, who the important people are, what the problems of rapport are likely to be, and whether the ideas one comes with actually have relevance to what is going on in the various communities. If areas or neighbourhoods selected for research are far apart, the researcher also gains valuable impressions about the town as a whole as he moves about within a larger area. Therefore, the final answer to the question of where to live and with whom to make initial contact is often determined by a knowledge of the town as a whole. Those who work "all over the place" might want to be located at critical points of contact between various communities or zones in the town. The advantage of this is that in multi-ethnic and multi-racial communities, or in towns where the rich live apart from the poor, or where slums and better residential areas jostle one another, the research worker ought to place himself at those strategic places which can allow him to observe what goes on on "both sides of the fence". Although a specific problem might concern the field worker, it is amazing how perspectives change, how unsolicited data can fill out interpretations, when an effort is made to observe behaviour over a wider area.

All these questions and considerations reflect a problem basic to all African urban research. Towns are large and highly complex entities: it is rarely possible to concentrate research on more than one or two areas or neighbourhoods unless the town is little more than a "township" (Abrahams 1961, Gappert 1968, Stryker 1968, Southall 1968); indeed the study of the smaller African towns is a much neglected subject (Gutkind 1968). The research worker, therefore, has no choice but to limit the unit of his observations – an inevitability based on some arbitrary decisions. Later on we shall suggest some simple ways out of this predicament, but in terms of the initial problems of settling into a neighbourhood, the rationale underlying its selection is clearly of great importance. Once contact is made, the information that a stranger has arrived will travel very fast and widely. To disentangle oneself from contacts once made may be a tricky matter and impede the course of later fieldwork.

In the last few years African urban research has become ever more demanding for the fieldworker. One indication of this is that initial contacts often take on a political flavour with the result that entry into various communities structures relations with informants from the very start (Gutkind 1969).

The days have long passed since the social researcher in Africa could assert his authority: he was white, and he worked under the protective umbrella of the colonial administration. Currently, the chances are very good that the initial contact will be converted into a minor political confrontation (as I described, 1969, when I began work among the unemployed in Lagos and Nairobi) forcing the researcher to "declare" himself on many burning social, economic and political issues. But fieldwork in the context of tense political situations also raises problems of identification with informants which is intensified, it seems, in the urban context. For the researcher this might result in particular problems of stress which can, perhaps, be avoided if he is not resident in the community being studied. This does cast less suspicion on the researcher *vis-à-vis* government officials (and the police!) but informants may literally demand that one live among them to see "how bad things are and how badly we are treated." Thus, when the author commenced his work among the urban unemployed he found himself surrounded by several dozen young men waiting outside the Lagos Labour Exchange where the following confrontation took place:

Young Ibo: You told us that you had come to this place to find out about men who are struggling to get work. I will tell you about that and so will all the other men here (and he cast his arms in all directions).

Another Ibo: Come to my house (interjections: And to mine, And to mine . . .) and you can meet all the men you want.

Author: Yes, I would like to come and meet as many of you as I can.

First Ibo: No, no, come to live in our house and then you will see how we suffer. I thought that you had come here to give us work (he held up his Labour Registration Card . . .).

Another Man: Give us work. Why did you come here if you cannot give us work.

First Ibo: Listen. I live in Mushin (a suburb of Lagos). I think that you should come there. I will show you men who are fighting for work and . . . (lost in shouting).

Author: If you tell me where you live I will come and see you and meet all the other men who are looking for work.

First Ibo: Ah, now you say you will come. But you will never stay.

Author: I will visit you as often as I can and stay as long as you will ask me to.

First Ibo: You see that Labour Officer there (he points to a young man with a white shirt sitting at a desk by a window). He lives in Ikoyi (a wealthy residential area) and he never comes to find out how we suffer ... You must come and stay with us and give us work ... you hear work. (Gutkind 1966)

No doubt not all first encounters in African towns are quite as aggressive and quite as demanding. Yet unusual as this episode might be, it illustrates how first contacts can produce hard and realistic demands which need to be taken into account as research proceeds. We are thus not only faced with problems due to the size of the town but also with a generally more militant atmosphere which seems to give some reality to the current view: If you are not part of the solution you are part of the problem. There can be little doubt that such confrontations are less likely to occur in a village context.

In short, the research worker in urban Africa steps into a complex ecological, social and political situation which produces uncertainty and a good measure of bewilderment. The time allowed him to "settle in" is probably far shorter than in the more relaxed life of the village; the decisions he has to make as to where to locate, and why, are probably more difficult and more critical than in a rural area; the political authorities he must deal with are also more important for his work, and the diversity of the urban population is such that he must maintain extensive and in depth contacts with people from widely different backgrounds. Making his decision as to where to locate, what neighbourhood or what group of people should form his primary anchorage, he must pay attention to the relevance of the major characteristics of the town as a whole so that concentration on a small segment of urban society does not become an end in itself. If it does, the complexity of micro unit or macro field, as they influence each other, will not have been adequately represented.

Of course, initial problems of contact are often the product of the particular personality of the fieldworker (Shelton 1964). Attempts to disguise one's true intentions and purpose, gratuitous comments offered as jokes, or efforts at ingratiation, can all substantially contribute to instant and lasting difficulties. While in a village such attitudes can damage field relations beyond repair, it is sometimes assumed that the greater heterogeneity of urban life makes it possible to change informants and in this manner constrained field relations can be avoided. It is true that in an urban area there is a larger potential group of informants, but it is perhaps equally true that complete integrity in field relations is of prime importance – the population is more sophisticated, politically more alive and, often, less tolerant. However, with real integrity and proper caution urban fieldwork is as rewarding an experience as fieldwork anywhere else.

3. *Problems of Definition and Selection of Topics*

In this section we will not be concerned with the interminable debate which has taken place over the years about "What is a Town?", "How is it to be defined?", and "What sort of Unit are we Looking at?" The variation of demographic definition is very wide, although the United Nations has suggested that the international community accept the figure of 20,000 people and above as comprising an urban area. When a small town turns into a big town, and a big town into a city, is not a matter which concerns us except for one consideration, namely, that urban anthropologists should make an effort to spread their skills over many different kinds of urban communities ranging from the smallest to the large metropolis. More fundamentally, however, demographic definitions alone are not wholly satisfactory. As we indicated in Chapter 1, people in a small rural community may all work in a nearby factory, and few of them grow their own food, while in a city such as Ibadan a large number of residents are farmers although they live under congested urban conditions. Definitions might usefully take account of what people do rather than, exclusively, the size of the population. This makes a distinction between urbanisation and urbanism. It is a distinction of less relevance to the demographer but of considerable importance to the urban anthropologist, because it simply accepts the fact that an urban style of life is now possible in Africa, as elsewhere, quite independent of either the size or the location of the city. Definitions are merely tools and they can be changed in the interest of the research worker and the particular problem which has been selected for research.

What is more important is the selection of the topic and clear definition of the problems. Gibbs (1961 : 14-15) had this to say about the above matter:

The definitive attributes of cities applied in a study should be closely geared to the theory being pursued and the nature of the research derived from it. If the concern is with types of governmental structure, political boundaries are of course relevant; but they may not be relevant when we view cities as economic entities, points of population concentration, etc. This is not to suggest that only one attribute should be used to define cities for a particular type of analysis. On the contrary, depending upon the nature of a given study, a configuration of attributes may be used. One can even concentrate on determining the extent of empirical correspondence between attributes. Thus, for example, with what frequency are "demographic cities" also "economic cities"? This sort of question is implicit in much urban research.

A relativistic approach to definition neither captures the essence of cities, if such can be said to exist, nor insures homogeneity in all of their characteristics. Cities defined in demographic terms, for example, may indeed manifest considerable political, economic, socio-cultural, and psychological diversity. However, this would be true for any definition of a city in terms of one attribute; in the final analysis, the matter of homogeneity is entirely relative to the problem at hand.

The selection and the definition of a problem "should be closely geared to the theory being pursued", Gibbs wrote. In this monograph we have suggested that an African urban area is a particular kind of unit within a larger national and regional society. Furthermore, we have indicated that the social, economic and political order in African towns differ in terms of complexity rather than in kind if compared to rural communities. Another view we have tried to put forward is that African towns are the loci for supra-urban organisations such as national governments, labour unions, political parties, ethnic voluntary associations and other specialised groupings. Although we have not put forward a theory of urbanisation and urbanism, we have pointed out that the study of African towns should concentrate on certain critical structural and processual features rather than being based on institutional analysis. We also share the views expressed by Horace Miner (1967) that the study of African towns offers an unusual opportunity to re-examine established theories, and evolve new models, in the context of a wide variety of environments. But even then urbanism, on any continent, is urbanism. In short, these are some of the theoretical points we have made out from which we must now distill some topics and problems linked to methodological considerations. Before we do this, though, we ought to remind the reader again that we suggested two important conceptual and methodological approaches: micro and macro analysis and situational and network analysis. The latter in particular has been discussed in great detail by Mitchell (1969) and Barnes (1968), the former concentrating on the towns of Central Africa and the latter on the political processes in the context of "local-level" politics.

In the first place much of our research should concentrate on urbanisation as a societal process.[1] This has at least two important dimensions: first, we must take account of the historical base on which African cities and towns have been built whether this is an indigenous or an imported colonial base. Particularly in the case of the colonial town, the history of colonial policies and structures can be, and usually are, of vital importance. Secondly, we must concentrate on the processes and structures which have produced, and continue to produce, the particular kind of urbanism unique to Africa and unique to each African town. The study of processes reveals sources of power and sources of change as these are generated both by internal transformations and external relations. Thirdly, we must concentrate more directly on how the urban fabric is built up. What are the key processes in expansion? Is it primarily by internal changes such as specialisation of occupations and the differentiation of the urban community into discrete units (classes), or is it by means of overall cumulative change brought about by massive migration into the cities? Is the speed of urbanisation brought about by rapid bureaucratisation, i.e. essentially by political processes? Urbanisation processes differ also in as much as sometimes the old is brought forward into the present, but transformed to serve the present, while at other times the old is totally rejected in favour of new structures and groupings which have few antecedents. The question to ask here is: what are the determinants of this selective process?

Methodologically, two approaches seem relevant to the study of urbanisation as a societal process. First, comparative perspective, and secondly, situational analysis. Few students of urban Africa have set up their problems on a

[1] In this section I have relied rather heavily on the proceedings of a conference on "African Urban Research Theory, Strategy, Utilization", held at the University of Wisconsin-Milwaukee, June 1966, written up by Professor George Jenkins, and published in mimeographed form. I participated in this conference.

comparative basis (although the work of Hanna and Hanna 1968, and Schwab 1954, 1965, 1970 are exceptions) in an attempt to isolate and determine the relevance and magnitude of basic processes of urbanisation and the resultant structures. Comparative studies should be based on significantly different histories, colonial policies, resource bases, size of population and its composition. Thus, studies should be set up which analyse specific processes and structures (for example, which processes create, and which slow down, the formation of socio-economic classes) in both the old and new towns of Africa. Such research should not be presented as "case studies" of towns but rather as studies in the comparative analysis of processes of urbanisation. Perhaps there is nothing much in a label, but there are differences in selective use of data for different purposes.

Secondly, greater use ought to be made of the method of situational analysis as a device to penetrate and expose the events, processes, and structures around which urban behaviour rotates. Thus almost any event, from a fight in a beer bar to a marriage ceremony, can lead the urban anthropologist to expose a large number of processes and conditions which make up the larger urban social system. Clearly, whatever urban Africans do, from trite and everyday affairs to the eventful and important, must always reflect that particular complexity which brings together many features of the urban system as a whole. Situational selection is designed to bring out the purpose and meaning of events and behaviour and the processes and structures on which these are based. Thus a series of such studies, in a comparative context, should be given priority.

Another series of problems should center around the relationship of the urban area to the hinterland, the region and the nation. Is it possible to restate the arguments and the conceptualisation of the rural-urban dichotomy? Has this dichotomy contributed to our understanding of either the processes of urbanisation or the qualities of urbanism? If an urban style of life is no longer restricted to urban residence, then this dichotomy has lost much of its usefulness. Furthermore, if African towns are merely units of a larger entity, i.e. the nation, then a great deal of research will have to be initiated (in which "social" geographers can make a major contribution) to try to reveal the impact of a "network" of towns in spatial relation and communication terms and how the towns, collectively, father a new style of life made available to an ever larger percentage of the total population (of a nation). This is facilitated partly because the towns are linked economically and politically via the increased mobility of Africans from one town to another (often across national boundaries).

Questions pertaining to the urban-hinterland complex can also be used to analyse, more perceptively, problems concerning migration and the migrant. Both have been treated as primary determinants in the growth of towns, in the processes of urbanisation and the quality of urban life. A new orientation might be to view migration and the migrant as of secondary importance simply because the towns are now established and a community of permanently resident Africans has come into being. This development raises the kind of questions put forward by Weiner (1967), Nelson (1970), and Pauw (1963), and Wilson and Mafeje (1963) who point to the more critical issues of the relationship between the established residents and the newcomers. This makes the migrants important not as migrants who circulate from village to urban area and back again but as economic and political competitors *vis-à-vis* the permanent residents.

On the other hand, some important questions do remain about migrants and their circular migration (Elkan 1967) which should be studied. For example, we still know very little about the selective factors in migration. What are the anthropological and psychological concomitants in the selective migration to cities of persons with urban-appropriate attitudes? Does migration increase rural homogeneity by removing dissident elements who should not be viewed as uprooted but as transplanted to a more favourable environment? Should characteristics of indigenous societies be spelled out in urban-relevant terms or is the urban habitat itself so dominating that the differential use of it by contributing societies can be given low priority?

There are no clear methodological models for the study of these questions. To penetrate the complexity of urban-hinterland relations requires a team approach involving geographers, economists and political scientists. It is a relationship of increasing importance and raises questions about the nation as a whole, the path of its development, the relevance of colonial policies which influenced the spatial distribution of towns, and how particular economic policies and factors structured this relationship. Thus, what is needed is a study, diachronically, of relevant aspects of rural and urban life, in a regional context, to determine the fission and fusion processes which are involved in this relationship.

At the level of migrancy and the migrant, while we know a good deal in general terms, it is only recently that we have any detailed case studies of particular migrants (Plotnicov 1967). As very few fieldworkers return to the venue of their research, most of the studies lack a diachronic base with the result that a large number of questions must remain unanswered.

Patterns of migrancy have their own dynamic over time; they involve more than mobility at any given moment. Thus it is questionable whether the term migrant has any meaning in the context of regular circulation when on each occasion the migrant stays longer in the town, adopts more determinedly urban habits and values and as such weaves himself into the political, economic and social fabric of the town. Yet because he was not born in the town we continue to refer to him as a migrant. Such conceptualisation prevents us from seeing the migrant as an urbanite because the temptation is great to treat him as a tribesman in town. This in turn has led some observers (Mayer 1961, Dubb 1966) to divide the urban population into two mutually exclusive categories of "modernisers" (the true established urbanites) and "conservatives" who, it is assumed, do not want to become urbanites. It was pointed out in the previous section that this was probably a false categorisation because what distinction did exist could be traced to economic inequalities rather than to a normative system which prevented full and active participation by a segment of the urban population. The so-called migrant is as much a part of the urban system as the more established resident but his incorporation in the urban system is at a lower level. This, of course, would be far clearer if we applied a class model to urban studies allowing us to sort out different groups at various levels of economic and political participation and power. In as much as the towns are dominated by various elitist groups, the poor (the migrants) are cast in the mould of being caught in a struggle between tradition and modernity. Because the urban poor lack economic and political power, they rely heavily on structures and associations which the elite define as traditional. But the migrant is no more "traditional" than other urbanites; what is more relevant is to find out who stands where and why in the urban system. As we shall see soon, the study of small urban neighbourhoods will help to throw much light on this question.

This discussion leads us to another set of problems which rotate around the definition of the city as a (colonial) social system not sealed off from its surroundings but with particular characteristics. Because most urban studies have dealt with particular aspects of urbanisation and urbanism, most researchers have lost sight of the relevance of the totality to the particular. Much time has been taken up with the study of ethnicity, voluntary associations, problems of adjustment and accommodation and basic survey work to establish fundamental characteristics of the urban population. In addition many students of urban Africa have concentrated on the study of the family unit, on the social functions of kinship, and on the emerging structures "beyond" kinship, on entrepreneurial activities and political organisation. However, few studies have approached the town as a system of economic and political power, where alliances are contracted for particular reasons, where lines of stratification emerge, where avenues of mobility are established and where particular groups exploit other groups. What we need, George Jenkins (1966) writes, is:

... more studies of how certain types of people lead other types of people in certain circumstances and fewer tabulations of figures demonstrating that some people have more education, money, cars, houses and medical care than others without demonstrating the social consequences of these differences.

Much of the literature looking at urban classes concentrates either on the new elites which have taken over from their former colonial masters or on chieftaincy, generally viewed as in a process of decay. Very little attention has been paid to the middle roles such as the foreman, or those who combine several roles such as the businessman who used his wealth to become a chief. We know too little about those crucial pivotal structures which Leo Kuper calls intercalary and Fred Riggs refers to as prismatic. Yet particularly in the cities the colonial situation created many such persons and structures, which are neither here nor there in terms of their antecedents. Kuper views the colonial system as one in which many sources of power (economic, political, and cultural) converge in a dominant group creating a class system of an administrative rather than capitalistic base, in which restricted opportunity for the disadvantaged group enhances the significance of small differences.

In Chapter 2 we put forward the view that an urban area should be analysed as a total system (which extends beyond its boundaries into the region and the nation of which it is merely a small part) in which various parts (sub-systems), be they discrete or overlapping, are collateral resulting in some measure of continuity and coherence in the system as a whole. So far few researchers have treated the data they collect in these terms; fewer still have collected the kind of data which would reveal how the system is put together; what the sub-systems are (ethnic groups, occupational or class groups, political groups, or neighbourhoods); how they are clearly identified; where their points of contact are, overlap or separate; and on what issues do they form alliances and what issues bring them into conflict. Furthermore, few studies have shown the methods and content of communication between various groups; how value systems make a "civic" culture or detract from it; how systems of sanctions operate to foster unity or competition; and what acts and ideas are translated into symbols understood by all, and what acts and ideas use symbolic forms particular to various groups. To this we might add such questions as how is a unified political administration achieved in a diversified urban area; how is political authority enforced; how are urban political leaders made; how do they "move over" from a local ethnic anchorage to the higher levels of urban administration (and from there on to the national level); and how are controversial political issues resolved under conditions of extreme inequalities of wealth, status and opportunity? Each of these questions is more than a mere enumeration of topics still to be explored. They are offered for consideration because they touch on matters central to an understanding of "how the system works." They take us far from the more conventional surveys and the institutional studies which are primarily focussed on some particular aspect of change and adaptation to urban conditions. Such research rarely exposes the critical features of the urban system, the strategies of power which hold it together, or the dialectic which "moves the system along." It is a challenge to urban anthropologists to distill out of this maze of questions which can be asked, problems which can be formulated, and propositions which can be tested. In Chapter 2 it was suggested that game theory might provide the conceptualisations and the definitions needed to tackle the topics set out above.

What appropriate methodology can be used to tackle these questions is likewise uncertain and, hence, open to a good deal of experimentation. What does seem certain, however, is that before we can embark on detailed studies it is essential that we have acquired a basic knowledge of the urban area as a whole. It is absolutely imperative that we become acquainted with the history of the area, its basic demographic features, the broad outlines of the political administration, a minimal knowledge of the composition of the population, what significant characteristics can be traced to the colonial legacy and, finally how the population makes its living. Having established these numerous parameters (which alone could be the basis of creative research), it is then possible to concentrate on one or more particular problems defining them in such a manner as to expose their relationship to the critical features of the urban system. This, again, shows the necessity of conducting micro studies.

Finally, we must make a brief comment about a subject dear to the heart of the social anthropologist, and that is the study of "social relationships" – urban social relations in our case. As we pointed out several times, the study of kinship is considered vital to the analysis of behaviour, social organisation and the relations between individuals and groups. However, it is rather unlikely that African urban social relationships, under present conditions, lend themselves readily to classical kinship analysis for the reasons listed as follows.

First, only very truncated segments of kin units are found in the urban community. Only in unusual circumstances is this not so (Schwab 1962). Secondly, kinship, as a system, is so embedded in the totality of African life that for it to function it must be reinforced by conditions which are commensurate with its purpose, i.e. a fairly high degree of social and cultural homogeneity, small-scale communities, and a normative system which is widely shared. While these conditions may not be totally absent in urban life, as in Yoruba towns, the extreme diversity, size of the city and particular attitudes and habits which usually accompany urbanisation, act as impediments to the operation of much that is demanded by the rules of kinship. Thirdly, it is not unreasonable to suggest that many migrants to the towns leave the rural areas because they wish to cut themselves free from some of the more burdensome demands of kinship obligations. This is not to suggest that the urbanite wishes to cut himself off irrevocably from the network which allocated to him rights and mutual aid. Rather it is to suggest that the most suitable social unit in an urban area is likely to be smaller, and that considerable value is attached to individual initiative and mobility. It is certainly a widespread fact in urban Africa that the established urbanite will look after the well-being of his wife and children first and foremost. At the same time, for as many people who can be found turning away their kin, as many others will share their earnings and facilities with those who camp on their doorsteps asking for help. But there is little doubt that many traditional rights and duties have lapsed. While the smaller kin unit might be more tightly knit than before, the extended kin group has little chance of surviving in urban Africa. It is true that certain entrepreneurial activities might lead to extensive kin cooperation (Marris 1968, 1968a); at other times, though, the view is frequently advanced by African entrepreneurs that many aspects of the kinship system are incompatible with modern business operations.

Although it will continue to be the task of the urban anthropologist, and sociologist, to study social relationships and, up to a point, to make this study a central concern (Southall 1961), the emphasis is likely to shift to the analysis of specifically *urban* facors as they modify and transform kinship links into associational ties (Gutkind 1965, 1965a) where such links play a lesser part. Both Southall (1959, 1961) and Mitchell (1958, 1960, 1966) have suggested approaches and theories in the study of urban social relations; Southall by using the concept of role (performance, distribution, density) and Mitchell by concentrating on internal and extrinsic factors. Mitchell suggests that urban social relations can be analysed in terms of three categories: structural relations, categorical relations and personal networks. He considers the former to be the dominant type of relations under urban conditions. They are, in his words (1967 : 51) "work relationships . . . [which] are probably the most tightly structured of all urban social relationships in the sense that the statuses and roles among workers are rigidly defined in terms of productive activity in which they are engaged." Kinship plays a minimal part in these relationships. On the other hand, categorical relationships "arise in situations where, by the nature of things, contacts must be superficial and perfunctory." These relationships are common, he writes (1966 : 52-53).

...in the daily life of a large town which [is] populated by people from many different tribes and where neighbourhoods are always changing in composition. They may occur in urban crowds, in beer-halls, in markets, and so on. Here town-dwellers tend to characterize people in terms of some visible characteristic and to organize their behaviour accordingly. ...It is an essential of categorical relationships that the internal divisions within a category should be ignored.

Southall (1961 : 39) makes the same point when he writes that: "It is rather a matter of external classification than of self-identification." While categorical relationships spring from urban "daily life" situations, Mitchell also points to two other significant conditions which influence these relationships: race and ethnicity. The former he cites as the "most striking type of categorical relationship" and of the latter that this relationship operates "as a way of simplifying or codifying behaviour in otherwise 'unstructured' situations." Jean Rouch (1956) refers to this type of categorisation as "super-tribalism" while Wallerstein (1960) has pointed to the same phenomena at the national level. But categorical relationships are more than a convenient way for the urbanite to bring order into the ethnic mosaic. Both Mitchell (1957) and Nkosi (1965) suggested that the etiology of these categorical relationships "may be related functionally to the sort of social situation which exists in African towns" (Mitchell 1966 : 54) and that they help to channellise conflict and hostility, between "categories" of the urban population, into acceptable expressions, i.e. the Kalela Dance practiced in the towns of Zambia; although at other times, and in more complex circumstances, they may take on more dramatic form as in urban South Africa where inter-ethnic Zulu fights are not uncommon. Nkosi (1965 : 8) offers this explanation of these fights:

The city has merely increased the pressures on the individual migratory labourer, thus making it even more necessary to find outlets for his aggression, while simultaneously increasing the penalty for engaging in tribal forms of combat. The ubiquitous police are ever ready to haul away anyone showing a propensity toward violence, which, in the urban areas, include most Africans forced to live abrasively on top of one another in squalid overcrowded conditions which help to produce maximum tension. At the same time tribal fighting in the urban community is stripped of much of the surrounding ritual, of the strict tribal code of conduct, and merely becomes brutal and cathartic. For the truly urbanized, sticks and clubs have been exchanged for more lethal weapons such as knives, iron bars, and even revolvers. For the less urbanized, clubs are still in fashion, for as the Zulus would put it, one does not walk the streets empty handed like a woman.

As urban conditions deteriorate for the masses of the poor and the unemployed, hostility and conflict between various categories of the population is likely to become more widespread as divisions are more sharply drawn. As competition increases so does the likelihood that conflict cannot be channellised into ritual and ceremonial expression or otherwise institutionalised, i.e. political or sporting activities (Scotch 1961). While the author carried out fieldwork in Nairobi and Freetown (Gutkind 1964 and 1966), he was a frequent witness on housing estates and in beer bars to various types of conflict (ranging from heated debates just on the point of turning into minor riots to cases of physical assault) between members of two or more ethnic groups who accused one another of political domination, and pointed to the corruption and nepotism this produced, charging that this was the source of the disadvantage suffered by others. As one might expect, on such occasions the air was filled with insults, obscene charges and threats of dire consequences to be suffered by each and everyone. While it is possible to suggest, as Nkosi (1965) has done, that such outbursts can perhaps be interpreted as an attempt to relive a glorious past, when viewed in the context of urban Africa it is more reasonable to suggest that the roots of such violence rest in economic, political and social conditions. Under such circumstances, categorical relations, which order the contacts between discrete ethnic and class segments of urban society, are turned into what might be called paroxymic relations which are produced by intense conflict, competition and agitation which arises frequently. Perhaps few other situations provide the urban anthropologist with richer data than the study of these relations and the events which brought them into being. The pioneering work done by Mitchell (1957), Nkosi (1965) and Scotch (1960, 1961) presents us with preliminary methodological and conceptual models.

Finally, Mitchell uses the label of personal network relations (which Plotnicov (1967) calls "Egocentric") "which individuals have built up around themselves in towns." The literature on this topic has recently been greatly refined with the publication by Mitchell (1969) on social networks in the towns of Central Africa. To date, the concept of social networks appears to be the most useful, and the most comprehensive, for the study of urban social relationships. It emphasises the "constructionist" and optative aspects of these networks, how they are built up and the specific purposes they serve. Furthermore, network analysis reveals not merely such matters as the degree of mobility of urbanites (Epstein 1961) but also where and how ethnic, occupational and class sub-systems overlap and where they do not and why. Thus the reconstruction of these personal and group networks (or the use of participant observation to observe their construction and use at any moment in time) combine, in rather subtle ways, micro and macro techniques. At the micro level, the network is constricted as it involves primarily kin and close friends (the effective network), and at the macro level, the extended level, the network can range (ecologically) over the whole urban area. In this manner the researcher can build up a fairly comprehensive knowledge of the town; the usefulness of the concept goes beyond the documentation of urban personal social relationships. As network "maps" (as it were) are drawn, the most critical points of urban systems are revealed which in turn can become foci of further studies. No doubt many anthropologists will be inclined to concentrate on small-scale relationships as these are considered to be more akin to those with which they have become acquainted in rural studies. However it is a matter for research to determine what kind of networks are of greater magnitude, i.e. close-knit or extended ones. In terms of the total urban situation non-kinship networks would appear to have greater importance in the long run, for the reasons advanced earlier. The social field in which the urbanite operates is a large one defined by the work situation, and even more so by his search for employment, the neighbourhood in which he lives, his participation in political activities and his search for relaxation. Although, according to Mayer (1961), some migrants restrict their social field of contact, the majority respond to the diversity of demands and conditions of urban life which involves them in interaction over a wide social field. However, Southall (1961 : 28) has pointed out that the

intensive study of small-scale relationships also provides a means of exploring the interstitial limbo in the more formal structure of society. The more formal the structure, the less extensive and significant is the limbo. It is at its maximum in many African towns because the formal structure is so wide or alien that it leaves great gaps in the social life of the masses of the people. It is of long-term importance in towns which continue to depend on a large population of temporary migrants and it is of transitional importance for both towns and individuals moving on to a more formally structured existence.

He concludes (p. 30) by suggesting that even face-to-face relationships "spring up without the conventional bases of kinship or neighbourhood [that] the full nexus of kinship and tribal obligations is often purposely evaded by town dweller... [yet] drawn upon and turned to new uses." In short, the principles and rules of kinship are altered, or exist in vacua, by (urban) situational circumstances and conditions and replaced by corporate groups such as voluntary associations, mutual aid societies, political parties, trade unions, guilds and professional associations. Thus each urbanite has to establish and define his own kinship and network ties. To establish how this is done requires more of the kind of case studies offered by Plotnicov (1967).

4. *The Town versus the Neighbourhood*

Many students of urban Africa have repeatedly pointed out that it is impossible to study *the* town in its totality. Although this clearly depends on its size, it is probably fair to suggest that any urban place over five thousand people presents the researcher with serious methodological problems. Nobody should be tempted to water down their research, to substitute extensive observation for intensive analysis, to the point that no clear picture of urban life emerges from a presentation. We are, therefore, left with very little choice but to concentrate on smaller units, hoping that we have made the right decision as to why we wish to study this area, or that unit rather than another. As we indicated earlier, it is a good investment, even if it does take time, to obtain basic knowledge about the town. Of course much time can be saved if demographic materials and maps are available. These should be studied very carefully. Air photographs are even more important, but they are rarely available. One should spend days walking around the town and keep a very careful record of where various communities are located, what their densities are, how the area is laid out, what facilities exist, what languages are spoken, what the basis of the livelihood is, what is the nature of the contiguous community, how is the town administered, what supra-urban agencies there are and, of course, as much as can be obtained about the history of the town. Many features will be easy to detect such as the racial composition of the urban population, whether it lives in racial or mixed enclaves, whether the residential lay-out is spatial or very congested, whether there is extreme ethnic heterogeneity, absence or presence of children, whether there are housing estates versus individual dwellings in slum areas, or the presence or absence of beggars. This device is perhaps no more than impression gathering which only a fool would dare to translate into explanations about social organisation and behaviour. But to gather these impressions is an important and vitally essential step. Even when there are publications about a particular urban area, because changes come with such speed it is wise to make this investment in time and effort.

All towns, whatever the size, however "atomistic" they are said to be, are composed of zones, segments, neighbourhoods, self-contained housing estates, courtyards, commercial and industrial areas, recreational complexes, markets, "the inner city" region, and the "suburbs", slum areas, green belts, service centers and numerous focal points where people reside, meet, and conduct their business. Thus any town has its particular social ecology, its distribution of the population, according to various criteria. These might be treated as natural units made up of people willing, if not always able, to live together who share a number of common characteristics such as religion, language and ethnic background, occupation, education and wealth. It is a pattern familiar to every urban dweller in North America. There are some locations which are considered desirable and others not so. The residents of African towns drift, in the same way as we do, to the location of their choice and to those in which they can afford to live. But wealth alone is probably not the main determinant of place of residence in African towns. More important is the ethnic and educational background of the urbanite. Wealthy men may elect to live in poor areas because they are occupied by members of the same ethnic group, while others pay less attention to this and move into ethnically mixed communities. In short, the social ecology of a town gives the lie to those who claim that African towns are one solid undifferentiated super slum. Neighbourhoods, large or small, mixed or heterogeneous, abound.

Although some problems of interest to the urban anthropologist cannot be anchored in a neighbourhood, such as the question. "What is the structure of urban local government?", or "How do voluntary associations contribute to urban integration?", a great many other problems can be investigated from this vantage point. It is the kind of "natural" unit which in size, and perhaps also in composition, is enough akin to a "tribe" so that the anthropologist may feel less confused and less threatened by urban conditions. But apart from making the research a little easier, the rationale for the selection of a neighbourhood is that it not only reflects, but in fact embodies, many of the characteristics and conditions extant in the town as a whole. For it must never be forgotten that neighbourhoods are merely segments of the larger urban totality, although they differ from one another significantly for reasons of their lay-out, their composition, the activities of the residents and their mobility.

Few urban neighbourhood studies have been conducted by anthropologists in Africa. Fraenkel (1964) concentrated on the Kru-speakers in Monrovia who are concentrated in a number of small areas. Gutkind (1957) studied a relatively small peri-urban area which, as seen below, was divided into four neighbourhoods; Hellmann (1948) studied a court yard in Johannesburg; Parkin (1969) focussed on two small African housing estates and Pons (1961, 1969) on all the residents along "Avenue 21" in Stanleyville (now Kinsangani), Zaire.

The analysis of structure and organisation of urban neighbourhoods reveals information at the micro and the macro level. At the macro level the neighbourhood reflects the most dominant characteristics of the urban area as a whole, and the region and the nation of which it is a small part, i.e. its resource base reflects the agricultural, entrepreneurial, commercial, and industrial activities of the nation as a whole, as do the earnings of the neighbourhood residents (as these reflect the general tempo of economic development; a slow rate of growth fills the neighbourhood with unemployed young men); its political administration as part of the administrative system of the national government which passes down its policies to the neighbourhood via a local government administration and/or a political party (or parties); and its composition as a reflection of both demographic and ethnic features of the nation as a whole. At the micro level a neighbourhood study reveals how a small community incorporates these extrinsic factors with or without loss of its autonomy, how its unique characteristics have come into being, and what extrinsic factors the residents accept, and why, and what they reject, and why. Furthermore, neighbourhood studies make it possible for us to turn away from the "impact theorists" (Bennett 1967) to the optative element in social orga- nisation or, as Barth (1967 : 662) has put it, "to describe how people in fact manage to arrange their lives." With this perspective neighbourhood studies allow us to determine why and how people make particular choices and how they allocate priorities among the choices. Though Fredrik Barth (1967) is not concerned with the study of urban neighbourhoods, he makes a significant point which adds a further rationale to our propositions (p. 668):

In our efforts to understand social change [we shift] our attention from *innovation* to *insti- tutionalisation* as the critical phase of change. People make allocations in terms of the pay- offs that they hope to obtain, and their most adequate bases for predicting these payoffs are found in their previous experience or in that of others in their community. The kinds of new ideas that occur can no more determine the direction of social change than mutation rates can determine the direction of physical change. Whatever ideas people may have, only those that constitute a practicable allocation in a concrete situation will be effected. And if you have a system of allocations going – as you always must where you can speak of change – it will be the rates and kinds of payoffs of alternative allocations *within that system* that determine whether they will be adopted, that is, institutionalised. The main con- straints on change will thus be found in the system, not in the range of ideas for innovation, and these constraints are effective in the phase of institutionalisation.

This poses new conceptual and methodological problems which cannot be worked out in a large-scale setting. Furthermore, nowhere can this kind of change be better observed than in an urban community; and nowhere is there a better comparative foundation than in an urban area where a series of neighbourhoods can be selected which are part of a single system. The study of a particular neighbourhood allows us to demonstrate how a particular ur- ban society develops a "system of strategies for acquiring its needed resour- ces, and also, for controlling the external agencies that provide them" (Ben- nett 1967 : 446). This is not to suggest that African urban communities are set on isolating themselves but rather to emphasise that local communities are not passive recipients. What is involved is a complex interplay, Bennett (1967 : 451) has suggested, between, in our case, the neighbourhood and the town as a whole; indeed the same is true between various neighbourhoods, i.e. there are economic and political relations between local urban neighbourhoods, between immigrant areas and those occupied by the permanent residents, between the suburbs and the inner city and between the slum dwellers and those in the better residential areas.

The lesson to be drawn from this for the urban anthropologist is simple: we need more and better small neighbourhood studies. These will have to reflect new analytical models and new methodologies. Experimentation is of the essence. We should not attempt to reproduce or adapt the conventional style of North American or European community study. African urban studies must pioneer new frontiers and new perspectives in social anthropology.

Finally, we mentioned earlier how important it is to gain some insights into the basic physical, organisational, structural, and institutional features of the urban area as a whole so as to be able to define and eventually to select contrasting neighbourhoods for further study. To show what can be done quickly, we now reproduce, from the author's fieldnotes, some passages about the peri-urban area of Mulago, Kampala, Uganda which was studied intensively between 1953 and 1957 (Gutkind 1963 and Southall and Gutkind 1957). Mulago contained 1,400 people and covered an area of some 74 acres; it was, thus, too large to be studied by one person. Although generalised surveys were initially conducted, with the help of two research assistants, more detailed work could only be carried out in smaller neighbourhoods.

There are four distinct areas in the suburb of Mulago which appear to be demarcated on the basis of density of population, ethnic composition and, it seems, occupational and "class" differences. The first of these, which I will now call the "inner core", has a density (according to a quick survey) of perhaps 70 persons per acre. It appears to be the main commercial centre and borders on the Municipality of Kampala and a large all-African teaching hospital connected with the local university. It is an area of great activity and a thoroughfare to the other areas. Those who live away from this inner core visit it frequently to make their purchases in the shops along the "main street". I have not seen many people from the other areas visit this place just to meet friends. Perhaps this is due to the fact that this area is almost totally occupied by Baganda. In addition the *muluka* (parish) chief resides here, who is a Muganda, and the weekly Saturday afternoon *lukiko* (council) is held just outside his house.

The second area, just to the west of the main street, has a slightly lesser density. I estimate between 50 and 60 per acre. It is a narrow belt some 90 yards wide and stretching some 400 yards due north and south parallel to the main street. Here are located many, perhaps 11, of the beer bars, and most of the charcoal and firewood sellers. There are virtually no shops. My first estimate suggests that at least 80% of the residents here are non-Baganda, and that over twenty different "tribes" are represented with the Rwanda and Toro in the majority. This alone makes this a very different neighbourhood. It is a much poorer area; the houses are in bad repair, several have burned down (how?), the paths are not well kept. The roofs of the houses are low, the doors narrow and few of them are plastered with white clay over the red mud. Occasionally there is a small cultivated plot but generally the houses are far too close. Almost all the migrants seem to be tenants (in contrast to the first area in which most homes are owned by the occupants) as both houses and land belong to the Ganda. In this area I have seen few material attributes of urban life such as radios, cars, bicycles, newspapers, good furniture ... Few residents here speak English and I think that illiteracy is high. It is, in a way, a depressing area. One gets the impression that the migrants try to humble themselves to their Ganda neighbours and that they move about with caution when they leave their neighbourhood. At the same time there are so many bars which are usually open with lots of people sitting either inside the room or on benches outside. There is a lot of social life in this place. People play drums, sing, dance, socialize, get too drunk and vomit on some open patch. I have seen lots of fights in this place in the span of just two weeks, and I am told that all the thieves live here. Occasionally one sees a better house under construction (an immigrant who has done well, perhaps) but on the whole it is a poor area. There do not seem to be separate kitchen and wash houses. In the late afternoon the place really comes to life as the single men come from work and start to cook their meals and wash their clothes. There seem to be very few women in this area – although all the beer sellers are and, they tell me, that most of them are Ganda women. They seem to have the economics of that tied up pretty well.

The third area is to the west and north and contrasts really strongly with both the inner commercial core and the migrant area. Here the density of population has dropped very sharply. I doubt whether it is more than 10 per acre. Hence the whole area looks different. It is more spacious, more rural in a way because there are lots of sizable *bibanja* (plots). Also the houses are much larger and often well plastered. Occasionally they are even painted with whitewash. The roofs are higher, there are windows (but not with glass) and nice doors. Here live many of the Ganda artisans and traders who work in Kampala, and one or two who have shops on the main street in the first area. There also seem to be one or two immigrants in this area. Their houses are not quite as good as their Ganda neighbours but they are far better than in the second area. There is no commercial life here. The touch of the urban is in the houses and in what is in them. Occasionally a car may be seen parked outside a house, but it is more likely to belong to a visitor than the occupant of the house. But there are lots of bicycles about. This is the area where many of the *batongole* (headmen who assist the *muluka* chief) live. They are really stewards who look after the land of absentee landlords and represent their interests. They also collect rent from roomers living in the second area. One has the impression that unlike the second area, there is some sort of family life here because there are women and children about the place. I have not seen any beer bars in this area, although I did discover two illegal *waragi* (Nubian gin) sellers. It is potent stuff. They seem to do well as they live in good houses. They are both Ganda. There are a number of people here who call themselves farmers, some grow food for sale and others have small patches of coffee trees. One man keeps five cows and sells milk and another goes to his market garden a little over one mile away. But most householders in this area seem to grow some of their food needs. But they often do not cultivate the plots themselves. Some of them employ migrants from the next area to help them. People have nice kitchen houses and almost everyone has a separate wash place. Women can often be seen preparing large meals (steaming *matoke*, plantain, in huge pans) for their family. In the afternoon they may sit outside the house, usually in the back courtyard sewing or weaving mats. People are quite well dressed, few torn shirts about the place. There are radios and gramophones. Compounds are well kept and rooms are large with concrete floors. Few women cook with firewood, they use charcoal or pressure stoves. I have not noticed many disturbances such as fights or heated arguments. I saw a suspected thief being arrested. Instead of being beaten by the locals he was taken quietly to the chief.

This is also the area whose inhabitants seem to take little notice of the people who live around them. Few of them seem to have much interest in the local administration of the parish – only the *batongole* have this interest. The area itself, because it is spacious, is divided into yet smaller units because paths seem to cut it up a bit. Two or three families live quite close together in sort of clusters. The residents certainly think of themselves as superior to the immigrants. They have more education and the menfolk can generally speak English quite well. But most of the people here seem to be somewhat more reluctant to talk. Women will say that they must wait until their husband comes home to answer any questions. Indeed men sometimes gave instructions not to answer any questions. Often, during the day, mothers will tend to their children, give them a bath or take them to a nearby health clinic for babies. Although breast feeding is the norm, this is the first area where I have seen some mothers use bottles.

Finally, there is a considerable area to the north, some 150 yards wide and running the whole length east and west of the northern part of Mulago. This area is a strange mixture of very large houses, well constructed with big rooms and panelled doors, glass windows and large court-yards, and poor dwellings. I am not sure who lives in the latter. The big houses are often closed because they belong to doctors, or Buganda Government officials, who spend a great part of their time on safari, and rich traders who own several houses both in the country and in other parts of Kampala. Houses and plots are spaced well apart and the average size of plot is at least two acres. The house owners usually own the land as well. It might be that the poorer houses are occupied by house servants and those who look after the plots on which some people grow a little food. It is the only part of Mulago where some people have flower gardens, small but nice. There is absolutely no commercial development here. I saw no shops of any kind. I would describe it as a sort of dispersed homestead area. This is really a different area but work here is not likely to be easy because few people are about. Yesterday I learned that some of the owners allow their relatives and friends from the rural areas to live in these homes. One young woman told me that the house belongs to her uncle, an Agricultural Officer, and that she had come to do some shopping in town but would only stay a few days. It was, she said, a very convenient place for her to stay.

These field notes are reproduced simply to indicate that a good deal of basic information can be gleaned in a very short time. The information reproduced above was obtained in just under two weeks, but this was preceded by three weeks intensive observation in and reading about the Municipality of Kampala. Air photographs, maps, historical accounts and statistical data and municipal records were consulted. The author was also given permission to read through a great deal of information in the archives of His Highness the Kabaka's Government. All this took about five weeks before work commenced in Mulago. In those early weeks impressions rather than hard data was obtained, but it was a vital period because it helped to define the area for subsequent concentration, but always with that vital background knowledge about the town as a whole, the region, the province in which Kampala was located and the country (Uganda) as major points of reference. Once the neighbourhoods in Mulago fell into perspective, smaller units yet were discovered which formed the core of some particular activities, such as the shopkeepers and the beer brewers. Other small units clustered around a courtyard, a section of a street, five houses whose occupants were close friends, a small ethnic association, and several other groupings which served as the basis for finding out how the whole matrix was held together.

5. *Heterogeneity as a Particular Problem in Methodology*

Every African urban study makes a special point of portraying the extreme diversity of the population, the ethnic mosaic which gives each town its particular pattern of social organisation and structure. Thus Leslie (1963 : 79-80) describing the occupants of *one* particular house in Dar es Salaam, notes:

There is the usual mixture of tribes: of the Arabs one, the owner, is a Seiyid from Shibam in the hinterland of the Eastern Aden Protectorate. The other Arabs are coastal men from tribes to whom it is traditional to come to Dar es Salaam as it is for the Nyamwezi; then there are the three Northern Rhodesians, come up here to get clerical work . . . ; a Makonde and a Yao sharing; a Sagara and a Luguru sharing; an Ngindo couple; and a Mwera pair of boys; the accent is thus predominantly southern. The Arabs all went only to Koranic School, but all are literate in Arabic. The three Rhodesians all completed the primary course and are literate in Swahili (Roman script); the same is true for the other southerners, the Mwera and the Makua, the Yao from Lindi, and the Sagara from Kilosa. But the Ngindo and the Makonde both from Lindi are uneducated and illiterate.

And in another house which Leslie (p. 73) describes as "in fact perhaps more homogeneous than most":

the owner is an Mbunga, his wife a Pogoro; next, a Zaramo couple; then, a Kutu man with a Zaramo wife; then a Zigua with a Luguru wife; a Haya with a Zaramo wife; a Pogoro couple; a Tonga with a Ngoni wife; a lone Rufiji, a lone Luguru, the two Pogoro brothers, and a lone Zigua. This is certainly quite a collection, ten tribes in eleven rooms, but when one looks more closely it is not as diverse as all that: for instance, the languages of Mbunga, Pogoro and Ngoni are more or less mutually intelligible; the Zaramo and Luguru tribes, though they cannot understand each other's languages, both speak Swahili fluently from boyhood and are in fact closely related tribes. The Tonga and Ngoni are also related.

Such ethnic heterogeneity is by no means exceptional. In Mulago (Gutkind 1957) the author counted representatives of some thirty-one ethnic groups. While the majority came from within Uganda, a good many had come to settle in the area from Kenya, Tanganyika, Rwanda, Burundi, Zaire, Sudan, Zanzibar, Malawi and Zambia. To be sure the ethnic mosaic was dominated by the Ganda and those groups living close to Kampala, but all the other groups were represented in sufficient number to be identifiable as a particular group, whose members perhaps lived close together or formed associations which kept them in regular contact. Yet, as one turns the pages of many urban studies, not a single author has raised the particular conceptual and methodological problems associated with the heterogeneity of the urban population. African urban studies are given no place in the recently edited papers by Kuper and Smith (1969) on *Pluralism in Africa*, in which heterogeneity and pluralism are most often treated as synonymous.

The implications for African urban studies are far reaching if we ignore, or otherwise find ourselves unable to deal with, the relevance of this phenomenon. In the analysis of African urban systems a basic decision will have to be made whether to concentrate on the cultural or the structural aspect of heterogeneity. While these two approaches are not mutually exclusive, and their relevance to each other should be brought out, not only will different data come to light as we concentrate on one approach or the other but, also, our interpretation will be rather different. Thus Smith (1969 : 34-35) warns:

> However, these social and cultural dimensions of heterogeneity and pluralism neither necessarily nor always correspond. This is so for two major reasons. Besides ideational and procedural correlates of social relations, culture includes such systems as language, aesthetic styles, philosophies, and expressive forms which may be transferred across social boundaries easily and with little social effect. Conversely, systems of social relations may perdure despite substantial shifts in their cultural content or explicit orientations. Thus, despite their common institutional basis and tendencies to congruence, culture and society may vary independently; indeed, their divergent alignments have special importance in contexts of pluralism ...

Although culture and structure are related through institutions, it is basically certain distinctive processes of interaction which regulate social relationships in heterogeneous societies. How these processes work, and the nature of interaction between various groups, are primarily determined by urban conditions rather than cultural differences. Thus the analysis of heterogeneity under urban conditions is best treated in structural terms. Structural analysis of heterogeneity will reveal how racial, ethnic, cultural, language *and* occupational and class differences are converted into particular types of personal and group relations; how economic and political inequalities emerge; around what urban conditions conflict arises (and whether the element of heterogeneity is significant and if so why), how political relations are structured, and what impedes or encourages the development of mechanisms of incorporation of various ethnic groups into the urban culture. It is, of course, possible that homogeneous and heterogeneous conditions do not pose basically contrasting patterns of interaction, particularly under urban conditions, because pressures toward consociational (Smith 1969 : 94) forms of interaction are considerable. Yet at what levels of the social order this takes place remains a major question to be answered.

Heterogeneity should not be defined, in the urban context at least, solely in terms of ethnic pluralism. Urban areas, be they in Africa or elsewhere, are invariably pluralistic if not in racial then certainly in cultural terms (although some towns are more pluralistic than others). In urban areas structural heterogeneity is reinforced by class, education, wealth, neighbourhood, political and religious affiliation (all of which might be linked to ethnic divisions). In such a model heterogeneity gives rise to a particular structure of social organisation – particularly urban social organisation, or as Kuper (1969 : 465) has put it, "Pluralism in a society refers then quite simply to a diversity of groups which sustain social relationships with one another." What the urban anthropologist should look for is more than the mere documentation of how many "tribes" live and work in a particular African town. It is particularly important to know how heterogeneity of urban populations has come about (obviously by migration of various groups), and it is equally important to analyse what Kuper (1969 : 473-479) has called the "Dimensions of Pluralism". By this he means that there are a number of mechanisms of incorporation, or exclusion, of diverse groups into a system. Unfortunately none of his models spring directly from African urban data, but these should be tested in future studies. All his models incorporate those aspects of social organisation we have previously termed "critical features" of the urban system, i.e. inequality-equality, continuity-discontinuity (tradition versus change), high-low mobility, cohesion-discohesion, occupational differentiation and class (stratification) differences.

Kuper (1969 : 479-480) concludes his skillful effort to synthesise the implications of the models put forward in *Pluralism in Africa*, by suggesting that two conditions can prevail: the polarisation of pluralism, and depluralisation. He suggests that:

polarization is marked by the heightened salience of sectional identity and the increasing perception of social relationships in terms of racial, ethnic, or other sectional conflict. Political reactions become polarized, as shown by antithetical interpretations of the same event . . . or by antithetical emotional responses . . .

At the objective level of polarization in social interaction, there is contraction of the middle ground of optional relationships, and sharpening of the qualitative contrasts between intersectional and intrasectional relationships. Lines and issues of cleavage are superimposed, and this is expressed in the rapid escalation of the most varied, and sometimes most minor local and specific disturbances to the level of general nationwide intersectional conflict. There is increasing violence, mounting by a dialectic of violence and counterviolence; and probably there are broad dialectical processes within the society, arising out of the distribution of land and of power, and driving toward more extreme polarization.

Depluralization, by contrast, indicates subjectively the diminishing salience of racial, ethnic, or other sectional ties. There may be explicit ideologies which assume the common interests of members of different sections, assert the efficacy of compromise and intersectional coopera- tion, and affirm the social ideal of assimilation (as in ideologies of the common society, or of the "melting pot"). Objectively, there is increasing continuity in the structures of the soci- ety, and the distribution of population in these structures. Other bases of association, hori- zontal linkages arising from common interests and functional differentiations, cut across ini- tial cleavages. Segregated, parallel, and intercalary structures dissolve, and there is increas- ing integration in institutional structures. Qualitative differences in intrasectional and inter- sectional relationships diminish. With the increasing significance of many diverse bonds be- tween people of different sections, lines of cleavage and issues of conflict become dissoci- ated, thus reducing the probability of escalation from minor disturbances. There is a commitment to compromise, and the cumulative experience of compromise and conflict res- olution may be expected to encourage further depluralization.

Whether the urban areas of Africa are in a process of increased ethnic polari- sation due to the heterogeneity of their population, or whether they are being depluralised (a process which can involve considerable violence), are questions which need a great deal of attention. To date a number of studies have focussed on various implications of ethnic diversity which has obscured an understanding of the processes of "homogenisation" as these are generat- ed under urban conditions. Whether environmental, economic, political and social conditions enhance or impede depluralisation should be a major topic for future African urban studies.

Because heterogeneity of the population is such a common characteristic of most towns, it is understandable that it is often treated as the most unique feature of urbanism. But this is not so. In the preceding pages we have repeatedly suggested that ethnicity, and its identifiable manifestations, as- sumes significance at particular times and under particular urban conditions. The various manifestations, therefore, of heterogeneity should be treated as dependent variables and urbanism (and urbanisation) as the independent variable.

In methodological terms, the heterogeneity of an urban population poses particular problems ranging from difficulties which arise in communication among people speaking many different languages, to the type of problems raised above. Problems of sampling are also compounded if the researcher wishes to obtain informants from a cross-section of the population. Possibly the best methodological approach is, once again, micro and macro analysis.

First, the range of heterogeneity needs to be established both from the point of view of ethnic diversity and in terms of diversity in occupation, education, wealth and class. Secondly, we need to retrace our steps to find out how, in general terms, the population did become ethnically diverse, i.e. when and what groups migrated to the town; how and what groups became established, where, and under what conditions, and in what occupations. Third, what is the relationship of particular colonial policies to the varied manifestations of urban heterogeneity (i.e. why colonial administrators treat-ed some tribes as "more honest " or "harder workers" than others)? Fourth, what is the relationship of economic changes, during the period of colonial-ism, to heterogeneity, i.e. what groups responded to what opportunities, and with what results? These, and numerous other questions, must be asked in an effort to piece together the circumstances which brought about the hetero-geneity of the urban population. The data obtained will lead to the recogni-tion that the diversity of this population reflects a similar diversity in the population as a whole. Trite as this observation might be, it in fact becomes the baseline for the analysis of numerous problems linking urban structures and behaviour to ethnic pluralism and other aspects of diversity. So much then for the macro approach.

At the micro level, several African urban studies offer insight into some basic aspects of heterogeneity, although direct concentration on this topic is rare. Most frequently, micro studies have concentrated on conflict aspects of urban heterogeneity (Nkosi 1965, Scotch 1964); the position of a particular ethnic group and its contacts and relationships with other groups (Fraenkel 1964); particular aspects of heterogeneity in an African housing estate (Par-kin 1969); the place of "strangers" in an African urban system (Cohen 1969, Plotnicov 1969); the ethnic and structural diversity of a particular African township, revealing distinctions between "conservative" and "modern" ur-banites (Mayer 1961, Powdermaker 1962; Wilson and Mafeje 1963); class analysis of urban systems (Gutkind 1970, Fraenkel 1964, Lukhero 1966); occupational prestige studies (Mitchell and Epstein 1959) and the micro analysis of small neighbourhoods (McVicar 1968, Pons 1961, 1969).

These studies have given us a good start. However, we now must concentrate more intensively on the relationships between pluralistic and structural diversity and various institutional and organisational patterns of towns, linking this diversity to change and modernisation generally. Thus, what is the relationship between urban heterogeneity and economic and social mobility, stratification, power, and authority, recruitment to and membership in various associations, basic characteristics of family and marriage, economic and religious institutions, employment patterns and entrepreneurial activities? Each of these should be treated in the context of models of change and modernisation to determine how plural and structural diversity increases or decreases, and under what conditions. Does the development of social classes in town (Plotnicov 1970) reduce integration and social participation resulting in greater segmentation, and increasing conflict potential inherent in ethnic and racial differences? On the other hand, the development of social class may be an indication, as well, of an expanding economy which allows a general participation in, and access to, new opportunities. This would also suggest that upward social mobility is possible and not invariably restricted to a particular segment of the population (Fallers 1963). If differential access to wealth and opportunity lead to a bifurcation of various exclusive, and possibly antagonistic, segments of the urban population, what then becomes the basis of group life? Does membership in ethnic associations assume greater significance? Is such membership a matter of choice, a natural drift by members of an "out" group who find protection and fellowship with one another? For example, the associations of unemployed in Lagos and Nairobi are ethnically very mixed, while employed men often hold membership in particular ethnic associations. Such a development seems to contradict a commonly held assumption that those in the lower stratum of society are more prone to join such associations while those in the middle and upper strata do not (Southall 1966, Lloyd 1966, 1966a).

The relationship between class and heterogeneity is cited as merely one example to indicate how changes in the political, economic, and social structure of African nations as a whole are likely to find particular expression in African towns. To date we have very few studies which indicate precisely how heterogeneity is manifest in urban life; how social classes are formed; whether groups relate to one another according to ethnic criteria or socio-economic position in the urban system. Because most studies have ignored the conditions and processes of change and modernisation, ethnicity has become the focus for analysis, treating it (falsely) as the independent variable. What kind of bias this reflects must be left to the reader to determine. To us it appears that the study of the relevance of heterogeneity in urban social organisation has been conceptualised as involving, essentially, the study of "tribesmen in town". This, of course, impedes any sort of understanding of the relevance of urbanism (and the particular style of life it creates) to social structure and social action patterns.

What we need, therefore, are comparative case studies of individuals (Plotnicov 1967), not randomly selected but using stratified sampling techniques, and obtain from them detailed accounts of their efforts to become established (over a period of time) in town. The towns selected for this purpose should likewise reflect a wide range of differences such as location, size, ethnic composition, function, economic base, impact of colonial policies, multi-racial and mono-racial characteristics and new and old towns (Southall 1961 : 6-13). From ethnic and non-ethnic associations we need to collect data on why and how they got started, and how they fit into the general urban order (and *not* what services they offer their members, or whether they provide an "adaptive mechanism" of one sort or another, for the emigrant – all of which has been repeatedly investigated). Such data as Fraenkel (1964) has collected from Monrovia on the urban social hierarchy, social mobility and the relation of social class to social origins, provides one model which needs further application.

To reiterate, heterogeneity in African towns is just one aspect of the total urban situation. The magnitude of its relevance and impact should be assessed in terms of urbanism and modernisation rather than abstracted from the matrix in which it operates.

6. *Participant Observation in an Urban Setting: The "Intensive" Anthropological Approach*

In the following sections we shall deal, briefly, with a number of research techniques, all of which have been used for many years, and which can be still used in African urban studies. Of course, these techniques will differ from one discipline to another. The excellent little volume edited by Hauser (1965) provides a useful statement on a wide variety of research methods used in urban studies. The reader should pay particular attention to the chapter by Matras (1965 : 73-87) who discusses various disciplinary approaches to urban studies ranging from historical to ecological approaches. We shall be concerned with basic anthropological techniques.

In an earlier section we quoted Philip Gulliver who expressed serious doubts concerning the use of standard anthropological research techniques in African studies (and one assumes from his comments that he would say the same to anthropologists working in towns elsewhere). In African urban studies, he writes (1965 : 97):

It was not possible for them to be of the kind of highly intimate, participant-observation project which has become the hallmark of most rural research. It was impractical, it was personally unsafe, and it was often disallowed by the local authorities. In any case, urban complexity, the absence of well-established cultural patterns and social structure, even the absence of a single language, made such intensive methodology unprofitable if not actually impossible. By necessity, recourse was had to extensive questionnaire techniques and statistical treatment with their obviously impersonal flavour, to the employment of numbers of field assistants who, despite their real worth, intruded between anthropologist and people in a way to which he was unaccustomed ... [Hence] some anthropologists, at least initially, have made no attempt to imitate orthodox anthropological methods when they study urban areas.

Before we go on to dispute much of what Gulliver says let us quote a few comments by the reviewer (Drake 1957 : 920) of *Townsmen in the Making* (Southall and Gutkind 1957):

Most anthropologists, too, will probably appreciate the vivid reports of conversations and brawls in beer-bars and on the streets; the interviews with a wide range of social types from chiefs to prostitutes ...

Because Gulliver has never conducted, at least not intensively, urban research, he is unaware of the fact that such studies are not, and rarely have been restricted to, the counting of heads and houses. Very few, if any, urban studies have made extensive use of questionnaire and statistical methods "with their obviously impersonal flavour", to the exclusion of in-depth participant-observations and anecdotal presentation. A quick review of eleven well-known African urban studies simply does not fit the characterisation which Gulliver has given them. Indeed, there are some very notable exceptions (Leslie 1963, Powdermaker 1962, Plotnicov 1967, Longmore 1959, Wilson and Mafeje 1963, and Southall and Gutkind 1957) which reflect deep involvement by the anthropologist and contain that "highly intimate" data Gulliver speaks about. In fact, the criticism has rather been that such urban studies lack a clear theoretical contribution which has been neglected in favour of simple accounts of the seamy side of everyday urban life.

There is no reason why "traditional" anthropological techniques cannot be used just as effectively in urban as in rural studies. Intensive observational techniques, i.e. participant-observation methods (Bruyn 1966, Babchuk 1962, Kluckhohn 1940, Miller 1952, Schwartz and Schwartz 1955, Vidich 1955, Becker 1958, Gold 1958, Trow 1957, Becker and Geer 1957) are possible as is intensive interviewing. Because the composition of the populations is more diverse, and the mobility of individuals rather higher than amongst the rural population, particular problems do arise. Nor must it be assumed that a few informants, however randomly selected, can provide in-depth and coherent information, or that participant-observation techniques, however skillfully used, provide the anthropologist with a magic which can tease the information out from anywhere and anyone. Depending on the topic and specific problem under investigation, it is possible that a smaller number of informants are required in village research on the assumption that the range of variation in structure and behaviour is somewhat narrower than in urban areas. Nor would it ever be disputed that urban research is perhaps more demanding and that participant-observation does not have about it that leisurely and relaxed quality as is usual in rural research. It might be more difficult to make friends (Shelton 1964) and ultimately to be trusted, among the people of a large city, although the recent works by Keiser (1969) and Liebow (1967) do not support this view. It is probably correct that those using participant-observation methods must learn to put up with certain pressures and difficulties rather different from those experienced in village research. For the urbanite time is money, and time spent with an anthropologist is money lost. Congestion and overcrowding make privacy in conversation with informants more difficult; the diversity of languages spoken in African towns may seriously interfere with close and prolonged contact: if the general speed of life is faster than in a rural area, and this is likely to be so, the researcher will find himself rushing about from place to place catching up with people who, having agreed to be at a given place at a given time, seem to be every other place at the same time! In a village one knows where people are, and the rhythm of life is not only somewhat slower but more predictable. These are part of the logistics of participant-observation and interviewing which need to be taken into account. What we might conclude from this is that fieldwork techniques, the standard participant-observation technique in particular, do not vary greatly, although the intensity of the field worker's involvement will vary from one situation to another. "When the anthropologist is in the field", writes Gulick (1970 : 124), "field work is his total life". He should know because he worked both in a village in Lebanon and in the town of Tripoli in Libya. He concludes (p. 151) that in "both studies, my methods were similar in that I relied primarily on my own powers of observation and anthropological skills in eliciting and recording information and feelings from other people."

There is no reason to suppose that the fieldworker cannot play an effective observational role (Gold 1958) in the course of his urban research although particular local and national conditions (Gutkind 1969) will strongly influence the role that he is to play. Furthermore, the method of participant-observation is not merely a tool used by the anthropologist, unlike all other methods it is closely related to his particular personality (Shelton 1964), his emotional stability and how he responds to stresses and strains (Wintrob 1969, Henry and Saberwal 1969, Freilich 1970, Bowen 1964, Spindler 1970). "In the final analysis", Henry (1969 : 46) wrote, "the success of fieldwork is largely the result of the unique interaction between the personality of the fieldworker, the nature of the research problem, and the socio-cultural environment in which research is undertaken."

The urban socio-cultural environment is, of course, different from that of a small village in the interior of an African nation. But as soon as the field-worker has become acquainted with the social contours of the town he can-not but fail to ease himself into the life of a particular family or neighbour-hood, into a particular set of circumstances, and establish relations with par-ticular individuals. He may not even be aware when and how his role changes from being a mere observer to being a participant-observer. Particu-lar situations will arise in which he may be one or the other, in which rela-tions will be distant, or intimate and prolonged. There is no evidence whatso-ever to believe that in a rural context the fieldworker is invariably, in all sit-uations, a complete participant (Gold 1958, Babchuk 1962) while in the town he is rarely more than just an observer. Whatever his role, by his own design or that which is assigned to him, Powdermaker (1968 : 420) has sug-gested:

There must be a high degree of reciprocal communication between him and the people he studies. This need represents an important difference between the methods of the social and the natural sciences. The chemist and the physicist do not communicate personally with molecules or atoms, but communication for the social scientist depends to a large degree on his psychological involvement. The fieldworker faces a special problem, however, for he must be both detached and involved. If this dual role is an inherent part of the anthropolo-gist's personality or self-image (strengthened by his training) he plays it spontaneously and easily.

It is true, as Gulliver (1965) has suggested, that in urban field studies the re-search assistant plays a somewhat larger part than in rural-based research, al-though this would only be true if the anthropologist is not prepared to learn the language of the people among whom he lives, an objective given rather low priority by Margaret Mead (1939) but high value by Lowie (1940). On the other hand, Audrey Richards (1935) has pointed out the usefulness of re-search assistants and the use of the questionnaire technique in village census research. Neither a poor language facility nor the use of research assistants impedes the use of participant-observation techniques in urban studies. What presents greater problems is the complexity of a town and its varied social life. If participant-observation is defined in terms of some kind of member-ship in, or close attachment to, one or more particular group, then urban con-ditions provide an ideal setting. Not only is the range of formal and informal, traditional and modern groups greater in towns than in rural areas (hence the anthropologist can match his inclinations, temperament and interests more smoothly by participating in congenial groups (Gulick 1970 : 143-145), but strangers are less conspicuous in town than in village life, a fact, which if true, facilitates observation and participation. To obtain membership in urban associations, political parties, welfare, sporting and religious groups is probably easier than participation in village-based groups which are primarily part of the kinship system. Thus Southall (1970) reports that he was a member of the Alur tribal association in Kampala, Uganda but makes no mention of a similarly close connection in rural Alurland. Whether such close connections provide more and better information, and what the consequences might be of "overrapport" (Miller 1952), cannot be predicted.

Clearly the method of participant-observation needs to be modified to suit each particular situation, be this in rural or urban research. However, in the latter context, modifications may have to be more extensive simply because this method was initially introduced, and subsequently refined, in the course of village research. Hence this technique for gathering information is based on certain premises about tribal social organisation. As a method it is thought to be particularly suitable in relatively small-scale and homogeneous societies. But such a connection is perhaps more a matter of accident than an indication that over time this method has been found uniquely suitable in the kind of research anthropologists normally do. Thus, Rosalie Hankey Wax (1968 : 239-240) points out:

Participant observation is essential to almost all branches of the social sciences that depend to any degree on understanding or meaning (Vidich 1955). Little can be accomplished in appraising or analysing data if neither the language in which they are expressed nor the point of view they reflect are understood by the analysts.

Like any other social research technique, participant-observation must be flexibly adapted to the procedures and values of the group being studied. It is not to be naively confused with the notion of "living like a native".

Some anthropologists are evidently reluctant to use this method on the grounds, as stated by Gulliver (1965 : 98), that urban societies are "unformed communities" and that urban research presents us with "a novel situation in Africa." The only thing novel is the inability of the anthropologist to accept the fact that urban life is as easily and readily researchable as community life anywhere, and that involvement in the life of the urbanite presents no greater problem than that portrayed in recent accounts by anthropologists working almost exclusively in rural communities (Freilich 1970, Spindler 1970). What differences there are, mostly of degree rather than of kind, should be a challenge to the anthropologist. True the urban anthropologists, most of whom are not troubled by such difficulties, are faced with a particularly complex social order and massive information which requires patient and systematic collection and analysis. To shy away from methodological challenges on the ground that urban studies are not really the bread and butter of the anthropologist can only project an image of our discipline which many of us want to change – permanently. If some urban anthropologists have thus far made relatively little use of the participant-observation method (which as we pointed out was basically not true), the reasons will be found to be rather different from those suggested by Gulliver. Indeed the argument could be made that the long neglect of urban studies has forced those who have eventually ventured into urban research to first do a great deal of groundwork: to answer such simple questions as who lives where, in what numbers, when did the migrants arrive and how do they make a living. It is for this reason that we must now turn briefly to the utility of survey techniques.

7. Survey Techniques: The Sociological Approach

The motto of North American sociology seems to be: when in doubt do a survey! Were it not for the often rather trite results which flow from this approach, to collect information so as to arrive at intelligent policy decisions, or to define a research question more precisely, such a motto makes good sense.

To the anthropologist social surveys are, generally, a new tool for research and most are ill equipped in using this technique. However, sociologists have conducted surveys (on most anything) for many years. Perhaps the first "scientific" survey, and also one of the most massive, was that conducted by Charles Booth who, before the turn of the century, initiated, at his own expense, a vast survey of "the whole of London society." When his data was finally published between 1889-1891, it was printed in seventeen volumes. His concern was primarily with the poor people of London whose living conditions he deplored and felt needed improvement. To be able to achieve this, he argued, required first "a true picture of the modern industrial organism." His aim was to combine observational with statistical research techniques. Most readers of these volumes seem to agree that what he set out to do, to collect as precise information as possible, was achieved with skill and insight.

Perhaps one of the earliest examples of the use of survey and census techniques in African (rural) anthropology comes from the research conducted by Dr. Audrey I. Richards (1935 and 1938) who, in the early 1930's, studied the Bemba of Zambia. Although she did not commence her work with a survey, she eventually designed a questionnaire and also collected individual case-records. She called the questionnaire "a useful weapon in the study of culture change", her main interest, and its use "nearly doubled the information ... previously obtained by the more pious resolution to 'ask as many people as I could'." The use of the case-records, utilising a questionnaire,

brings the anthropologist into individual contact with each member of a village for perhaps half an hour in the solitude of his or her own hut, and the individuals interviewed are thus a representative collection and not merely a set of the most voluble informants who are only too ready to haunt the tent door. (1938 : 53)

Dr. Richards clearly found this relatively new technique very useful not merely because she managed to gather more data with the use of the questionnaire than she might otherwise have obtained, but primarily because she collected *particular* information in a *standardised* manner. The information obtained helped her to learn more about the "extent and the variety of contact change." But she also offered a word of caution.

Nor is this work which could be successfully done by a novice, or even a new-comer in any one area. It needs a good knowledge of the language, and experience in dealing with each particular tribal type, as well as experimentation with the problems suitable for examination in this way. I would prophesy that the first sociological censuses undertaken by the anthropologist would be found to be completely worthless after a few weeks' further work. Nor ... do I think the collection of vital statistics throughout a tribal area is a job which the anthropologist should undertake, as well as his sociological inquiries. He has neither the time nor the qualifications for such work. (1938 : 58)

The use of survey methods, and the quantification of data, is viewed by many anthropologists as a threat to their long established fieldwork tradition in becoming deeply involved with people among whom they live. Survey techniques are treated as "sociological", as lacking in personal participation and detailed observation; anthropological techniques involve "a high degree of reciprocal communication between [the anthropologist] and the people he studies." However since the end of the Second World War, an increasing number of anthropologists have used survey and statistical techniques during some stage of their field work. This is particularly so in urban studies. Yet rarely (Acquah 1958) have survey methods taken the place of participation, intensive observation and interviewing. Urban studies have not yet, though, reached the stage described by Nathan Glazer (1964 : 43-44).

The sociologist today — whether his field of interest is the community, criminology, marriage and the family, world politics, social classes, housing — is a man who asks people questions and then statistically analyzes the answers to them. If he does not ask the questions himself, he hires someone else to ask them; or, if not that, he analyzes the statistics gathered by those who *have* asked questions – census-takers, social workers and others.

There are several reasons why the anthropologist, particularly the urban anthropologist, has turned cautiously to the use of survey and quantification methods. The anthropologist in the rural areas has slowly discovered that he is not working in static and custom bound societies and that neither social organisation, behaviour nor values are standardised to the point that all people conform to a single pattern. Belatedly we have recognised that "exceptions" cannot be set aside, because they are not exceptions, rather they reflect variability of social organisation and behaviour along a range from the ideal to the real. We are, therefore, interested in establishing the parameters of behaviour and values. To achieve this we need to study a larger number of cases (of people and events) drawn from a larger universe (Hanna 1966). This is not easily done if the anthropologist works in a large village or town.

We cannot participate in all social activity and we cannot interview all villagers. We therefore turn to some form of sampling and survey method. But what troubles the anthropologist is what kind of data can be treated in this way. Progressively the view is that almost any kind of information can be collected in this way – at least as it supplements data gathered in other ways.

Today many anthropologists are working in larger and what has come to be known as more complex societies. This allegedly increased complexity (as we have defined this in Chapter 2) has taken two forms: social organisational and material culture complexity. The former, under the impact of change and modernisation has dramatically increased the variability of behaviour and values and the latter has changed from simplicity to modern technology. Whether the anthropologist studies a small rural pre-industrial community or a modern town he cannot ignore the significance and implications of variations as these have become more widespread during the last hundred years. If this is not disputed, then we need the kind of data which documents these changes as they are spread throughout society. While one hundred years ago we might have been able to correctly say that all the people in a village ordered their lives in a very narrow range of permissible behaviour, today this would be an impossible statement to make. The response to, and adaptation to, change are as variable as responses and adaptation to fashions. We simply can no longer say that all village or town people react in a certain way because they all hold this or that view in common. What we need, therefore, is some way to document and measure variability. That is what surveys and questionnaires are designed to do. But having collected information about variability of organisation and behaviour, we suddenly find a great deal of data on our hands which need to be put into some kind of order and analysed. One way to do this is to apply quantitative techniques which are primarily measures of distribution, frequency, intensity and variability. On this basis we can determine what the relationship might be between characteristic A and B, what the frequency and variability of certain behaviour is (involving a particular category of people) and a great deal of other information about the distribution of a wide range of characteristics, both social and material.

It is perhaps reasonable to suggest that the variability brought about by change is more clearly evident in African towns than in African villages.

Furthermore, over the years many anthropologists have studied the rural people of Africa with the result, among others, that the information we have (be it accurate or not) about village life is far greater than what we know about town life. While in the latter this is not invariably a disadvantage, it does mean that the urban anthropologist cannot "read up" all the previous studies which have been published so that he can define a new interest and suggest a clearly stated problem. In most cases, the urban anthropologist steps into a situation about which he knows little. Hence simple fact finding, i.e. to establish parameters of this or that, becomes vital to his subsequent work. Some kind of simple survey, therefore, may often precede more intensive work although it is rather more common to conduct it at a later stage or even as a final effort. The urban anthropologist does this because he needs information, and not because he has changed and forsaken his approach which in the past brought such rich results. Surveys and quantification are merely additional tools added to his "bag of tricks." To be sure he might apply these new techniques in the collection of data which some colleagues (Gulliver 1965) do not consider vital (or information that should really be collected by sociologists), but in the long run it must be left to the urban anthropologist to determine what data is relevant to his work. If demographic and vital statistics are collected a clear purpose underlies such a decision, namely to see what the relationships might be between size, composition, and age of the population and some other data, i.e. some qualitative aspect of urban life such as neighbourhood relations. The same might be said if, at one stage, the urban anthropologists collect information about housing, sanitary conditions, over-crowding, household possessions and income (Batson 1949). All of these have a bearing in one way or another on the more qualitative and critical aspects of social organisation and behaviour which have been of such major interest to anthropologists. Let us cite another example of the relationship of "cold" data to, shall we say, cultural patterns such as kinship. The nature and operation of urban kinship is clearly related to the size of the household, the incomes received by its members, their education, and the kind of housing available to them. All this kind of information can only be collected in more standardised form.

In short, survey and quantification techniques should be treated not merely as supplementary (we use them if we have time and feel inclined to a little experimentation!) but as an integral part of good anthropological research. No anthropologist gives up his birth-right merely because he designs a questionnaire. The latter is merely a tool; what does matter are the kinds of questions he wants answered (indeed what is more critical is whether he can design an intelligent question) and for what purpose. The skilled anthropologist will know how to mix judiciously participant-observation and questionnaire techniques; and even more so, he will know what he can expect to obtain from either one, what can be intelligently quantified, and what is better treated otherwise. At present African urban studies are in an experimental period in both conceptualisation and methodology. Professor Clyde Mitchell in particular has applied new techniques (Mitchell 1966a, 1969; Mitchell and Epstein 1957). Of course, we must be careful to avoid blind alleys, but neither should we mark time.

8. *Inter and Multi-Disciplinary Approaches and Research Techniques*

"A team", Hortense Powdermaker (1968 : 421) writes, "has obvious advantages in working on complex problems and in large societies." But, she also adds, "As yet there have been relatively few field teams initiated by anthropologists which cover a large number of disciplines."

With the exception of work done by members of the Natal Regional Survey in South Africa, which included at least one study of an African urban community (University of Natal 1959) carried out by a team of two sociologists, two psychologists and one social anthropologist, no other team research of African towns has been published — although a good deal has been done. The publication on the *City of Ibadan* (Lloyd, *et al* eds. 1967) is a collection of papers by individual scholars who organised a seminar at the University of Ibadan, Institute of African Studies, in 1964. Although the members did not collaborate closely in their fieldwork, anthropologists, historians, statisticians, political scientists, geographers, economists, and scholars of Islam and Christianity came together to present their research results gleaned from the study of a single town.

Multi-disciplinary and team research is rather rare in anthropology, although in the last few years some attempts have been made to bring together a group of people who can collectively define a problem and then apply their own particular specialisation. Perhaps the best example of this is the team effort directed by Dr. Audrey Richards (1960) which involved twelve social scientists (ten anthropologists, one historian and one political scientist) studying the status and functions of chiefs in two countries of Eastern Africa, Uganda and Tanzania. They met frequently to discuss theoretical and methodological problems – but they all worked independently in the field. No similar effort has been attempted (if so, it has not been published) in the study of African towns. The need to do so is very great – although the personal, intellectual, conceptual and methodological hurdles and pitfalls are great. Of course several different kinds of teams could be put together; one which comprises only anthropologists (representing such sub-disciplinary specialisations as political, economic and social anthropology); another made up of an anthropologist, an economist, a political scientist, an historian and other social scientists; yet another team could comprise an anthropologist, a doctor, an environmental ecologist and a geographer. All of them would have something to say about a wide variety of aspects of urban life – communication between anthropologists would be easier (hopefully) than between an anthropologist and a doctor. The further one crosses disciplines the more difficult, but not the less desirable, communication between members of a team becomes. If an anthropologist attempts to deal with a problem outside his training and competence he would have to "trespass beyond the limits of [his] competence, and that to exercise this competence one must abstain from becoming involved in the problems of others" (Devons and Gluckman 1964 : 18). If we were to take this point of view really seriously, the future of urban studies would not be particularly bright.

It is clearly impossible for a researcher, be he anthropologist or psychologist, geographer or historian, to collect data outside of his own field. But other data, indeed virtually all data, is relevant for a more comprehensive understanding of *his own data*. Thus the anthropologist can collect as much data as possible on the structure and operation of kinship in town, but unless a psychologist, or social psychologist, works alongside (and together they study the same unit, but from different perspectives) his particular analysis and interpretation will not only lack in depth and breadth, but more seriously his analysis might be seriously deficient, and hence, false. If this is the case, it might then be argued that the anthropologist was not a highly trained person – but the fault might not be his. The basis of different social science disciplines is not so much different "fields" of human thought and action as different perspectives on the *relationships between phenomena*. Unfortunately, but perhaps inevitably in the social sciences, we tend to categorise data into cultural, social, economic, or political realms. There is a "natural" order in these categories, and between them; it is the social scientist who attempts to find out what this order is and how it works, and in the process introduces confusion and disorder. While this is clearly not his intention, it is brought about because the anthropologist defines his research interests in anthropological terms, and the geographer in his own terms. There is no easy answer although this inevitable compartmentalisation is wholly at odds with the way the human group is organised.

One way to correct this is simple enough: cooperation between the disciplines and those social scientists who are "with it" and have got the "message". A simple example can be cited. Until fairly recently few anthropologists paid any attention to the history of colonialism and its impact on the people they studied. We now realize that in many cases our neglect of the historical events which engulfed the colonial people often distorted our analysis and interpretation (Alkalimat 1969; Hare 1969; Gough 1968, 1968a; Guillermo 1966; Magubane 1968, 1969; Onwuachi and Wolfe 1966; Worsley 1964, 1964a). In fact, on several occasions in this monograph we pointed out how important it is in urban studies to take into account the impact of colonial ideology and policies if and when they have some bearing on urbanisation and urbanism.

Ideally, all social science research should at least be set up in such a way to facilitate multi-disciplinary research. Not only will the wisdom of this be questioned, but the hope of achieving such close cooperation in the near future is rather remote. Yet we ought to recognise that certain research interests, and particularly the locale in which we work, should give high priority to a team and multi-disciplinary approach. One such locality is an African urban area.

The *raison d'être* behind this approach should by now be fairly clear. The kind of complexity we have attempted to describe is such that few, if any, characteristics of urbanisation, or the activities of those who live in a town, can be reduced to a single research perspective. While this should apply to most research done by anthropologists, it is particularly important for urban research. One reason for this is that the growth of towns, and the activities of urbanites, are linked to a vast number of relatively recent developments in Africa as a whole and to a particular nation where urban studies are conducted. Thus, for an anthropologist to study the organisation of entrepreneurial activities (be it of big businessmen or small traders) in towns requires not only a knowledge of economic theory (and as such the help of an economist) but also an acquaintance with, at least in general terms, the main trends of economic change and development in the nation as a whole. Of course, what data he is able to collect even within the framework of the conventional interest of anthropologists, will be of interest and can be used to graft on to the research carried on by others. This is what normally happens. In an urban situation it is easy to go off the rails rather early in the research, and never to get back again on the right track.

Unless the problem selected by the anthropologist is so highly specialised (i.e. symbolism in ritual activity in towns – Tiger 1967) that its significance in a broader context is not very great, most topics of interest require close cooperation with researchers in other disciplines. After all we want to obtain as much information as possible, in depth, over the shortest time, which is as *comprehensive* as possible. Because urban areas are large, and the size of the population considerable, we are faced with special methodological and conceptual problems. Our research should not proceed in a piecemeal fashion. We cannot blindly assume that urban studies are similar to tribal studies. Urban anthropological research in Africa must be moulded into a comprehensive and coordinated approach (Jenkins 1966, 1967a).

Such coordination is based not only on solid theoretical argument: it is further dictated by the fact that African urban studies have attracted a very large number of research workers with the consequent danger of duplication of effort. Thus Jenkins (1967 : 70) reports that

At least 300 scholars are presently engaged in African urban studies. Some twenty-five books are scheduled for publication in the next two years by Americans alone and recent conferences have recommended more research into the urban aspects of unemployment, migration, geography, psychology. Concurrently, interest in traditional disciplinary preoccupations is declining in the light of a continually widening discussion about appropriate kinds of theory and the kinds of phenomena about which we should theorize.

The need for cross-disciplinary cooperation is also strongly emphasised by Jenkins (1967 : 77-78) who points out that:

There are many independently initiated studies of urbanizing Africa which reveal a number of common traits: they are increasingly historical and developmental; increasingly marked by prior theoretical guidelines; and increasingly concerned with studies of social systems as they urbanize rather than merely with cities. It is from this quarter, then, that we may hope for a link between urbanists and those who view integration and development solely at the national level. It might also be added that African urban scholars are increasingly utilizing research methods used elsewhere. Historians employ massive documentation, sociologists utilize random sampling and computer techniques, and political scientists administer attitude questionnaires. Developing systems no less than developed ones require sophisticated theory and methods. Together these characteristics are providing the basis for a newly emergent cooperation among African urbanists.

No doubt African urban studies will have a future in whatever manner they are conducted. Yet if coordination among scholars is not achieved, we shall end up knowing more and more about less and less.

9. Recapitulation and Synthesis

In this chapter we have attempted to set out some of the major methodological problems which the urban anthropologist, working in African towns, will have to face. In our presentation we have tried to show how particular urban characteristics and conditions produce special methodological problems for the researcher. In fact we have gone one step further indicating how various conceptual approaches, problems of definition, and the selection of topics are linked to research approaches and techniques. We have not attempted to produce a how-to-do-it outline because urban anthropologists are still feeling their way; most of the time they proceed in a rather hit and miss way (which is dignified with the label experimental) hoping that the kind of techniques employed will tease out the kind of information sought. Fortuitous circumstances sometimes work in our favour, while at other times we soon reach a dead end.

In this chapter we have tried to show how we might avoid dead end research. Of course, not all aspects of our urban research will be highly creative, nor do we always have to try new methods because a good deal of any research, anywhere, calls for no more than slow, patient, and systematic collection of information. Much of our work, the techniques we use, is not very spectacular; and to try new techniques merely for the sake of them is often not very rewarding. The point that we have tried to make, however, is really quite simple: urban research, be it in Africa or elsewhere in the Third World, offers a unique and creative opportunity to try something new because town life, in most regions of Africa, has gathered together totally new kinds of communities. As such we study more than just a town, its lay-out, the composition of its population, and the social life of its inhabitants. Throughout this monograph we have suggested that the study of African towns brings into sharp relief many important characteristics of the major changes which have taken place in Africa over a considerable period of time. These changes have produced very complex patterns and results which, we have suggested, call for new research techniques to detect and analyse them, using the town as a kind of natural laboratory. The reason why the anthropologist needs to apply new research techniques is due to the fact that until quite recently he worked almost exclusively in a rather different setting, although many would argue that the kinds of problems and questions of interest to him are basically not very different from what they were in the past. This is no doubt true, but what is left out of this view is that the setting in which the urban anthropologist works is not the same as that of a village or a group of scattered homesteads.

We indicated this before because the urban environment contrasts very sharply (even if nothing else does) with the ruralscape. There is something overwhelming about density and congestion of a population and provides a new experience to most anthropologists (Spindler 1970). Almost immediately the anthropologist is faced with the reality of certain logistic and practical fieldwork problems which, if they are not handled correctly, might be a burden for the rest of the fieldwork period. To know where to settle, and why, is surely a rather more complex matter than to pitch one's tent in or near a small settlement. Moreover, to make friends in a town, to ask people to give of their valuable time, might be a bigger task than to ease oneself gradually into the life of a village. It need not be so, but it usually works out that way. Thus, almost from the start, fieldwork appears more demanding and rather more hectic. In political terms the sheer number of officials and important leaders of various segments of the urban community is far larger. To ignore them is fatal, to meet them all is nearly impossible.

Perhaps the most fundamental problem we have discussed in this chapter is, no doubt, one which has concerned anthropologists for a long time. What is the appropriate unit for our observations? In this regard can we transfer our past experiences, and the way in which we have defined these units, to urban research? It is perhaps the most controversial question we face. We have suggested that an African urban area is a particular kind of unit in a larger regional and national setting. This view suggests that before we define this unit we must pay attention to such items as the history of a town, where its residents came from and why they came. We pointed out that it was vital to obtain as much general information about a town as possible before making a final decision on what to study and where to settle. Only when such questions (and others) have been asked and answered is it possible to determine what is the most important unit for study.

How will this unit help us to understand some important features of a town? Will our research reveal a great deal of particular data about one small segment of the population, or is it representative of more widespread characteristics? Above all, how is this particular unit related to other units; to the town as a whole, and to the region and the nation of which it is a part? Can we, by extension, learn something about the hinterland in which the town is located; about the motive as to why people migrate or translocate? Further, will our concentration on a small segment of a town, a small neighbourhood, tell us anything about those major characteristics which we have called "critical features", such as social and economic mobility, stratification, and the formation of socio-economic classes? Does our unit for study allow us to test certain propositions which have been advanced about the effects of urban life on kinship organisation, about the effects of heterogeneity on social structure and inter-personal relationships? These and many other questions should be asked first before our research begins. Our definitions and decisions are bound to reflect some measure of arbitrariness, but by asking the right questions first we can avoid many subsequent failures. We ought to avoid being trapped by current academic "fads" which attempt to analyse and explain the patterns of social organisation of African urban life in terms of a single characteristic, albeit an important one, that of ethnicity. We put forward the view that patterns of urban social organisation are determined more by urban conditions than by cultural differences. The reason why we took this position is simple: the determinants must be analysed in the situational context in which they arise. Thus, at times, ethnicity will play a vital part while at other times the processes of "depluralisation" will be more important. We concluded by saying that heterogeneity should be treated as a dependent variable, and urbanisation and urbanism as the independent variables. We have suggested that micro and macro analysis (which should always be used to complement each other) are the most suitable conceptualisations and research techniques in the collection and analysis of urban data. Utilising such an approach we can find out, for example, how social classes are formed in African towns; whether groups relate to one another according to ethnic criteria or socio-economic position in the urban system. If we make ethnicity the independent variable we have implicitly accepted the view that we are studying tribesmen in town rather than townsmen in town.

In the latter part of this chapter we concentrated somewhat more on the relevance of some standard research techniques, participant-observation, survey research, quantification of data, and multi-disciplinary and team research. We pointed out that there is no reason why participant-observation cannot be used in urban studies, although the researcher must adapt this approach to suit the particular conditions which prevail in urban areas. On the other hand we also pointed out that it is quite likely that the participant-observer will find himself in a rather more complex and tense position because urban conditions reflect many of the serious dilemmas which currently beset many African nations. But perhaps more fundamentally, the participant-observer must ask himself the question: In what neighbourhood and in what situations is it possible to be a participant-observer? But even then, what differences there are as compared to rural research might not be as great as some anthropologists have suggested.

In the section on survey techniques we pointed out that for a number of years now many anthropologists have used simple techniques of quantification as a supplement to their more conventional means of collecting data. The reasons for using these techniques are manifold, but a major purpose is to establish the ranges and variations in behaviour, attitudes and values. To discover what the parameters are calls for the study of a large number of "cases" and the establishment of some measure of controlled   experimentation. Furthermore, anthropologists are turning to the study of complex societies (such as towns) thereby increasing the urgency of collecting information from a larger social field (Bailey 1964). In addition, the anthropologist may wish to collect information about material possessions and relate their ownership to a variety of social and economic characteristics. For such a purpose in particular (or such matters as income distribution), survey techniques are most useful. Such techniques are also useful when in urban research it becomes necessary to collect simple but basic information before more detailed research commences (Spindler 1970). Survey techniques, therefore, are an integral part of much social science research. We should not be hesitant to use these methods simply because we do not know the answer to the question of what can, and what cannot be, meaningfully surveyed and or quantified. There is still so much about Africa's urban areas that is little known or unknown that we will have to use every means available in the collection of information. The skilled anthropologist will know how to judiciously mix various techniques.

Finally, one way to learn how to use new techniques is to work in a team with other social scientists. Cross-fertilisation of research methods is not the only gain; different approaches, perspectives, and definitions will also help the anthropologist (as he can help others) to better understand his own data. Thus multi-disciplinary research, even if it involves little more than research workers from different disciplines occasionally talking together (which is not too unusual these days) will generate, perhaps, alternative and more compre-

hensive explanations on the basis of which generalisations can be more firmly drawn. African urban research is badly in need of such an approach. We
have made a good start, but we seem to be hesitant to go on still further.

V   *Urban anthropology:*
the future of a pioneer

1. *Introduction*

There comes a time when a changing intellectual "climate" forces us to take a close look at what we, anthropologists, are doing; why we are doing what we are doing, how well we have done our work in years past and, more fundamentally, what we ought to be doing.

Those who have committed their intellectual life to the study of the "hard" sciences may feel that there is a "natural" and "logical" unfolding of what phenomena must next be studied; there is no need to look back because in these fields ideas and techniques have a natural way of staying up-to-date. There is a logical sequence which guides their research. This might be so for the physicists who understand much about the structure of the atom and are now "logically" led to the study of yet smaller particles, or the biochemists who, knowing the vital part which protoplasm plays in the world of living organisms, are now engaged in disentangling the complex chemistry of the source of all living things.

Those in the humanities, the arts, and the more recent social sciences cannot claim that their ideas and methods are as firmly rooted and as constantly being refined in a logical progression. The world of ideas, and the vast variation in the behaviour of man, have compelled the behavioural scientist to spread himself very thinly over a huge field of knowledge. There are vast gaps in our knowledge about man's life in years gone by, gaps which we may never be able to fill, and there are huge areas of research before us which we may never be able to tackle. More complicated yet is the answer to the question: what ought behavioural scientists do in the years ahead? We are literally dazzled by the range of tasks to which we ought to devote our limited manpower and, some would say, our limited competence. Should we as anthropologists respond to the pressures on our discipline to drop what we have always done and get into the uncharted seas of data with which many of us are not familiar? To do better what we have done in the past is, of course, as scientific as responding to new ideas and demands. Where, exactly, does our future lie? The past was secure and cozy; the future might be paved with pitfalls. The past was secure because we thought we knew what anthropology was all about. We all looked to the "fathers" of our discipline who established the guidelines of our field of interest. But our fraternity is no longer composed of "members only". We now work in the harsh glare of world opinion, and our acts are being judged by the younger members of our profession whom we have recruited into our ranks.

That anthropology has now become a "popular" subject among university students does not seem in doubt any longer; enrolment in both undergraduate and graduate courses has risen very steeply. As a result we have incorporated into our profession a very large number of young people who, having been born just before or after the Second World War, have a very different perception of world affairs and the human condition than those "elders" who, in the inter-war years, set the pace. But even more, anthropology has acquired some "natural enemies", namely the very people we used to "study"; the people whom we so glibly called "simple" and "primitive". Whether these adjectives ever had any meaning is no longer a relevant issue. What is now fact is that the so-called simple people have called a halt to our traditional activities. Social anthropologists in particular are not too welcome in many parts of the "underdeveloped" world. While the reasons for this development (which we could have anticipated if we had more often asked ourselves some searching questions about our profession) do not concern us directly in this monograph, the emergence of urban anthropology is not unrelated to the criticism levelled at us. Thus, in the preface to a symposium on urban anthropology, sponsored by the Southern Anthropological Society in 1968, the Series Editor (Hudson 1968:v) commented:

Thus, at the very time when the number of anthropologists is increasing rapidly, the traditional objects of our study are decreasing with comparable rapidity; this accounts for some of the necessity for anthropologists to do urban research. But there is another kind of necessity for urban research in anthropology ... anthropology has been accused of having an almost grotesquely primitive or rural image of man, and this at a time when both industrial and industrializing societies suffer almost insoluble urban problems caused by people moving into (and out of) the city. Without relinquishing our primary concern with primitives and peasants, anthropologists must of necessity round out their picture of man by becoming more knowledgeable about city people.

While the emphasis on what our "primary concern" ought to be is not shared by this author, the above quotation at least asks us to take note of what is also taking place in the real world – the rise of urbanism. But, as we have pointed out at various times in the previous chapters, urban anthropology should not be based only on the grounds that we are forced to change direction, or that we reluctantly must acknowledge the fact that rural people are now migrating in vast numbers into what were once small urban areas. The rich literature from urban Africa alone precludes the possibility that our "elders" treat the urban anthropologist as a stray who has wandered into the profession and now begs to be taken into the fold. While such sentiments will linger for a time yet, the contributions made by urban anthropologists in the past, and those still in store, will stand entirely on their own and be judged on their own merit. As urban anthropologists we do not merely react to the past; we like to think that we have opened a new future for anthropology. Just at present this might indeed seem an extravagant claim. But nobody can doubt the dramatic force behind urbanisation which has so remarkably transformed large sections of the "primitive" world. For, as we pointed out before, urbanisation should not be seen only in simple demographic form, i.e. the high concentration of people in towns and cities, but rather as an agent of a more widespread transformation which reaches into villages and hamlets and progressively sets the pace for rural change.

We may have a fight on our hands. As John Gulick (1963) has pointed out, the "phrase 'urban anthropology' may seem like a contradiction in terms". Contradiction, however, for whom? Surely only for those who are encapsulated in the immutability of a professional tradition. If the study of the urban environment is somehow not part of anthropology, we must then assume that somehow anthropologists have discovered over time that the only natural habitat for pre-industrial man is in a sea of rurality. Hence the existence of urban man provides us with evidence of some sort of social aberration, a study of which is best placed in the hands of those concerned with deviance! Clearly, such a view is absurd. Yet, even some urban anthropologists, particularly those working in the low-income countries of the Third World, seem to insist that their studies must take place in a truly "anthropological setting". Thus, at a recent *Conference on Anthropological Research in Cities* (1970), one of the participants pointed out that urban anthropologists tend to concentrate on non-Western and pre-industrial towns; in effect they look for those towns, and those groupings within towns, which are as far removed from Western types as possible. This, then, satisfies the "anthropological perspective". Why this should be so reveals a great deal about anthropologists. Perhaps it is for this reason that "real" anthropologists have yet to attempt the kind of work published by Liebow (1967) and Keiser (1969). The only way for anthropologists to shed the encapsulation of their traditions and ethnocentricity is to engage in far reaching comparative studies – an honourable and creative tradition first pioneered by anthropologists. Thus Clyde Mitchell, one of the contributors to the above named conference, suggests that urban anthropologists are passing through an "identity crisis", to which we would add that this is true for all of social anthropology. If there is indeed such a crisis its etiology does not rest in anthropology as a discipline but has been produced by its practitioners. Rather than bury all of anthropology, why not just bury those caught up in this crisis! There is no need for the latter if we respond naturally to the new opportunities which lie before us. This means that the anthropological perspective should not be competitive with sociology, our closest sister discipline, but complementary to it. It is a matter which we raised in the last chapter.

Perhaps the problems faced by the profession are more fundamental. Do we understand the nature of social change – for that matter does anyone? Anthropologists claim that they do, that they pay attention to this vital characteristic of all types of societies and all forms of social organisation. However, the topics which anthropologists select for study generally relegate a close look at social change to a low level of importance. Thus Magubane (1968, 1971) has shown, with some penetration, how students of Africa, and in particular anthropologists, have failed to give due weight to the impact of colonialism, how it penetrated the total fabric of African society and, as such, accelerated change on a broad front. While many studies try to find out how a particular society "has changed", or how specific institutions are changing, the anthropologist has rarely departed from the cornerstone of his main concern, tradition. We have been more concerned with the modification of tradition rather than with the significance of social change. This appears to be a perspective which has made many anthropologists immune to alternative frames of reference. As recently as 1965 in a series of ethnographic studies on the *Peoples of Africa* (J.L. Gibbs, ed.), the various contributors only paid passing reference to the impact of colonialism on African societies. The student is left with the totally false impression that in Africa indeed "custom is king". The point we made in all the previous chapters is that urban anthropology must begin with a new baseline in its analysis be it of African, Asian or Latin American societies. We gave our reasons for this point of view.

Furthermore, anthropologists seem to have experienced some difficulty in accepting the view that it is just as legitimate to study large-scale societies as small-scale and "traditional" societies· What might be considered illegitimate about the study of the former is rarely made clear other than to suggest that such societies are best studied by sociologists. This appears to be based more on a defensive reaction, or some rationalised form of romanticism, than on the view that the human group, whatever its size, complexity, or wherever it is to be found, always was and always will be of interest to the anthropologist. True enough, since the end of the Second World War, some anthropologists have courageously moved into these large-scale and allegedly more complex societies. But when they do this their work comes, legitimately, under very careful, but also rather critical, scrutiny (Devons and Gluckman 1964; Gutkind 1966a). It is then often suggested that anthropologists have exceeded the range and level of their competence. While this might be true, the lesson to be learned from a "failure", if failure it is, is not to retreat into the past and do what we have always done, but to look forward; we should ask ourselves the kind of questions with which we began this chapter. Our refusal or inability to do so will relegate us to the kind of "scrap heap" Dr.

Audrey Richards (1961) has written about. While some anthropologists might believe that the study of the urban environment falls more appropriately into another discipline, the point must be made again that rural life is now strongly influenced by urban conditions; much of what anthropologists used to do, they must now do from a different perspective. Rather than being driven into a reluctant acceptance of such a position, we can ease the "transition" by a greater willingness to incorporate new areas into our enquiries. Perhaps we have an advantage over other disciplines because over time we have learned how to combine the cultural, the historical, the sociological and the ecological perspectives. If we have achieved this much, there is no reason why we should impose on our work a wholly unnatural constraint. While it might be an exaggeration to argue that urban anthropology will "save" the discipline from eventual extinction, it is certainly not unreasonable to suggest that much of what is "new" in anthropology has been contributed by some urban anthropologists. Some of the creative work done by Philip Mayer and Clyde Mitchell (1969) on "social network" theory promises new and different analytical models which need a great deal of further exploration. While some of our colleagues suggest that these approaches are not really new, they have thus far not been able to support this assertion.

2. *The Need to Change Direction: From Traditional to Modern Studies*

To "change direction" does not imply that we ignore the creative efforts of the past, or that we cease doing what we have always done – although, perhaps, we can try to do better than we have done in the past. The reason why we ought to consider a "change of direction" is really rather simple: the people we have always studied in the past, the "simple" and "primitive" people, are no longer either primitive or simple. What is transforming such societies is not, of course, urbanisation alone: it is a transformation which began a long time ago and was hastened by the onset of colonialism, the impact of Western ideas and technology and, more recently, by a determination of ex-colonial people to take a major role in shaping their own life and thought. It is as much the latter, as anything else, which ought to force the pace, and supply the logic, for a change of direction. Of course, there will always be those societies whose transformation is a little slower and it is largely to them that the "Urgent Anthropologist" turns to for his field of research. But even for such societies the pace has quickened; they are being forced into the so-called modern world either by simple extermination or coercion. While some of these societies are putting up a gallant fight, others retreat still further into a wild hinterland and a few decide to give up the fight. All such people command our respect and our help and many anthropologists have, in recent years, mobilised what resources and skills they have to represent the interests of those who lack the power and the means to defend themselves. It is a worthy battle which will and must continue – although "victory" is a rather remote possibility.

Few people of the Third World have either been able to resist, or have rejected outright, the new ideas and conditions which have so obviously engulfed them. We are not saying here that Westernisation is the fountainhead of transformation, for many ideas and conditions which make up change stem from other, and quite different, sources. But the fact remains that there are certain key transformational forces which are laid like a blanket over the "developing nations". Whether this is desirable or not, is not directly relevant to the subject under discussion. In this monograph we have concentrated on urbanisation as one of the key transformational forces. One reason why we call for a change of direction is suggested by Hutchinson (1968 : 27):

The point is that urbanization as it occurs today is quite probably a different phenomenon than it was in previous times, such as in preindustrial, prescientific societies. The study of urbanization in contemporary societies by the anthropologist must be carried out within the context of the concomitant social and cultural forces. The interrelationship of urbanization as concentration and scientific rationalism will most probably provide the nexus for future studies, since this is what population concentration is primarily linked to.

What Hutchinson seems to suggest is that to study the urban environment is to unlock all manner of other changes which are taking place. Are we ready, then, for such a macro perspective? There is now at work, so it seems, a new strategy and a new dynamism which guides change. We are, in short, confronted by a new kind of organised complexity. If this is so then we had better move from the anthropology of small-scale societies to the anthropology of large-scale and complex organisations. We need not build the bridge from one to the other, it is being built largely by people themselves. The peoples of some societies have acquired this new complexity more rapidly than others; so the anthropologist might then ask himself, "What accounts for the faster or more rapid speed of change?". At present we cannot be sure what *the* most important agent, or agents, of change might be. Professor Lucy Mair (1964 : 315) has suggested that even small-scale societies undergo constant change, however small.

I have tried ... to argue that the social changes we are witnessing today are effected by social forces that have been in operation in all times — the manipulation of whatever areas of free choice there may be by people who are able to calculate where their advantage lies. When new opportunities present themselves, many people will hesitate to take risks with them, and some will perceive that their advantage would lie in the maintenance of the status quo if this were possible: they are the conservatives. Both types of person have always existed in all societies. What is peculiar about the changes of the present day in the non-western world is simply the breathless speed with which historical circumstances have extended the room for manoeuvre.

Unless we change direction, if tradition continues to be the bedrock and the yardstick against which we "measure" change, we shall never clearly understand the reasons for the "breathless speed"; nor will we be able to put our finger on the particular "historical circumstances" which lie in back of the new social forces to which millions of people are now exposed.

It is not unreasonable to suggest that all social anthropologists today, whatever types of communities they select for study, must pay attention to the increasingly important relationship between the people of the local community, and the regional and national context in which they find themselves. The recently published essays edited by Swartz et al (1966) and Swartz (1968) attest to the importance of this approach which was first initiated by Epstein (1958) in his study of *Politics in an Urban African Community* and, outside of Africa, by F.G. Bailey (1963,1964) in his brilliant analysis of the *Politics and Social Change, Orissa in 1959*. More recently, Mazrui and Rotberg (1970) edited a set of papers under the title *Protest and Power in Black Africa* which, although broadly set in the discipline of political science, indicates how much the anthropologist has "missed" in his study of alleged "traditional" societies. African urban studies, indeed urban studies anywhere, have revealed how important it is not to abstract the urban environment from the regional and national matrix in which it is located. Anthony Leeds (1968 : 32) in his search for more creative models in the study of the anthropology of cities has this to say on this vital issue:

... anthropologists have tended to perpetuate traditional concerns – kinship, the community, child training, study of associations, etc. – transferring these, first, forty to fifty years ago, to the quite different societal context of rural communities and then, to the drastically different context of the city in large-scale society. Some of the methodological problems regarding tribal societies were never resolved, and sometimes never even raised, though they closely involved both theoretical models and field work procedures. In this transference of traditional concerns from tribal experience to city studies, these problems were perpetuated and intensified.

Leeds goes on to point out that the exact variables involved in the study of the urban environment are not merely those unique to urban life but also those which indicate how the city is linked to macro processes in the nation as a whole. To transfer traditional anthropological models to the study of the city produces "a yet greater failure" because.

... the justification for treating the units under description as autonomous is still less self-evident, while the blindness to the complexity of interrelation within the encompassing social entities (e.g. city, nation) which includes the unit as one of its variables is even vaster. In the case of the city, the blindness leads to its atomized treatment, as if these variables (kinship, associations, housing, etc.) were separable, discrete, and unrelated elements — as it were, *accidents* of the city rather than caused and linked manifestations *of* the city (and national) process.

As we have tried to point out in earlier chapters, urban populations are highly diverse in their composition and character, a fact which is also the case in rural communities but at a lower level of magnitude. It is not just the fact that a heterogeneous urban population presents the anthropologist with a setting with which he is not familiar, more fundamentally he is not accustomed to spreading his research net over wider areas. The study of African urbanism might realistically be approached from the perspective of political economy; and here we could point to the contributions by such authors as Baran (1957), Buchanan (1963), Frank (1967) and Fanon (1959, 1964, 1966), writings which are highly relevant to the study of the Third World city and the processes of urbanisation as these are closely linked to colonial and imperialist policy and doctrine. It is significant that thus far few scholars, be they anthropologists or otherwise, have explored the relationship between imperial policy and urban growth and structure. It is a task in which the anthropologist can contribute a particular perspective. The anthropologist must accept the fact that the city, and the urban environment, is part of a far larger social, economic and political field. However, when he "defines the unit for observation", he does so in an abstract and largely arbitrary manner. Michael Olien (1968 : 83), drawing on his experience in Costa Rica, suggests a four dimensional model for the study of the urban environment: intra-community relations, urban-rural relations, urban-national relations and urban-international relations. His model is based on the premise that:

The city is not an isolated community. Instead the urban community lies in a *nexus of interrelationships* [my italics]. Not only are there relations between the sub-cultures of the community, but there are also relations between the city and the rural areas, between the city and the nation, and even international relations. In part, it is this very network of relationships which makes an understanding of the city possible. Describing the context in which an urban area exists may allow anthropologists to approach the same level of totality in their studies of cities as has been reached in the studies of isolated primitive groups.

It has frequently been suggested that the unique contribution of anthropology lies in intensive rather than extensive studies. This might be so. But at the same time we are equally committed to extrapolate from the data we have collected broader and wider generalisations. We do just this when we study, comparatively, kinship or economic or political organisation. Our focus thus far has been on a highly restricted set of phenomena which, as Leeds (1968) suggested, we have reduced to still more highly specialised problems resulting in knowing more and more about less and less. Thus, Lewis Mumford (1968 : 81) writing about the late Patrick Geddes says that he

... sought to demonstrate the constant interplay of ideas, forces, functions, groups, and institutions, all of which are usually treated by the specialised sciences as if they were independent and isolated.

More broadly-based urban studies may not be the antidote to arrest further over-specialisation, but such studies may well point the way to the anthropologist to take account of the fact that now more than ever the study of the community must reflect that "wide nexus of interrelationships" which alone gives meaning to its peculiarities and those features it has in common with communities elsewhere. Not only must urban anthropologists apply a regional and national perspective to their studies (on careful reflection it will be found that almost all of the traditional concerns of the anthropologist can be creatively cast in such a mold), but also anthropologists must extend their research to Western towns and cities where, it might be argued, the relevance of this frame of reference provides the ideal training.

Of course much of what we have said may seem somewhat apocalyptic to some anthropologists, while to others we are saying nothing new. This will be a matter for critics to resolve in the years that lie ahead. Perhaps, more fundamentally, the ideas put forward in this and the preceding chapters, assume that we know more than we actually do about urbanisation and the urban environment in the Third World. The only reasonable comment that can be made is that perhaps we know more than we think, but also that we ought to know more than we do at present. Or, perhaps, we might say that whatever we do know, in factual terms, is not as important as knowing what to do with the information, how to analyse and interpret it. While such a statement can be applied to almost any scholarly effort, the study of Third World urbanism is perhaps an interesting case which allows us to test certain basic assumptions which students of urbanism have made.

If we ask the question: "What is the future for urban development in the Third World?", the answer surely is that the present cities and towns will get larger and ever more congested. But if we ask: "What type of urbanism is likely to emerge?", we are less certain of the answer. There appear to be two alternatives. Firstly, all Third World cities and towns will, before long, be like most Western cities — an assumption sometimes implicit in the thinking of those sociologists who have worked in both Western and non-Western urban areas. They might be right. The second alternative is that Third World urbanism might turn into a very different entity, quite different from our experience in the West. It is a view strongly held, and strongly implied, by those urban anthropologists who have worked exclusively in non-Western urban areas. They too might be right or both views might be wrong on the ground that neither sociologist nor anthropologist have a full command of the facts.

In a very stimulating paper by Aidan Southall (1970) the following point of view was expressed:

Nobody can doubt the dramatic rise in urbanization throughout the world. One aspect of it is now popularly referred to as the population bomb. This is the demographic aspect, which is rapidly imposing upon millions and millions of more human beings levels of density in occupation which can only be described as urban. The demographic effect, of sheer increase in numbers of living bodies, is greatly intensified by what may be called the technological factor, whereby methods of production and distribution, of transport and communication, induce further population concentration.

Most general statements about this galloping world urbanization are made in terms of these two composite factors of population and technology. Since there is also no doubt that these two factors are new and ubiquitous in their operation, with quite minor exceptions, the initial impression is already implicitly conveyed that contemporary world urbanization is a basically homogeneous process and indeed becoming more and more so. If population increase and the spread of technology are taken as the main factors in rapid urbanization, then it appears that the Third World is catching up on the West in the first respect and certainly hastening after the second, even if the technological gap is absolutely growing. The central problem ... to raise is how far this implicit or explicit assumption of increasing homogeneity is true.

Urban studies by anthropologists are still mainly of non-Western cities, while Western cities are still mainly studied by sociologists. The two frames of reference are not the same and those well read in the one are often not in the other. Most urban sociologists assume that if Western and non-Western cities are not basically alike it is only a matter of time before they will be. There may be a backlog of traditional culture but it will soon be caught up and washed away by the advancing tide of modernization.

In contradiction to their view it is ... [suggested] that most cities of the Third World are in significant respects condemned to move in a direction opposite to that of Western cities. A fundamental relationship is reversed in that urban population is rising far and away faster than industrial expansion. In certain respects population growth hinders industrial growth in the Third World instead of being stimulated and matched by it.

Here, then, is one of the first controversial issues raised in urban research. In this monograph we cannot offer an answer, although by implication we have made some suggestions which may help to throw some light on this controversy. But to suggest that urbanisation and urbanism in the Third World is likely to move "in a direction opposite to that of Western cities" would suggest that the anthropologist has the interest to raise new questions and the skills to encompass a very wide set of data. This is good and should be encouraged. That we are not quite ready yet, both methodologically and conceptually, to carry out research over a wider field of data should be viewed as a challenge rather than a handicap. The correct emphasis which Southall gives to the relevance of technology and population for the study of urbanism is not a new idea (Gutkind 1969a; Toynbee 1970; Mumford 1970). It underlines the need for anthropology to take account of the interstitial and converging fields which have now become so relevant to anthropologists asking new questions and penetrating areas not hitherto considered relevant to them. It is in this sense too that there is some meaning behind the suggestion that we ought to change direction. In doing so some older problems (Gutkind 1969b) in anthropology might suddenly be looked at in a new light and, as a consequence, be resolved.

What we are suggesting is not really a plea that we should look at "new" data; many anthropologists have for long suspected that our data was being analysed in terms of categories of phenomena too narrowly defined. By extending our field of observation we shall allow ourselves to penetrate in greater depth the areas and problems about which we feel anthropologists might have something to say. To reject this is to insist that our first priority is to do better what we have always done, or to suggest that our data can somehow be more effectively, and more logically, abstracted than the data collected by other social scientists. This is false and if accepted will relegate us still further to the very peripheries of social science research. Southall's paper (1970) suggests the following creative role for anthropology, particularly in its relation to sociology:

By its commitment to understanding other cultures, or simply other situations, on their own terms, intensively and at length, anthropology can correct the dangerous tendency for the increasing elaboration of technique in sociology, combined with the inertia resulting from the enormous accumulation of Western data, to force data from non-Western countries into the same precoded molds. Anthropology can do this if it not only continues to collect empirical data fully checked by face to face observation and involvement, but also relates intensive local data to its wider framework through its capacity to transcend narrow intellectual disciplinary boundaries between categories such as economic, political, kinship and religious data. *Since it is recognized that no urban situation, or community, can be bounded in the sense of the mythical tribe, it is essential to recognize the extent to which local situations are determined by distant and large-scale forces.* [My italics]

This summarises as clearly as any statement we have seen the view expressed in this monograph and in particular in the last few pages. To suggest that we change direction is, perhaps, too strong a prescription. Or is strong medicine really required?

3. *Being Trapped by "Pure" versus "Applied" Studies: A False Dichotomy*

All scientific effort rests on the pillars of "model building" and on the application of knowledge to the affairs of everyday life. When we refer to "theory building", we are engaged in the construction of "conceptual models" or, as the jargon goes, in the design of a "frame of reference". Both our models, or our frame of reference, are put together by relating certain "variables" to each other, or to be more specific, to test how a number of variables are related to each other. Variables are observable, at least this is so in the social sciences, and may be of a qualitative (urban ethnic associations) or a quantitative (the age composition of an urban population) nature. The theoretical urban anthropologist attempts to ferret out all manner of variables, both obvious ones and those which appear to him more subtle. Having selected a whole range of variables he then attempts to combine these in particular (model) ways in order to test out some idea or proposition (such as the one put forward by Professor Southall on p. 207). "Concepts," R. K. Merton (1957 : 89) writes, "constitute the definitions . . . of what is to be observed; they are the variables between which empirical relations are sought" such as status, role, social distance and anomie. Thus variables can be classified not only as to their formal content but also according to their relationship with one another. These relationships are generally of two types: independent or dependent variables. In urban anthropology we can treat ethnicity, in the urban environment, as the independent variable and try to find out how and why this phenomenon changes when related to (measured against) the dependent variables such as education and wealth. All science proceeds in this way. It is the basis of all knowledge. It is generally referred to as "pure" science on the ground, as much as any other, that we are "testing" ideas; ideas which first and foremost are designed simply for the sake of obtaining information and also of solving a problem which has troubled us intellectually and not, necessarily, in practical terms. Such "pure" research must continue, unless we as anthropologists, or the human community for that matter, have decided that we know all that there is to be known and that all that remains for us to do is to "apply" whatever knowledge we have. Should that day ever come, we will have ceased to be human beings!

Men are constantly concerned with application. Indeed, the trouble with the modern world might be that we no longer know how to intelligently apply all the knowledge we have (Peattie 1970). Rather than allowing knowledge to serve us in practical ways we seem to be bent on devising ways which will make sure that our collective destruction is made ever more certain. We can sum up this view with the well-worn cliché which says that the machines have run away with the men. It is surely not unreasonable to suggest that this is our trouble in the modern world (Mumford 1970).

The sane application of knowledge to human affairs is, of course, not new. We are all impressed with the rapid march of technology from the days when the Egyptians built their pyramids to the time when men began to walk on the surface of the moon. To apply theory to practical problems is not an easy task; the first question to ask is, in human affairs at least, whose theory? While we can produce better products, make better medicines and build larger bridges, we find it more difficult to build better men. We may never succeed. The application of theories to the life and labour of the human group are very diverse; and what is more serious still, we have little in the way of "tests" to find out if our theories are correct, i.e. is it possible to apply what we have learned, were our original premises correct — if they were not, it is sheer waste of time to think about the problems of application. We cannot afford to do too much experimentation with people.

The fact of the matter is that we now have a huge body of knowledge (and let us assume that what we know is more or less "correct"), as well as the technical skills to translate much of what we have learned into a service to mankind. After all we have now learned, on the basis of a vast amount of "pure" research, to increase rice and wheat yields. The question which ought to concern us as urban anthropologists is how we can apply our knowledge to improve the urban environment. There is a great temptation in thinking that our knowledge about urbanisation and urbanism in the Third World is still too much in its infancy to start experimenting with the lives of innocent people. After all, we might argue, those who live in these cities and towns know better than we, the academics, what urban life is all about; they also know better than we, the theoreticians, what ought to be done ease the burdens of their life. This might indeed be so, but does this absolve us from the social responsibilities of action and application of our skills?

In this brief section we want to make a very simple point. Unlike the study of the more "traditional" concerns of anthropology (myths, ritual, kinship, culture and personality), the urban anthropologist has the unique opportunity to combine theory and application (unless he should be concerned with the study of myth and ritual in the urban environment!) as long as he accepts the premise that there is theory in application and application in theory. This is more than just a piece of intellectual gimmickry because it is based on the premise that the study of the urban environment brings the anthropologist closer to the fundamental realisation of the enormous discrepancy between theory and reality (Peattie 1970). It is a recognition made real by the uniqueness of urban life, by the complex composition of its population, the scale and diversity of its operation and the fact that the urban community, and the behaviour of the individuals who make up the community, are not "bounded in the sense of the mythical tribe" (Southall 1970). What we are saying is that the study of "practical problems" faced by the people living in a city may provide the urban anthropologist not merely with a "legitimate" base for his presence but, more significantly, with a rich potential to test various "models". We are not suggesting that urban anthropologists should stay away from "pure" research, there is no reason why we should not tackle some rather esoteric topics, but at the same time we should recognise that such an approach may take us back to those things we have always done, using more often than not rather overworked ideas and models. We cannot, and should not, preclude such research but we should also be sure that we understand the limits of creativity which seem to be inherent in this perspective.

Urban anthropologists, like other anthropologists, want to study something that is, perhaps, "new" and certainly something that is "significant" (Gulick 1968). To argue like this involves us in rather complex subjective assessments, which can be the most creative part of our thinking, but what is probably more important is that we study what is "real". We know that reality is perceived differently by different people and groups. But in the last few years we have come to understand more about what is real to people; and what is real to people brings us closer to an understanding of "how the system really works". This is controversial and as yet such thoughts are not very sophisticated. They need refinement. It is all too easy to see such prescriptions as little more than the hot air which comes from the ideologies of the "left"; the ideologues who pressure us to accept their views of what the "real" world is all about. But before we glibly reject their views as contrary to the free spirit of inquiry, and contrary to science, we would do well to at least experiment with the views which they have laid at our door.

We may think that some aspect of ethnicity is more significant than the study of an urban baby health center. But how can we be so sure that a study of the latter does not directly or indirectly lead us to an understanding of the former. Or we may feel that the study of social class and stratification in an urban community is a more "promising" line of inquiry than the study of what goes on in a beer bar or on a housing estate. Yet Parkin (1969) has shown very clearly how fruitful it can be to look at the latter (in Kampala) in order to understand the operation of the former. The research done by Marris (1961) sprang directly from a concern with the consequences of slum clearance and urban planning in Lagos. The study of young men and women attending a youth club can form the basis of testing various models concerned with social mobility and various other features of change and transformation. Or at an even more "practical" level, there are many features of community and neighbourhood projects be they concerned with water supplies, the construction of schools or the building of recreational facilities which can, and do, lead directly to the collection and subsequent analysis of rather more complex data. The list could be extended endlessly.

It is a simple point which we have tried to make, but because it is simple we have been inclined to ignore it. We subscribe too easily to the axiom that if we take a simple idea, or a simple event (if any event is ever simple), and talk about it in a sophisticated and complicated manner, we are being profound. Likewise, we seem to assume that unless we engage only in pure research we are neither good scholars nor advancing the cause of science. While this might be so in some fields, let us say in theoretical physics, it does not invariably apply to the social sciences. In anthropology and sociology in particular we ought to ask the question often — what is knowledge for? True enough, these sciences like others are still striving to understand some basic fundamentals in the composition and structure of (human) phenomena. But the point is frequently overlooked that we can also examine these fundamentals by studying the practical. Indeed the researcher who selects a practical problem faced by members of an urban community does so because he knows that the circumstances underlying the real world will naturally lead him to understanding the kind of organised complexity which we have discussed in previous chapters. And once he has reached this level of exposing the complexity of everyday situations and events, he then stands a far better chance of putting his finger on a wide range of variables and selecting from them those with which he can construct his "models".

4. *Urban Studies: Some Simple Research Proposals*

Research on various aspects of urbanisation and urbanism in the Third World, although not new to social scientists, has greatly increased in the last few years. In Africa alone Jenkins (1967a : 70) estimated that by 1967 there were "At least 300 scholars . . . engaged in African urban studies" and that "some twenty-five books [were] scheduled for publication in the next two years by Americans alone . . . ". Recently, Gutkind (1973) put together a bibliography on (non-Western) urban anthropology containing almost one thousand items. Such a bibliography could be at least twice as long if we added to it studies of Western cities and towns. There is certainly not a dearth of information to draw on. While the *field* of urban anthropology might be new, a lot of people, the majority not anthropologists, have studied many features of urbanism. We have collected a lot of information, spread very unevenly over a vast area of the world, and still know so little! This is frustrating to recognise, while it is pleasant to know that there is still much that needs to be done. No urban anthropologist should go hungry in the next fifty years!

Scholars do not want to be told what to do. Each one of us, while always building on the work done by others before us, feels that our research proposals and designs are, perhaps, unique and likely to "fill a gap in the literature". Many of us fail to achieve that vital contribution, that important intellectual breakthrough, which moves us forward and opens up new fields for investigation and new ways of looking at data. Many of our urban studies have been repetitive or have harped too long on a single theme, i.e. the study of voluntary associations seen as "adaptive mechanisms." Sometimes we have searched along dead ends, while at other times we have succumbed to the fads of the moment, i.e. studies of tribalism. Of course, hopefully, each piece of research has added something new – however small the contribution. When all is said and done, urban anthropologists of the future together need to put their minds to work and try to find some direction in their research. Are there any priorities to be tackled? Few scholars are willing, however, to put their weight behind an overall plan of research. Although we are willing to go to conferences designed to take stock and assess where we stand, once we are back in our offices we dream up unique lines of inquiry which once again send us scrambling in all directions. This is the nature of the beast and we had better all learn how to live with each other.

Nevertheless some suggestions for further research might be appropriate. We have already made a number of these, indirectly, in the pages of the previous chapters. We are constrained to give these ideas any order of priority, in part because no one urban anthropologist has a comprehensive view of so vast a field as urban anthropology is, or might become, but also because there is still need for far more discussion over what we should theorise about.

Perhaps the most fundamental question which should be raised in the years ahead concerns the whole approach to the study of Third World urbanism. What kind of urbanism are we studying, and how should we go about our research? Are cities and towns of the Third World going to take on the same characteristics as those of the Western world? Can we look forward to megalopolises – those vast mechanised entities which, despite concentration of population, stretch for endless miles over the landscape? Or will the urbanism of Africa, Asia and Latin America turn into itself and hence produce an urbanism of a quite different variety? Apocalyptic predictions are hazardous. Yet conceptions of the future course of events, i.e. how strongly the Western model of urbanism has already imposed itself on Third World towns, will strongly influence the premises on which our research is designed. On the other hand, we can take the view (which is thought to be based on solid empirically obtained data) that the values and structures of traditional African societies will for years to come play a major part in African towns, a point of view recently put forward by Schwab (1970a). These approaches are clearly somewhat incompatible; but more significantly they lead the research worker to look for different data and such data is analysed according to mutually exclusive models. This very basic question gets close to the heart of the matter. We can only resolve it by very extensive comparative fieldwork in non-Western towns (we know how Western towns function and how they have evolved so comparative fieldwork will not necessarily have to include the latter).

Another way to resolve the problems posed by this question is to set our research on Third World urbanism in the context of development theory which is designed to analyse total system change. Only then can we be sure that we have considered urbanisation and urbanism in relation to economic and political transformation. Setting the study of urbanism in such a context brings us back to some of the points we made in earlier chapters when we discussed the relevance of scale, organised complexity, the force of migration and the critical points of social systems all in relation to the study of urbanisation. Third World cities, as cities everywhere, reflect the expanded scale of operations at regional, national and international levels. This in turn requires that we pay increasing attention to the historical evolution of urban areas in the pre-colonial and colonial periods. Regional and national history in the Third World can, perhaps, become the foundation for the study of urbanism. Thus in the next few years we ought to pay far closer attention to the study of the relationship between imperial policy and urban development. This has yet to be explored.

Another area for more penetrating studies is presented by the unresolved controversy about continuity or discontinuity between rural and urban life. Scholars such as Gluckman (1961), Mitchell (1966) and Epstein (1958 and 1961) have strongly argued for an analytical separation of these fields, one rural and one urban, although recently modifications have been discussed (Epstein 1967) for a continuum from one to the other – a view also shared by the present author although modified somewhat by suggesting that it is the task of the urban anthropologist to determine what the functions of rurality really are in an urban context, i.e. what is its true degree of magnitude. Schwab (1970a), on the other hand, has strongly argued in support of a rural-urban continuum. Jenkins (1967a : 72-73) has legitimately raised some questions which he says spring from the "unarticulated premises about non-urban life" and, he might have added, about urban life.

One of the problems in [urban] research lies in unarticulated premises about non-urban life. It is assumed that kinship created a cohesive unit in which the strong, the wealthy, and the clever willingly provided for the weak, the poor, the shiftless – regardless of their willingness to reciprocate. It is more likely that kinship and reciprocity were rarely this congruent. Reciprocity opportunities were extended to non-kin such as wives, clients, and slaves and were withdrawn from kin sold as slaves or as bond-servants. Formalized lineage councils and courts were required to resolve conflicts in lineages large enough to have social differentiation, competition and conflict. It was the conditions of a levelling subsistence economy that required reciprocity while kinship institutions provided a useful set of lasting relations in which the intermittent patterns of reciprocity could function over time.

As long as the economy and technology made it difficult for individuals to accumulate permanently disproportionate advantages, reciprocity worked, but the system could break down, with fission producing new non-reciprocating groups. Thus, Ibadan was founded in the nineteenth century and grew to a population of 50,000 in two decades on an influx of migrants who left their families to form a pre-European, preindustrial city in which traditional patterns remained vulnerable. A chronicle of Ibadan history lists fifteen lineages out of a hundred which can no longer be traced. Another six are the result of kinship disputes resulting in fission and non-reciprocating groups. The assumption that voluntary associations were created because tensions and schism suddenly entered African life in the twentieth century ignores the somewhat tenuous nature of African family life prior to Western impact and suggests that much of our thinking about urban life requires an examination, *within a single frame of reference* [my italics], of the rural mode with which it is contrasted.

It is clear that Schwab (1970a), who bases his argument on the continuity of corporate groups in urban areas, is not aware of this analysis by Jenkins although both authors write in relation to the urbanism among the Yoruba of Western Nigeria.

There are, of course, numerous ways to attempt to resolve the complex issues which are raised. For some years to come anthropologists will ask themselves to what extent can a system of ritual and ceremonial, its symbols and meaning, which are an integral part of a (rural-based) tribal system survive in the context of the institutions, the interaction and the values commensurate with urbanism? Clifford Geertz (1957) has pointed to the incongruities which might result from a clash of different styles of life when the meaning and symbols of ritual and ceremonial turn out to be dysfunctional, to be out of place, in an urban setting. On the other hand Robert W. Wyllie (1968) has shown that in the small town of Winneba, Ghana, a communal ritual, of rural origin, persists because it is "congruent with the [urban] sociocultural system of which it is a part". Likewise, Clyde Mitchell (1957) has sought to demonstrate how a ceremonial can be skillfully adapted to generate new meaning and symbols directly related to an urban situation. It appears clear from some of this literature that ritual and ceremonial reflect as much a need to cope with change as does a "static" cultural item which is only functional in a rural context. Geertz has insisted that we pay attention to the "inherent incongruity and tension" between the "logico-meaningful and the causal-functional" modes of integration. To this we would only add that we need also to take into account, more than we have done in the past, the relevance of size, composition and economic and political features of urban areas as these might throw some light on what are now seen as incongruities and tensions. In exactly the same way in which we have questioned the relevance of the concept of tradition which anthropologists find so vital to their thinking, we ought to likewise question the view that the transition from a rural to an urban style of life invariably produces incongruities and tensions. If the latter were really inherent in the transformation we would also have to accept a high degree of determinism and as such reject the very adaptive mechanisms which we have insisted exist.

We ought to relegate the concept of tension to a lower level of magnitude and treat its reality as part of everyday life. To do otherwise invariably takes us back to the view that as long as men lived in a rural environment harmony prevailed while the urban environment generates tensions and strains. We ought to concentrate far more on the operational aspects of social systems, from the small village to the nation, in terms of their functional continuity and the processes which contribute to the working of these systems rather than to label, quite often arbitrarily, some of the former as dysfunctional. But even if we continue to do so, we ought to ask ourselves, particularly in urban studies, what is functional about dysfunctional processes and relationships. The recent literature on urban gangs and protest movements strongly emphasises this point. We could reformulate many of these issues in terms of standard typological constructs, i.e. from tribal sacred ritual orientation to an urban profane and secular one, but to do so raises the analysis to an unnecessarily high level of abstraction.

Much of the literature on urbanisation deals with what Little (1957) has called "adaptive mechanisms" and Imoagene (1967, 1968) refers to as "Urban Involvement and Rural Detachment" and Mayer (1961, 1962, 1964) speaks of as "in-town" and "extra-town" ties. The language, all describing much the same phenomena, is varied but not very clear. So much that passes for intellectualism is no more than analytical gimmickry to which we are all so addicted. The past should stimulate us to ask new questions. Thus another fertile field for future research is to assess from new perspectives the present functions of voluntary associations and those groupings which have replaced the more conventional associations. Even more important, we ought to ask why some immigrant groups form such associations and others do not – a question once posed by Southall as far back as 1956. While the Igbo form such associations (as well as a vast number of other people in Third World towns) when they are away from their homeland, the Hausa in Ibadan generally do not (Cohen 1965 : 19). Why is this so? A variety of explanations have been offered ranging from strictly cultural data to a demonstration that "joining" and associations are related to the growing socio-economic differentiation which has gradually become established in the towns. The question, therefore, to be answered is whether the migrant is predisposed to join and form associations with others or does the need for this arise in the town? Mitchell (1966 : 47-48) puts the matter this way:

The individual does not bring his social institutions with him to the town. The institutions are part of different social systems and the individual moves from one into the other. It is fallacious, therefore, to think of rural institutions changing into urban types of the same institutions. The fact is rather that urban dwellers develop institutions to meet their needs in towns and these, because of their different context, differ from rural institutions meeting the same need in the tribal social system.

Jenkins (1967a : 73-74) sums up the controversy by saying:

What is needed, then, is a framework which accounts for those who migrate, and those who do not, for those who utilize adaptive organizations, and those who do not, and for those who experience disorganization, and those who do not.

To resolve the matter we might adopt the view that joining urban-based organisations might be related to factors other than ethnicity, namely those socio-economic and political criteria which are part of a broader and more complex set of development processes. This suggests that we ought to take into account the relevance of historical factors, the "scale" of the urban system, the resource base of the urban area and its hinterland, colonial policies and the evolution of political consciousness and activities. Whether we talk about adaptive mechanisms, or any other formulation to highlight the same phenomenon, we are dealing with certain basic societal processes which are part of more macro-sociological structures and organisational principles.

Finally, in this brief set of suggestions for further research to which a large number of new ideas ought to be added, the student of Third World urbanism must surely recognise that not only is there a great variety of cities, large and small, but also a great variety of urban subcultures. This in turn suggests a great variety of urban experiences (Arensberg 1968 : 4). It is, therefore, quite fallacious to assume that there is, as yet, one common urban culture. Not only is this likely to be a highly ethnocentric point of view, but more fundamentally to hold it removes the researcher wholly from an understanding of the subtleties of individual and group perceptions and motivations as these are rooted in a complex of conditions and circumstances which most often defy clear categorisation and analysis. What urban life is all about must take into account the cognitive and perceptual dimensions which influence and guide the relationships between the individual and his urban environment, i.e. the manner in which the individual responds to various cultural and social categories and gives meaning to the objects and relationships in the "external" world, the interpretation of symbols, and how decisions are made in the context of knowledge, experience and thought. Put in a somewhat simpler way, we ought to ask ourselves constantly how the urbanite "perceives" the urban world. An early effort at this kind of approach, in terms of cultural "categories", was attempted by Bascom (1963). Using this approach, urban anthropologists must be fully conversant with recent writings in structural linguistics, social psychology, experimental psychology, componential analysis and the theory of cognitive dissonance.

Linked to these new conceptual approaches are those which have come more directly from sociology and anthropology such as network and situational analysis (Mitchell 1969) and the experiments using quantification methods (Mitchell 1969a; Mitchell and Epstein 1957, 1959). Clyde Mitchell's recent theoretical contribution on the theory of social networks applied to the urban areas of Central Africa plus the case studies collected under his editorship, make an assessment of these approaches and models now possible. A whole range of new problems are raised by this approach, the most fundamental one being, perhaps, whether the very orthodoxy of structuralism which it was designed to replace will in turn be replaced by another. It is also clear that network and situational analysis has raised new methodological questions (Garbett 1968; Barnes 1969) which remain largely unresolved. While the techniques of micro and macro sociological analysis might come to our aid, to resolve some methodological problems, they in turn raise new issues which rotate round a clear definition of the unit under study.

Jenkins (1967a) attempts a summary of the many independent strands in African urban research and Gulick (1968) sets out three "Research Strategies". Turning first to the latter he suggests that the first strategy is to apply "traditional" anthropological methods and to turn to more conventional topics, although these "must take into account [the urbanite's] relationships to the total city environment". However, Gulick (p. 96) warns that some kinds of traditional anthropological concerns, i.e. "the formal analysis of kinship terms used by city dwellers could quite conceivably be done in such a way that it would contribute little or nothing 'to a better understanding of the complexities of the urban environment' " (Gulick 1963 : 445), and adds that "only urban field work which makes such a contribution is 'urban anthropology' ". For his second strategy he suggests "an institutional inventory of the city" on the ground that such "macrocosmic information . . . is essential raw material for comparative analysis". This strategy emphasises the need for descriptive material, a point which we have also made in this monograph. His final strategy is to give support to a suggestion made by Arensberg (1968) who recommends studies of the "deployment" of institutions over a given area. These appear to be studies which "concentrate . . . on institutional networks" independent of "rural or urban boundaries". Arensberg (1968 : 11) himself has summed up this research strategy as follows:

The empirical task of cultural comparison, therefore, means separating out the institutions and specifying their different lacings or integration without assuming them to take nucleated, urban form. How they are deployed in the constituent communities of a society or how they are gathered into centers to be labelled either urban or something else is an inductive question of best range and best fit in crosscultural data. For example, is the royal capital of Dahomey a city? The question is real, much hinges in anthropology on our understanding of native sub-Saharan African 'urbanism', a touchstone of civilization, like literacy.

Jenkins summarizes his "Overview of Current [African urban] Research" as follows:

. . . there are many independently initiated studies of urbanizing Africa which reveal a number of common traits; they are increasingly historical and developmental; increasingly marked by prior theoretical guidelines; and increasingly concerned with studies of social systems as they urbanize rather than merely with cities. It is from this quarter, then, that we may hope for a link between urbanists and those who view integration and development solely at the national level. It might also be added that African urban scholars are increasingly utilizing research methods used elsewhere. Historians employ massive documentation, sociologists utilize random sampling and computer techniques, and political scientists administer attitude questionnaires. Developing systems no less than developed ones require sophisticated theory and methods. Together these characteristics are providing the basis for a newly emergent co-operation among African urbanists.

In this monograph we have attempted to set out some theories, models and methods, but whether they are "sophisticated", new or creative will have to be judged by the critics.

5. Conclusion

The field of urban anthropology is relatively new and, as Gulick (1963 : 445) has pointed out, to some the phrase "may seem like a contradiction in terms". It will take a fair amount of time yet before the frontiers of our discipline have been destroyed so that we can incorporate in our field topics and interests which are not viewed as "antithetical" and contradictions in terms of our traditional concerns. There is no reason why the field of urban anthropology cannot live in harmony with whatever traditional interests remain in the years to come. At the same time, there is equally no reason why urban anthropologists should not be in the vanguard of the destruction of artificial boundaries which have kept us from looking over the fence. There are those who feel, rather smugly perhaps, that urban anthropologists have no claim to such a point of view because they have yet to succeed in defining what the urban environment is. How we can know this until we devote ourselves to the necessary tasks demanded by this challenge, is a matter which seems to escape the critics. The implication seems to be that in as much as the sociologists have worked in the urban environment they should be encouraged to continue to do so. But we have started a new task and we must continue with it. Even if we lack as yet that much sought after entity, a clear conceptual framework for the study of the urban environment (the implication being that we have mastered these matters for the study of the rural environment), we cannot deny that we have made a reasonable start, particularly in the field of African urban studies while anthropologists working in Latin America, Asia and the Middle East are increasingly concerned with urban research. Thus far we may know more specifically about African urbanism than urbanism elsewhere in the Third World, but this cannot be converted into a charge that we still flounder in a sea of conceptual confusion. Those who elect to argue this way seem to want us to generalise before we are ready to do so. Is that not rather what far too many anthropologists have done whose interest is in the rural environment? Perhaps our greatest contribution will be to go slowly, create our models with caution, become genuinely comparative in perspective and method and explore the realms beyond our traditional frontiers. "There are", Gulick (1963 : 453) writes

no theoretical or methodological tenents of the discipline which keep the anthropologist outside the city gates. Yet there, for the most part, he is, while others are doing an increasingly large amount of business inside. Why? One explanation is the possibility that anthropology as a profession tends to attract individuals who by temperament are inspired to live among and study people about whom no one else cares, at least not enough to undergo the inconveniences which the anthropologist often undergoes in getting his material.

To pretend that the social sciences, and in particular anthropology, do not attract particular kinds of personalities would be rather foolish although to prove this contention is another matter. Likewise, if anthropology does indeed attract those of a particular, although unspecified temperament, then urban anthropology has a very bright future because the city is full of people about whom other fellow citizens seem to care but little. If we are the only social scientists who care about the neglected and the downtrodden, we seem to have been slow in mobilising this in respect to city people. Indeed, today a small number of anthropologists seem to have committed themselves to working for the interests of the rulers rather than for the benefit of the downtrodden (Wolf and Jorgensen 1970). But these alone are not considerations which should either attract fellow anthropologists into urban research or on which we can build specialisation. Instead of attracting to anthropology those with "certain temperamental sets", it might be wiser to make the field more attractive to the more hard hitting policy thinkers whose sentiments and perspectives are not so easily swayed by an unconscious struggle with a false and often quite hypocritical romanticism. For some reasons, which are not easily explainable, the anthropologist has (at least until quite recently) found greater emotional satisfaction among rural people (Spindler 1970). It is a satisfaction (but not without agony as Bowen, 1964 and Powermaker, 1966 have shown) enhanced by the smaller scale of rural societies, their allegedly greater homogeneity and a characteristic known as being closer to nature. This satisfaction is the kind of illusion which has also led some anthropologists to feel that urbanism is destructive of all that is good and noble in man. We may be forgiven if we suggest that anthropologists seem all too willing to escape from reality. Turning once again to Gulick (1963 : 454-456), he neatly portrays the fanciful world of the anthropologist.

The anthropologist likes to gather his material so that he can portray to others the reality which he has experienced and studied. For this he needs some sense of completeness or pattern, and one of his weaknesses is that if he does not readily find this in the external situation, he may inadvertently find it in his own fertile mind. Much of his pedantic, but none too clear, talk about holism, functional context, and model formation derives from his inclination and his semi-conscious struggle with it. It is also what accounts for his readiness to generalize from a small-scale situation to what he "intuits" to be patterns of a culture as a whole, without bothering with intermediate steps of testing. It further accounts for the fact that anthropologists are often irritated by sociological findings not so much because they are "quantified", but because they are abstracted so far from the behavioural context and from situations that can be visualized.

The inclination to visualize is one of the sources of the anthropologist's tendency to over-generalize, sometimes so vividly and convincingly that he eventually accepts his own general portrayals as established facts rather than as what they, at best, actually are, hypotheses. I have already mentioned cases in which preconceptions of certain cultural patterns are in effect assumed to be established facts, and I have suggested that the nature of cities is such that one is likely to be able to find in them by chance examples of anything one is looking for. The visualizer is sorely tempted to take this tack and anthropologists have often succumbed. Urban anthropologists must resist the temptation, even if it means tempering the vividness of their portrayals, for otherwise they are likely to complicate, rather than simplify, the problems of urban research.

The study of the urban environment, created by man and now approaching a respectable age, may be just what anthropologists have been waiting for to give expression to their particular "temperamental sets" and their dedication to go where nobody else dares to go — among people and their troubles and their joys. Trite as it is to say so, the urbanite is no less "real" than his country cousin; for the sake of fairness we ought to consider paying more systematic attention to him. We might even then be able to use our skills to assist in the creation of urban conditions which, as more and more rural people drift to the city, are fit for all men.

Toynbee (1970) has warned of the imminent coming of "Ecumenopolis" which will encompass the land-surface of the globe. He insists that the question is not whether Ecumenopolis is going to come into existence, "it is whether its maker, mankind, is going to be its master or to be its victim".

For much of the rich industrial world, Ecumenopolis has arrived. For the poor and downtrodden part of the world this development may be more than an apocalyptic warning.

I, for one, will not reject the birth of *apocalyptic anthropology.*

References Cited

Abiodun, J.O., "Central Place Study in Abeokuta Province, Southwestern Nigeria," *Journal of Regional Science*, VIII (1968), 57-76.

Abrahams, R.G., "Kahama Township, Western Province, Tanganyika," in Southall A.W. (ed.), *Social Change in Modern Africa* (London, 1961), 242-53.

Acquah, I., *Accra Survey* (London, 1958).

African Urban Notes, African Studies Center, Michigan State University, East Lansing (commenced publication irregularly in April 1966).

Aldous, J., "Urbanization, the Extended Family and Kinship Ties in West Africa," *Social Forces*, XLI (1962), 6-12.

Alkalimat, Abd-l Hakimu Ibn (Gerald McWorter), "The Ideology of Black Social Science," *The Black Scholar*, I (1969), 28-35.

Ardant, G., "Automation in Developing Countries," *International Labour Review*, XC (1964), 432-71.

Arensberg, C.M., "The Urban in Crosscultural Perspective," in Eddy, E.M., (ed.), *Urban Anthropology: Research Perspectives and Strategies* (Athens, Georgia, 1968), 3-15.

Babchuk, N., "The Role of the Researcher as Participant Observer and Participant-as-Observer in the Field Situation," *Human Organization*, XXI (1962), 225-28.

Bailey, F.G., *Politics and Social Change, Orissa in 1959* (Berkeley, 1963).

—, "Two Villages in Orissa," in Gluckman, M., (ed.), *Closed Systems and Open Minds: the Limits of Naivety in Social Anthropology* (Chicago, 1964), 52-82.

—, *Stratagems and Spoils. A Social Anthropology of Politics* (Oxford, 1969).

Banton, M., *West African City: a Study of Tribal Life in Freetown* (London, 1957).

—, "The Restructuring of Social Relationships," in Southall, A.W., (ed.), *Social Change in Modern Africa* (London, 1961), 113-125.

Baran P.A., *The Political Economy of Growth* (New York, 1957).

Barnes, J.A., "Marriage in a Changing Society," *Rhodes-Livingstone Papers*, XX (1951).

—, "Networks and Political Process," in Swartz, M. J., (ed.), *Local-Level Politics: Social and Cultural Perspectives* (Chicago, 1968), 107-30.

—, "Graph Theory and Social Networks: a Technical Comment on Connectedness and Connectivity," *Sociology*, III (1969), 215-32.

Barth, F., "On the Study of Social Change," *American Anthropologist*, LXIX (1967), 661-69.

Barth, H., *Travels and Discoveries in Northern and Central Africa*, 5 vols. (London, 1857-1858).

Bascom, W., "Urbanization among the Yoruba," *American Journal of Sociology*, LX (1955), 446-54.

—, "Urbanism as a Traditional African Pattern," *The Sociological Review*, VII (1959), 29-43.

—, "The Urban African and his World," *Cahiers d'Etudes Africaines*, IV (1963), 163-85.

Batson, E., "Socio-Economic Problems: Techniques and Results of Surveys," African Regional Scientific Conference, No. E(n) 6 (1949).

Beattie, J., *Understanding an African Kingdom* (New York, 1965).

Becker, H.S., "Problems of Inference and Proof in Participant Observation," *American Sociological Review*, XXIII (1958), 653-60.

Becker, H.S. and B. Geer, "Participant Observation and Interviewing: a Comparison," *Human Organization*, XVI (1957), 28-32.

Beckman, G., "Spatial Aspects of the Interaction of Industrial and Urban Development in Ghana," *African Urban Notes*, V (1970), 35-37.

Bendix, R., "Tradition and Modernity Reconsidered," *Comparative Studies in Society and History*, IX (1967), 292-346.

Bennett, J.W., "Microcosm-Macrocosm Relationships in North American Agrarian Society," *American Anthropologist*, LXIX (1967), 441-54.

Berreman, G.D., *Behind Many Masks: Ethnography and Impression Management in a Himalayan Village*, Society for Applied Anthropology, 4, 1962.

Blanksten, G.I., "Transference of Social and Political Loyalties," in Hoselitz, B.F. and W.E. Moore (eds.), *Industrialization and Society* (Paris, 1963), 175-96.

Bowen, E.S., *Return to Laughter: an Anthropological Novel* (Garden City, N.Y.), 1965.

Bowen, T.J., *Central Africa: Adventures and Missionary Labors in Several Countries in the Interior of Africa, from 1849 to 1856* (Charleston, S.C., 1857).

Bruyn, S.T., *The Human Perspective in Sociology: the Methodology of Participant Observation* (Englewood Cliffs, 1966).

Buchanan. K., "The Third World — its Emergence and Contours," *New Left Review*, XVIII (1963), 1-19.

Buchler, I.R. and H.G. Nutini (eds.), *Game Theory in the Behavioral Sciences* (Pittsburgh, 1969).

Caldwell, J.C., "The Erosion of the Family: a Study of the Fate of the Family in Ghana," *Population Studies*, XX (1966), 5-26.

Callaway, A., "Nigeria's Indigenous Education: the Apprentice System," *ODU*, I (July 1964), 1-18.

Chambers, M., "Jesus of Oyingbo," *New Society*, LXXX (1964), 13-15.

Childe, V.G., *Man Makes Himself* (London, 1936).

Chombart de Lauwe, P.H., "Field and Case Studies," in Hauser, P.M., (ed.), *Handbook for Social Research in Urban Areas* (Paris, 1965), 55-72.

Clapperton, H., *Journal of a Second Expedition into the Interior of Africa, from the Bight of Benin to Soccatoo* (Philadelphia, 1829).

Clignet, R., "Urbanization and Family Structure in the Ivory Coast," *Comparative Studies in Society and History*, VIII (1966), 385-401.

Cohen, A., "Politics of the Kola Trade: some Processes of Tribal Community Formation among Migrants in West African Towns," *Africa*, XXXVI (1965), 18-36.

—, *Custom and Politics in Urban Africa: a Study of Hausa Migrants in Yoruba Towns* (Berkeley, 1969).

Cohen, Y.A., (ed.), *Man in Adaptation. The Cultural Present* (Chicago, 1968).

Colson, E., "Family Change in Contemporary Africa," *Annals of the New York Academy of Sciences*, XCVI (1962), 641-52.

Conference on Anthropological Research in Cities, University of Wisconsin-Milwaukee, June 8-13, 1970, mimeo.

Coser, L., *The Functions of Social Conflict* (Glencoe, 1956).

Davidson, B., "Pluralism in Colonial Societies: Northern Rhodesia/Zambia," in Kuper, L. and M.G. Smith (eds.), *Pluralism in Africa* (Berkeley, 1969), 211-45.

Davis, J.M., *Modern Industry and the African* (London, 1933; Reprint 1966).

Denham, D., H. Clapperton and N. Dudney, *Narrative of Travels and Discoveries in Northern and Central Africa in the Years 1822, 1823 and 1824*, 2v (London, 1826).

Despres, L.A., "Anthropological Theory, Cultural Pluralism, and the Study of Complex Societies," *Current Anthropology*, IX (1968), 3-26.

Devon, E. and M. Gluckman, "Introduction," in Devon, E. and M. Gluckman (eds.), *Closed Systems and Open Minds: the Limits of Naivety in Social Anthropology* (Chicago, 1964), 13-19.

Diamond, S., "Modern Africa: the Pains of Birth," *Dissent*, X (1963), 169-79.

Drake, St.C., "Review of *Townsman in the Making* by Southall, A.W., and Gutkind, P.C.W., *American Anthropologist*, LIX (1951), 919-20.

Dubb, A.A., "Red and School: a Quantitative Approach," *Africa*, XXXVI (1966), 292-302.

Dumont, R., *False Start in Africa* (New York, 1962; 2nd ed. 1966).

Du Sacre-Coeur, M.A., *The House Stands Firm* (Milwaukee, 1962).

East Africa Royal Commission Report 1953-1955 (London, 1955).

Eisenstadt, S.N., "Anthropological Studies of Complex Societies." *Current Anthropology*, II (1961), 201-22.

—, "Some Observations on the Dynamics of Traditions," *Comparative Studies in Society and History*, XI (1969), 451-75.

Elkan, W., *An African Labour Force: Two Case Studies in East African Factory Employment*, East African Studies VI (Kampala, 1956).

—, *Migrants and Proletarians. Urban Labour in the Economic Development of Uganda* (London. 1960).

—, "Circular Migration and the Growth of Towns in East Africa," *International Labour Review*, XCVI (1967), 581-89.

Epstein, A.L., *The Administration of Justice and the Urban African*, Colonial Research Studies VII (London, 1953).

—, *Politics in an Urban African Community* (Manchester, 1958).

—, "The Network of Urban Social Organization," *Rhodes-Livingstone Journal*, XXIX (1961), 29-62.

—, "Urban Communities in Africa," in Gluckman, M. (ed.), *Closed Systems and Open Minds: the Limits of Naivety in Social Anthropology* (Chicago, 1964), 83-102.

—, "Urbanization and Social Change in Africa," *Current Anthropology*, VIII (1967), 275-95.

Evans-Pritchard, E.E., *The Nuer* (Oxford, 1950).

Fallers, L.A., "Equality, Modernity, and Democracy in the New States," in Geertz, C. (ed.), *Old Societies and New States; the Quest for Modernity in Asia and Africa* (New York, 1963), 158-219.

Fanon, F., *A Dying Colonialism* (New York, 1959; 2nd ed. 1965).

—, *The Wretched of the Earth* (New York, 1966).

—, *Toward the African Revolution* (New York, 1964; 2nd ed. 1967).

Firth, R., *Elements of Social Oganisation* (London, 1951).

Flegg, H. and W. Lutz, "Report on an African Demographic Survey," *Journal for Social Research*, X (1959), 1-24.

Fortes, M., *The Dynamics of Clanship among the Tallensi* (London, 1945).

Fraenkel, M., *Tribe and Class in Monrovia* (London, 1964).

Frank, A.G., *Capitalism and Underdevelopment in Latin America* (New York, 1967).

Freilich, M. (ed.), *Marginal Natives: Anthropologists at Work* (New York, 1970).

Gamble, D.P., "Sociological Research in an Urban Community (Lunsar) in Sierra Leone," *Sierra Leone Studies*, XVII (1963), 254-68.

—, "The Temne Family in a Modern Town [Lunsar] in Sierra Leone," *Africa*, XXXIII (1963), 209-25.

Gappert, G., "Preliminary Outline for Investigating the Function, Structure and Growth of Small Towns in Tanzania," *African Urban Notes*, III (1968), 32-38.

Garbett, G.K., "The Application of Optical Coincidence Cards to the Matrices of Digraphs of Social Networks," *Sociology*, II (1968), 313-31.

Geertz, C., "Ritual and Social Change: a Javanese Example," *American Anthropologist*, LIX (1957), 32-54.

—. "Primoridial Sentiments and Civil Politics in the New States," in Geertz, C. (ed.), *Old Societies in New States* (Glencoe, 1963), 105-57.

Germani, G., "Migration and Acculturation," in Hauser, P.M. (ed.), *Handbook for Social Research in Urban Areas* (Paris, 1965), 159-78.

Gibbs, J.L. (ed.), *Peoples of Africa* (New York, 1965).

Gibbs, J.P. (ed.), *Urban Research Methods* (New York, 1961).

Glazer, N., "The Rise of Social Research in Europe," in Lerner, D. (ed.), *The Human Meaning of the Social Sciences* (New York, 1964), 43-72.

Gluckman, M., *Custom and Conflict in Africa* (Oxford, 1955).

—, "Analysis of a Social Situation in Modern Zululand," *Rhodes-Livingstone Papers,* XXVIII (1958).

—, "Tribalism in Modern British Central Africa," *Cahiers d'Etudes Africaines,* I (1960). 55-70.

—, "Anthropological Problems arising from the African Industrial Revolution," in Southall, A.W. (ed.), *Social Change in Modern Africa* (London, 1961), 67-82.

—, *Politics, Law and Ritual in Tribal Society* (Oxford, 1965)..

—, "The Utility of the Equilibrium Model in the Study of Social Change," *American Anthropologist,* LXX (1968), 219-37.

Gold, R.L., "Roles in Sociological Field Observations," *Social Forces,* XXXVI (1958), 217-23.

Golde, P. (ed.), *Women in the Field* (Chicago, 1970).

Gough, K., "Anthropology and Imperialism," *Monthly Review,* XIX (1968), 12-27.

—, "New Proposals for Anthropologists," *Current Anthropology,* IX (1968a), 403-07.

Green, L.P. and T.J.D. Fair, *Development in Africa: a Study in Regional Analysis with special reference to Southern Africa* (Johannesburg, 1962).

Gugler, J., "Life in a Dual System," East African Institute of Social Research Conference Papers (Kampala, 1965), mimeo.

—, "On the Concept of Urbanization," East African Institute of Social Research Conference Paper, 363 (Kampala, 1966), mimeo.

—, "The Impact of Labour Migration on Society and Economy in Sub-Saharan Africa: Empirical Findings and Theoretical Considerations," *African Social Research,* VI (1968), 463-86.

Guillermo, B.B., "Conservative Thought in Applied Anthropology: a Critique," *Human Organization,* XXV (1966), 89-92.

Gulick, J., "Urban Anthropology: its Present and Future," *Transactions of the New York Academy of Sciences,* XXV (1963), 445-58.

—, "The Outlook, Research Strategies, and Relevance of Urban Anthropology: a Commentary," in Eddy, E.M. (ed.), *Urban Anthropology: Research Perspectives and Strategies* (Athens, Georgia, 1968), 93-98.

—, "Village and City Field Work in Lebanon," in Freilich, M. (ed.), *Marginal Natives: Anthropologists at Work* (New York, 1970), 123-52.

Gulliver, P.H., "Anthropology," in Lystad, R.A. (ed.), *The African World: a Survey of Social Research* (New York, 1965), 57-106.

Gusfield, J., "Tradition and Modernity," *American Journal of Sociology,* LXXII (1967), 351-62

Gussman, B., "Industrial Efficiency and the Urban African," *Africa*, XXIII (1953), 135-44.

Gutkind, P.C.W., Unpublished Field Notes from Kampala, Lagos, Freetown, Ibadan, Salisbury, Nairobi, Lusaka and Accra (1953-1966).

—, "Four Neighbourhoods in Mulago," (1957), mss.

—, "African Urban Family Life," *Cahiers d'Etudes Africaines*, X (1962), 149-72.

—, *The Royal Capital of Buganda* (The Hague, 1963).

—, "African Urbanism, Mobility and the Social Network," *International Journal of Comparative Sociology*, VI (1965), 48-60.

—, "Network Analysis and Urbanism in Africa: the Use of Micro and Macro Analysis," *Canadian Review of Sociology and Anthropology*, II (1965a), 123-31.

—, "African Urban Family Life and the Urban System," *Journal of Asian and African Studies*, I (1966), 35-42.

—, Review of Devon, E. and M. Gluckman (eds.), *Closed Systems and Open Minds: the Limits of Naivety in Social Anthropology*, *Anthropologica*, VIII (1966a), 363-66.

—, "The Energy of Despair: Social Organization of the Unemployed in Two African Cities: Lagos and Nairobi – a Preliminary Account," *Civilisations*, XVII (1967), 186-214; 380-405.

—, "Orientation and Research Methods in African Urban Studies," in Jongmans, D.G. and P.C.W. Gutkind (eds.), *Anthropologists in the Field* (Assen, The Netherlands, 1967), 133-69.

—, "The Small African Town in African Urban Studies," *African Urban Notes*, III (1968), 5-10.

—, "African Responses to Urban Wage Employment," *International Labour Review*, XCVII (1968a), 135-66.

—, "The Social Researcher in the Context of African National Development," in Henry, F. and S. Saberwal (eds.), *Stress and Response in Fieldwork* (New York, 1969), 20-34.

—, "Tradition, Migration, Urbanization, Modernity and Unemployment in Africa: the Roots of Instability," *Canadian Journal of African Studies*, III (1969a), 343-65.

—, "Urban Anthropology: Creative Pioneer of Modern Social Anthropology — the African Case," *Proceedings 8th International Congress of Anthropological and Ethnological Sciences* (Tokyo and Kyoto, 1968), v.2 (1969b), 77-81.

—, "The Socio-Political and Economic Foundations of Social Problems in African Urban Areas: an Exploratory Conceptual Overview," *Civilisations*, XXII (1972), 18-34.

—, "Bibliography on Urban Anthropology," in Southall, A. (ed.), *Urban Anthropology; Cross-cultural Studies in Urbanization* (New York, 1973), 425-89.

Hanna, W.J., "The Cross-Cultural Study of Local Politics," *Civilisations*, XVI (1966), 1-15.

Hanna, W.J. and J.L. Hanna, *Polyethnicity and Political Integration in Umuahia and Mbale* (Washington, 1968).

Hare, N., "The Challenge of a Black Scholar," *The Black Scholar*, I, (1969), 58-63.

Harries-Jones, P., "Marital Disputes and the Process of Conciliation in a Copperbelt

Town," *The Rhodes-Livingstone Journal*, XXXV (1964), 29-72.

Hauser, P.M., "The Social, Economic and Technological Problems of Rapid Urbanization," in Hoselitz, B.F. and W.E. Moore (eds.), *Industrialization and Society* (Paris, 1963), 199-215.

—, (ed.). *Handbook for Social Research in Urban Areas* (Paris, 1965).

Hauser, P.M. and L.F. Schnore (eds.), *The Study of Urbanization* (New York, 1965).

Hellmann, E., "Methods of Urban Field Work," *Bantu Studies*, IX (1935), 185-202.

—, *Rooiyard: a Sociological Survey of an Urban Native Slum Yard*, Rhodes-Livingstone Papers, XIII (Capetown, 1948).

Henderson, R.N., "Generalized Cultures and Evolutionary Adaptability: a Comparison of Urban Efik and Ibo in Nigeria," *Ethnology*, V (1966), 365-91.

Henry, F., "Stress and Strategy in Three Field Situations," in Henry, F. and S. Saberwal (eds.), *Stress and Response in Fieldwork* (New York, 1969), 35-46.

—, and S. Saberwal (eds.), *Stress and Response in Fieldwork* (New York, 1969).

Howard, C., "The Rise of Alice Lenshina," *New Society*, IV (1964), 6-8.

Hudson, C., "Preface," in Eddy, E.M. (ed.), *Urban Anthropology: Research Perspectives and Strategies* (Athens, Georgia, 1968), v-vi.

Hutchinson, H.W., "Social Anthropology and Urban Studies," in Eddy, E.M. (ed.), *Urban Anthropology: Research Perspectives and Strategies* (Athens, Georgia, 1968), 24-30.

Imoagene, S.O., "Mechanisms of Immigrant Adjustment in a West African Urban Community," *Nigerian Journal of Economic and Social Studies*, IX (1967), 51-66.

—, "Urban Involvement and Rural Detachment," *Nigerian Journal of Economic and Social Studies*, X (1968), 397-411.

Izzett, A., "Family Life among the Yoruba, in Lagos, Nigeria," in Southall, A.W. (ed.), *Social Change in Modern Africa* (London, 1961), 305-15.

Jahoda, G., "Boys' Images of Marriage Partners and Girls' Self-Images in Ghana," *Sociologus*, VIII (1958), 155-69.

—, "Love, Marriage and Social Change," *Africa*, XXIX (1959), 177-90.

—, "Witchcraft, Magic and Literacy," *New Society*, XVI (1963), 15-17.

Jenkins, G., "African Urban Research: Theory, Strategy, Utilization," Proceedings of a conference held at the University of Wisconsin-Milwaukee (1966).

—, "Government and Politics in Ibadan," in Lloyd, P.C., A.L. Mabogunje and B. Awe (eds.), *The City of Ibadan* (Cambridge, 1967), 213-33.

—, "Africa as it Urbanizes: an Overview of Current Research," *Urban Affairs Quarterly*, II (1967a), 66-80.

Jongmans, D.G. and P.C.W. Gutkind (eds.), *Anthropologists in the Field* (Assen, The Netherlands, 1967).

Keiser, R.L., *The Vice Lords: Warriors of the Streets* (New York, 1969).

Kilson, M., "African Political Change and the Modernization Process," *The Journal of Modern African Studies*, I (1963), 425-40.

Kluckhohn, F.R., "The Participant-observer Technique in Small Communities," *American Journal of Sociology*, XLVI (1940), 331-43.

Krapf-Askari, E., *Yoruba Towns and Cities* (London, 1969).

Krige, J.D., "The Social Function of Witchcraft," *Theoria*, I (1947), 9-21.

Kuper, L., "Structural Discontinuities in African Towns: some Aspects of Racial Pluralism," in Miner, H. (ed.), *The City in Modern Africa* (New York, 1967), 127-50.

—, "Ethnic and Racial Pluralism: some Aspects of Polarization and Depluralization," in Kuper, L. and M.G. Smith (eds.), *Pluralism in Africa* (Berkeley, 1969), 459-87.

Kuper, L. and M.G. Smith (eds.), *Pluralism in Africa* (Berkeley, 1969).

Lander, R. and J. Lander, *Journal of an Expedition to Explore the Course and Termination of the Niger* (New York, 1832; 1854).

Leeds, A., "The Anthropology of Cities: some Methodological Issues," in Eddy, E.M. (ed.), *Urban Anthropology: Research Perspectives and Strategies* (Athens, Georgia, 1968), 31-47.

Leslie, J.A.K., *A Survey of Dar es Salaam* (London, 1963).

Lewin, K., *Field Theory in Social Science* (New York, 1951).

Lewis, O., *Five Families: Mexican Studies in the Culture of Poverty* (New York, 1959).

—, *The Children of Sanchez: Autobiography of a Mexican Family* (New York, 1961).

Liebow, E., *Tally's Corner: a Study of Negro Streetcorner Men* (Boston, 1967).

Little, K., "The Role of Voluntary Associations in West African Urbanization," *American Anthropologist*, LIX (1957), 579-96.

Lloyd, B., "Indigenous Ibadan," in Lloyd, P.C., A.L. Mabogunje and B. Awe (eds.), *The City of Ibadan* (Cambridge, 1967), 59-83.

Lloyd, P.C., "The Yoruba Town Today," *The Sociological Review*, VII (1959), 45-63.

—, "Introduction," in Lloyd, P.C. (ed.), *The New Elites of Tropical Africa* (London, 1966), 1-85.

—, "Class Consiousness among the Yoruba," in Lloyd, P.C. (ed.), *The New Elites of Tropical Africa* (London, 1966a), 328-41.

Lloyd, P.C., A.L. Mabogunje and B. Awe (eds.), *The City of Ibadan: a Symposium on its Structure and Development* (Cambridge, 1967).

Longmore, L., *The Dispossessed: a Study of Sex-life of Bantu Women in and around Johannesburg* (London, 1959).

Lowie, R.H., "Native Languages as Ethnographic Tools," *American Anthropologist*, XLII (1940), 81-89,

Lukhero, M.B., "The Social Characteristics of an Emergent Elite in Harare," in Lloyd, P.C. (ed.), *The New Elites of Tropical Africa* (London, 1966), 126-38.

Mabogunje, A.L. *Yoruba Towns* (Ibadan, 1962).

—, "Urbanization in Nigeria — a Constraint on Economic Development," *Economic Development and Cultural Change*, XIII (1965), 413-38.

—, *Urbanization in Nigeria* (London, 1968).

MacGaffey, W., "Afterthoughts by an Anthropologist: Field Research in Kongo Central,"

Cahiers Economique et Social, IV (1966), 211-15.

Mafeje, A., "A Chief Visits Town," *Journal of Local Administration Overseas,* II (1963), 88-99.

Magubane, B., "Crisis in African Sociology," *East Africa Journal,* V (1968), 21-40.

—, "Pluralism and Conflict Situations in Africa: a New Look," *African Social Research,* VII (1969), 529-54.

—, "A Critical Look at Indices used in the Study of Social Change in Colonial Africa," *Current Anthropology,* XII (1971), 419-45.

Mair, L., *Primitive Government* (London, 1962).

—, *New Nations* (London, 1963).

—, "How Small-Scale Societies Change," *The Advancement of Science,* XXI (1964), 308-15.

Malinowski, B., *A Diary in the Strict Sense of the Word* (New York, 1967).

Marris, P., *Family and Social Change in an African City* (London, 1961).

—, "Individual Achievement and Family Life," *African City Life, Nkanga,* I (1968), 20-26.

—, "The Social Barriers to African Entrepreneurship," *Journal of Development Studies,* V (1968a), 29-39.

Marwick, M.G., "The Continuance of Witchcraft Beliefs," in Smith, P. (ed.), *Africa in Transition* (London, 1958), 106-14.

—, "The Sociology of Sorcery in a Central African Tribe," *African Studies,* XXII (1963), 1-21.

Mathew, G., "The East African Coast until the Coming of the Portuguese," in Oliver, R. and G. Mathew (eds.), *History of East Africa,* v. I, (Oxford, 1963), 94-127.

Matras J., "Other Social Research Approaches," in Hauser, P.M. (ed.), *Handbook for Social Research in Urban Areas* (Paris, 1965), 73-87.

—, "Social and Personal Disorganization," in Hauser, P.M. (ed.), *Handbook for Social Research in Urban Areas* (Paris, 1965a), 179-91.

Mayer, P., *Townsmen or Tribesmen: Conservatism and the Process of Urbanization in a South African City* (Cape Town, 1961).

—, "Migrancy and the Study of Africans in Town," *American Anthropologist,* LXIV (1962), 576-92.

—, "Labour Migrancy and the Social Network," in Holleman, J.F. *at al* (eds.), *Problems of Transition* (Pietermaritzberg, 1964), 21-34.

McClelland, D.C., *The Achieving Society* (New York, 1961).

McNulty, M.L. "Urban Structure and Development: the Urban System of Ghana," *The Journal of Developing Areas,* III (1969), 159-68.

McVicar, K.G., *Twilight of an East African Slum: Pumwani and the Evolution of African Settlement in Nairobi,* (University of California, Los Angeles, 1968), Ph.D. dissertation.

Mead, M., "Native Languages as Fieldwork Tools," *American Anthropologist*, XLI (1939), 189-205.

Merton, R.K., *Social Theory and Social Structure* (Glencoe, 1957).

Middleton, J., *The Study of the Lugbara: Expectation and Paradox in Anthropological Research* (New York, 1970).

Miller, S.M., "The Participant Observer and 'Overrapport'," *American Sociological Review*, XVII (1952), 97-99.

Miner, H., *The Primitive City of Timbuctoo* (Princeton, 1953).

'—, "The City and Modernization: an Introduction," in Miner, H. (ed.), *The City in Modern Africa* (New York, 1967), 1-20.

Mitchell, J.C., "The Kalela Dance: Aspects of Social Relationships among Urban Africans in Northern Rhodesia," *Rhodes-Livingstone Papers* 27 (Manchester, 1957).

—, "Types of Urban Social Relationships," in Apthorpe, R. (ed.), *Present Interrelations in Central African Rural and Urban Life* (Lusaka, 1958), 84-87.

—, "The Causes of Labour Migration," *Bulletin Inter-African Labour Institute*, VI (1959), 12-46.

—, "The Anthropological Study of Urban Communities," *African Studies*, XIX (1960), 169-72.

—, "Social Change and the Stability of African Marriage in Northern Rhodesia," in Southall, A.W. (ed.), *Social Change in Modern Africa* (London, 1961), 316-29.

—, "Theoretical Orientations in African Urban Studies: Methodological Approaches," in Banton, M. (ed.), *The Social Anthropology of Complex Societies* (London, 1966), 37-68.

—, "Aspects of Occupational Prestige in a Plural Society," in Lloyd, P.C. (ed.), *The New Elites of Tropical Africa* (London, 1966a), 256-71.

—, (ed.), *Social Networks in Urban Situations: Analyses of Personal Relations in Central African Towns* (Manchester, 1969).

—, "African Images of the Town: a Quantitative Exploration," Manchester Statistical Society (1969a).

Mitchell, J.C. and A.L. Epstein, "Power and Prestige among Africans in Northern Rhodesia," *Proceedings and Transactions*, XLV (1957), 13-26.

—, "Occupational Prestige and Social Status among Urban Africans in Northern Rhodesia," *Africa*, XXIX (1959), 22-40.

Mitchell, R.C., "Religious Protest and Social Change: the Origins of the Aladura Movement in Western Nigeria," in Rotberg, R.I. and A.A. Mazrui (eds.), *Protest and Power in Black Africa* (New York, 1970), 458-96.

Morrill, W.T., "Immigrants and Associations: the Ibo in Twentieth Century Calabar," *Comparative Studies in Society and History*, V (1963), 424-48.

Mumford, L., "Patrick Geddes," in Sills, D.L. (ed.), *International Encyclopedia of the Social Sciences*, VI (New York, 1968), 81-83.

—, "Reflections: the Megamachine," *The New Yorker*, XLVI Part I (10 Oct. 1970), 50-131;

Part II (17 Oct. 1970), 48-141; Part III (24 Oct. 1970), 55-127; Part IV (31 Oct. 1970), 50-98.

Nadel, S.F., "Witchcraft in Four African Societies: an Essay in Comparison," *American Anthropologist*, LIV (1952), 18-29.

Nelkin, D., "The Economic and Social Setting of Military Take-overs in Africa," *Journal of Asian and African Studies*, II (1967), 230-44.

Nelson, J., "The Urban Poor: Disruption or Political Integration in Third World Cities?" *World Politics*, XXII (1970), 393-414.

Nkosi, L., "Zulu Tribal Fights," *New Society*, V (18 Feb. 1965), 6-9.

Okediji, F.O. and O.O. Okediji, "Marital Stability and Social Structure in an African City," *Nigerian Journal of Economic and Social Studies*, VIII (1966), 151-63.

Olien, M.D., "Levels of Urban Relationships in a Complex Society: a Costa Rican Case," in Eddy, E.M. (ed.), *Urban Anthropology: Research Perspectives and Strategies* (Athens, Georgia, 1968), 83-92.

Oliver, R. and G. Mathew (eds.), *History of East Africa* 3 v. (Oxford, 1963).

Ominde, S.H., *Land and Population Movements in Kenya* (Evanston, 1968).

Onwuachi, P.C. and A.W. Wolfe, "The Place of Anthropology in the Future of Africa," *Human Organization*, XXV (1966), 93-95.

Parkin, D.J., "Types of Urban African Marriage in Kampala (Uganda)," *Africa*, XXXVI (1966), 269-85.

—, *Neighbours and Nationals in an African City Ward* (London, 1969).

Parrinder, G., *Religion in an African City* (London, 1953).

Patch, R.W., "Life in a Callejon," *American Universities Field Staff, Report Service*, VIII (1961).

Pauw, B.A., *The Second Generation: a Study of the Family among Urbanized Bantu in East London* (Cape Town, 1963).

Peattie, L., "Pure and Dirty Research on Public Programs," Conference on Anthropological Research in Cities, University of Wisconsin-Milwaukee (1970).

Peil, M., "Methodological Lessons of the Medina Survey," *Ghana Journal of Sociology*, II (1966), 23-28.

Phillips, A. (ed.), *Survey of African Marriage and Family Life* (London, 1953).

Phillips, R.E., *The Bantu in the City: a Study of Cultural Adjustment on the Witwatersrand* (Lovedale Press, ca. 1939).

Plotnicov, L., "Going Home Again - Nigerians: the Dream is Unfulfilled," *Trans-Action*, III (1965), 18-22.

—, *Strangers to the City: Urban Man in Jos, Nigeria* (Pittsburgh, 1967).

—, "The Modern African Elite of Jos, Nigeria," in Tuden, A. and L. Plotnicov (eds.), *Social Stratification in Africa* (New York, 1970), 269-302.

Polanyi, K., *Dahomey and the Slave Trade* (Seattle, 1966).

Pons, V., "Two Small Groups in Avenue 21: some Aspects of the System of Social Relations in a Remote Corner of Stanleyville, Belgian Congo," in Southall, A.W. (ed.), *Social Change in Modern Africa* (London, 1961), 205-16.

—, *Stanleyville: an African Urban Community under Belgian Administration* (London, 1969).

Powdermaker, H., *Copper-Town: Changing Africa* (New York, 1962).

—, *Stranger and Friend: the Way of an Anthropologist* (New York, 1966).

—, "Field Work," in Sills, D.L. (ed.), *International Encyclopedia of the Social Sciences*, V (New York, 1968), 418-24.

Rapoport, A., " Game Theory and Human Conflict," in McNeil, E.B. (ed.), *The Nature of Human Conflict* (Englewood Cliffs, 1965), 195-226.

Reich, C.A., "Reflections: the Greening of America," *The New Yorker*, XLVI (Sept. 26, 1970), 42-111.

Richards, A.I., "The Village Census in the Study of Culture Contact," *Africa*, VIII (1935), 2-33. (Reprint of above: International African Institute, Memo 15, 1938.)

—, "Anthropology on the Scrap Heap?", *Journal of African Administration*, XIII (1961), 3-10.

—, (ed.), *East African Chiefs: a Study of Political Development in some Uganda and Tanganyika Tribes* (London, 1960).

Roberts, A.D., "The Lumpa Church of Alice Lenshina," in Rotberg, R.I. and A.A. Mazrui (eds.), *Protest and Power in Black Africa* (New York, 1970), 513-68.

Rotberg, R.I., "The Lenshina Movement of Northern Rhodesia." *Rhodes-Livingstone Journal*, XXIX (1961), 63-78.

Rotberg, R.I. and A.A. Mazrui (eds.), *Protest and Power in Black Africa* (New York, 1970).

Rouch, J., "Migrations au Ghana," *Journal de la Société des Africanistes*, XXVI (1956), 33-196.

Rudolph, L.I. and S.H. Rudolph, *The Modernity of Tradition* (Chicago, 1967).

Ryan, B.F., *Social and Cultural Change* (New York, 1969).

Schwab, W.B., "An Experiment in Methodology in a West African Urban Community," *Human Organization*, XIII (1954), 13-19.

—, "Social Stratification in Gwelo," in Southall, A.W. (ed)., *Social Change in Modern Africa* (London, 1961), 126-44.

—, "Continuity and Change in the Yoruba Lineage," in Furness, F.N. (ed.), *Anthropology and Africa Today, Annals of the New York Academy of Sciences*, XCVI (1962), 590-605.

—, "Looking Backward: an Appraisal of Two Field Trips," *Human Organization*, XXIV (1965), 373-80.

—, "Oshogbo, an Urban Community," in Kuper, H. (ed.), *Urbanization and Migration in West Africa* (Berkeley, 1965a), 85-109.

—, "Comparative Field Techniques in Urban Research in Africa," in Freilich, M. (ed.), *Marginal Natives: Anthropologists at Work* (New York, 1970), 73-121.

—, "Urbanism, Corporate Groups and Culture Change in Africa below the Sahara," *Anthroplogical Quarterly*, XLIII (1970a), 187-214.

Schwartz, M.S. and C.G. Schwartz, "Problems in Participant Observation," *American Journal of Sociology*, L (1955), 343-53.

Scotch, N.A., "A Preliminary Report on the Relation of Socio-Cultural Factors to Hypertension among the Zulu," *Annals of the New York Academy of Sciences*, LXXXIV (1960), 1000-9.

—, "Magic, Sorcery and Football among the Urban Zulu: a Case of Reinterpretation under Acculturation," *Journal of Conflict Resolution*, V (1964), 70-74.

Shelton, A.J., "The 'Miss Ophelia Syndrome' as a Problem in African Field Research," *Practical Anthropology*, XI (1964), 259-65; 276.

Silberman, L., "Social Survey of the Old Town of Mombasa," *Journal of African Administration*, II (1950), 14-21.

—, "The Urban Social Survey in the Colonies," *Zaire*, VIII (1954), 279-99.

Singer, M., "The Modernization of Religious Beliefs," in Weiner, M. (ed.), *Modernization: the Dynamics of Growth* (New York, 1966), 55-67.

Skinner, E.P., "Labour Migration and its Relationship to Socio-Cultural Change in Mossi Society," *Africa*, XXX (1960), 375-99.

—, "Labor Migration among the Mossi of the Upper Volta," in Kuper, H. (ed.), *Urbanization and Migration in West Africa* (Berkeley, 1965), 60-84.

Smith, M.G., "Institutional and Political Conditions of Pluralism," in Kuper, L. and M.G. Smith (eds.), *Pluralism in Africa* (Berkeley, 1969), 27-65.

—, "Pluralism in Precolonial African Societies," in Kuper, L. and M.G. Smith (eds.), *Pluralism in Africa* (Berkeley, 1969a), 91-151.

Smith, R.S., *Kingdoms of the Yoruba* (London, 1969).

Sofoluwe, G.O., "A Study of Divorce Cases in Igbo-Ora," *The Nigerian Journal of Economic and Social Studies*, VII (1965), 51-62.

Soja, E.W., *The Geography of Modernization in Kenya* (Syracuse, 1968).

Southall, A.W., "Determinants of the Social Structure of African Urban Populations, with Special Reference to Kampala (Uganda)," in Forde, D. (ed.), *Social Implications of Industrialization and Urbanization in Africa South of the Sahara* (Paris, 1956), 557-78.

—, "An Operational Theory of Role," *Human Relations*, XII (1959), 17-34.

—, "Introductory Summary," in Southall, A.W. (ed.), *Social Change in Modern Africa* (London, 1961), 1-66.

—, "The Concept of Elites and their Formation in Uganda," in Lloyd, P.C. (ed.), *The New Elites of Tropical Africa* (London, 1966), 342-66.

—, "The Pattern of Migration in Madagascar and its Theoretical Implications," *African Urban Notes*, III (1968), 14-22.

—, "Trends in Third World Urbanization: a Point of View and a Factor in the Relation between Anthropology and Sociology," Conference on Anthropological Research in Cities, University of Wisconsin-Milwaukee (1970).

Southall, A.W. and P.C.W. Gutkind, *Townsmen in the Making: Kampala and its Suburbs* (Kampala, 1957).

Sovani, N.V., "The Analysis of 'Overurbanization'," *Economic Development and Cultural Change*, XII (1964), 113-22.

Spindler, G.D. (ed.), *Being an Anthropologist: Fieldwork in Eleven Cultures* (New York, 1970).

Stryker, R.E., "Local Politics in the Ivory Coast: 'Modernization' and the Atrophy of Public Life," *African Urban Notes*, III (1968), 11-14.

Sundkler, B.G.M., *Bantu Prophets in South Africa* (London, 1961; 1st ed. 1948).

Swartz, M.J. (ed.), *Local-Level Politics* (Chicago, 1968).

Swartz, M.J., V.W. Turner and A. Tuden (eds.), *Political Anthropology* (Chicago, 1966).

Taylor, J.V. and D.A. Lehmann, *Christians of the Copperbelt* (London, 1961).

Thomas, B.E., "On the Growth of African Cities," *African Studies Review*, XIII (1970), 1-8.

Tiger, L., "'Bureaucracy and Urban Symbol Systems," in Miner, H. (ed.), *The City in Modern Africa* (New York, 1967), 185-213.

Toynbee, A., "The Coming World-City," *The Times*, (18 July 1970), 5. (Extract from: *Cities on the Move* (London, 1970).

Trow, M., "Comment on 'Participant Observation and Interviewing: a Comparison'," *Human Organization*, XVI (1957), 33-35.

Turner, H.W., *African Independent Church. History of an African Independent Church of the Lord (Aladura)*, v.1; *The Life and Faith of the Church of the Lord*, v.2 (Oxford, 1966).

Tylor, E.G., *Primitive Culture*, v.1 (London, 1873).

University of Natal (Department of Economics), *The African Factory Worker: a Sample Study of the Life and Labour of the Urban African Worker* (Cape Town, 1950).

University of Natal (Institute for Social Research), *Baumannville: a Study of an Urban African Community* (Cape Town, 1959).

Vidich, A.J., "Participant Observation and the Collection and Interpretation of Data," *American Journal of Sociology*, LX (1955), 354-60.

Wallerstein, I.M., "Ethnicity and National Integration in West Africa," *Cahiers d'Etudes Africaines*, I (1960), 129-39.

Watts, H.L., *Durban: a Study in Racial Ecology* (London, 1959).

Wax, R.H., "Participant Observation," in Sills, D.L. (ed.), *International Encyclopedia of the Social Sciences*, V (New York, 1968), 238-41.

Weinberg, S.K., "Culture and Communication in Disorders and Psychotherapy in West Africa," *African Urban Notes*, V (1970), 22-28.

Weiner, M., "Urbanization and Political Protest," *Civilisations*, XVII (1967), 44-52.

West Africa, No. 2747 (January 24 1970).

Whiteford, A.H., *Two Cities of Latin America: a Comparative Description* (New York, 1964).

Williams, T.R., *Field Methods in the Study of Culture* (New York, 1967).

Wilson, M.H., "Witch Beliefs and Social Structure," *American Journal of Sociology*, LVI (1951), 307-13.

Wilson, M.H. and A. Mafeje, *Langa: a Study of Social Groups in an African Township* (Cape Town, 1963).

Wilson, G. and M.H. Wilson, *The Analysis of Social Change* (Cambridge, 1945).

Wintrob, R.M., "An Inward Focus: a Consideration of Psychological Stress in Fieldwork," in Henry, F. and S. Saberwal (eds.), *Stress and Response in Fieldwork* (New York, 1969), 63-76.

Wirth, L., "Urbanism as a Way of Life," *American Journal of Sociology*, XLIV (1938), 3-24.

Wolf, E.R. and J.G. Jorgensen, "Anthropology on the Warpath in Thailand," *The New York Review of Books*, XV (Nov. 19, 1970), 26-35.

Worsley, P., *The Third World* (London, 1964).

—, "The End of Anthropology," Working Group of the 6th World Congress of Sociology (1964a).

Wyllie, R.W., "Ritual and Social Change: a Ghanian Example," *American Anthropologist*, LXX (1968), 21-33.

Young, P.V., *Scientific Social Surveys and Research* (Englewood Cliffs, 1956), 3rd ed.

Tables

TABLE 1

World population, rural and urban (towns and cities) 1800-1970 (in millions)

Year	World Total	Rural	Urban	Towns 20,000+	Cities 100,000+
1800	978	948	29	23	16
1850	1,262	1,181	80	54	29
1900	1,650	1,425	224	151	90
1950	2,502	1,795	706	566	406
1960	3,013	2,018	993	809	592
1970	3,628	2,229	1,399	1,169	863
% increase					
1800-1850	5.2	4.5	22.5	18.2	11.8
1850-1900	5.5	3.8	22.7	22.8	25.6
1900-1950	8.7	4.7	25.8	30.1	34.9
1950-1960	20.4	12.4	40.7	42.9	45.9
1960-1970	20.4	10.4	40.8	44.4	45.9

Source: Davis, K. *World Urbanization 1950-1970*. Volume II: *Analysis of Trends, Relationships, and Development*. Population Monograph Series no. 9 Institute of International Studies, University of California, Berkeley, 1972, p. 56.

TABLE 2

Census and projected urban populations by continents and size of groups, 1960, 1975, 2000

Continent 1960	1,000,000 +	500,000 999,000	300,000 499,000	100,000 299,000	100,000 and over	20,000 99,000
N. America	67 M	18 M	12 M	22 M	119 M	47 M
Latin America	25	8	6	13	51	41
Europe	80	35	21	53	189	152
Asia	102	25	22	55	204	151
Africa	6	2	4	8	20	18
Oceania	4	1	1	1	7	3
World total	284	89	66	152	590	412
1975						
N. America	84 M	22 M	14 M	24 M	144 M	60 M
Latin America	61	18	15	24	118	48
Europe	113	60	38	60	271	180
Asia	221	66	66	33	486	221
Africa	12	12	9	15	48	27
Oceania	5	3	1	1	10	2
World total	496	181	143	257	1,077	538
2000						
N. America	125 M	37 M	31 M	47 M	240 M	41 M
Latin America	148	47	41	59	296	59
Europe	189	114	66	85	454	208
Asia	774	232	194	310	1,509	425
Africa	41	31	21	36	129	36
Oceania	8	4	2	2	16	3
World total	1,285 M	465 M	355 M	539 M	2,644 M	772 M

Source: *United Nations Yearbooks.*
　　United Nations, Growth of the World's Urban and Rural Population 1920-2000, New York, 1969.

TABLE 3

World's rural and urban populations 1960, 1975, 2000 (in millions)

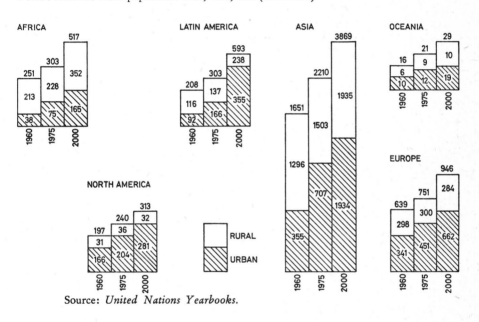

Source: *United Nations Yearbooks.*

TABLE 4

Rural and urban population (whole world)

	1950 - 1970 (in millions)		
	1950	1960	1970
World	2,501,894	3,012,659	3,604,518
Urban[1]	706,383	993,718	1,371,378
Rural	1,795,511	2,018,941	2,233,140
%			
World	100.0	100.0	100.0
Urban	28.2	33.0	38.0
Rural	71.8	67.0	62.0

[1] 20,000 and above

Source: Davis, K. *op.cit*. p. 11.

TABLE 5

Percentage increase (or decrease) per decade of total, rural and urban population 1950-1960 and 1960-1970.[1]

1950-1960	Total	Rural	Urban[2]	City[3]
N. America	20.0	0.4	31.2	38.1
L. America	31.9	16.1	55.3	74.1
Asia	21.3	14.2	60.2	68.1
Africa	29.9	24.0	66.3	76.3
World	20.4	12.4	40.7	45.9
1960-1970				
N. America	15.1	—5.4	24.0	32.7
L. America	32.5	15.0	51.9	69.3
Asia	20.3	12.8	49.8	53.2
Africa	29.7	23.2	59.9	65.4
World	19.6	10.6	38.0	43.1

[1] Includes estimates
[2] 20,000-99,000
[3] 100,000 and above

Source: Davis, K. *op.cit*. p. 179.

TABLE 6

World cities in 1970 — distribution according to size

Size of cities	Number of cities
12,800,000	1
6,400,000	14
3,200,000	18
1,600,000	61
800,000	128
400,000	232
200,000	479
100,000	711

Source: *United Nations Yearbooks.*

TABLE 7

Town and city population (whole world) in percentages
1950-1970

	1950	1960	1970[1]
Urban			
Town[2]	42.5	40.4	38.2
City[3]	57.5	59.6	61.8
World			
Town	12.0	13.3	14.5
City	16.2	19.7	23.5
Rural	71.8	67.0	62.0

[1] Includes estimates
[2] 20,000-99,000
[3] 100,000 and above
Source: *United Nations Yearbooks.*

TABLE 8

Percentages of urban and rural populations in developed and underdeveloped regions, 1950-2000

Year	Less developed region		%	More developed region		%
	Urban	Rural		Urban	Rural	
	Millions			Millions		
1950	265	1,363	16	439	418	51
1960	403	1,603	20	582	394	60
1970	635	1,910	25	717	374	66
1980	990	2,267	30	864	347	71
1990	1,496	2,623	36	1,021	316	76
2000	2,155	2,906	43	1,174	280	81

Source: United Nations, *A Concise Summary of the World Population Situation in 1970.*
New York, 1971.

TABLE 9

Rural and urban population increase (or decrease) 1950-1970[1] of less developed regions (selected) in percentages.

Region	Total	Rural	Urban[2]	City[3]
N. America	17.5	—2.6	27.6	35.4
Western Africa	38.2	31.0	88.3	122.9
Eastern Africa	27.5	24.6	69.7	140.8
Central America	39.4	22.6	62.2	87.1
Caribbean	25.8	18.6	38.2	50.8
Tropical S. America	33.9	14.5	62.9	88.4
East Asia	16.6	7.5	68.7	64.9
	(Japan: —42.5)			
Southeast Asia	29.1	24.2	56.7	68.3
Southwest Asia	29.4	19.4	56.7	86.0
Southern Asia	23.5	21.7	32.9	44.3
Oceania	29.3	27.3	62.6	0.0

Source: Davis, K. *op.cit.* p. 200.

[1] Includes estimates
[2] 20,000-99,000
[3] 100,000 and above

TABLE 10

Population growth of some major urban areas in less developed regions

Dar es Salaam	1900 =	20,000	Nairobi	1906 =	11,500
	1970 =[1]	353,000		1970 =	507,300
Ibadan	1890 =	200,000	Calcutta	1920 =	1,820,000
	1967 =	720,000		1960 =	5,810,000
Dakar	1904 =	18,400	Tehran	1940 =	625,000
	1969 =	677,000		1960 =	1,840,000
Kinshasa	1908 =	4,700	Djakarta	1930 =	525,000
	1970 =	1,200,000		1960 =	2,850,000
Abidjan	1910 =	1,000	Lima	1940 =	600,000
	1968 =	400,000		1960 =	1,575,000
Addis Ababa	1908 =	35,000	Mexico City	1920 =	675,000
	1967 =	637,000		1960 =	4,825,000
Lagos City	1901 =	41,000			
	1969 =	842,000			

[1] Figure after 1967 maybe estimates if censuses were not held or details not yet available.

Sources: United Nations, *Growth of the World's Urban and Rural Population, 1920-2000.* ST/SO A/series A/44, 1969.

Rosser, C. *Urbanization in Tropical Africa: a Demographic Introduction.* International Urban Survey, Ford Foundation, New York, 1973, pp. 38-39.

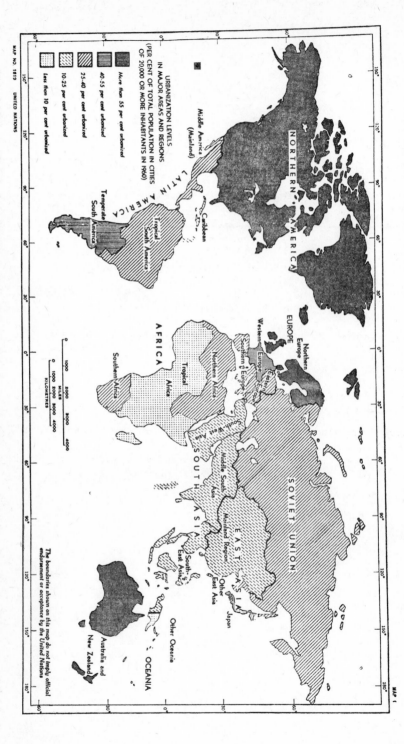

Map 1. Urbanization levels in major areas and regions of the world (percentage of total population in cities of 20,000 or more inhabitants in 1960)

URBANIZATION LEVELS
IN MAJOR AREAS AND REGIONS
(PER CENT OF TOTAL POPULATION IN CITIES
OF 20,000 OR MORE INHABITANTS IN 1960)

More than 55 per cent urbanized
40-55 per cent urbanized
25-40 per cent urbanized
10-25 per cent urbanized
Less than 10 per cent urbanized

MAP NO. 1819   UNITED NATIONS

The boundaries shown on this map do not imply official
endorsement or acceptance by the United Nations

MAP 1

Source: United Nations, *Growth of the World's Urban and Rural Population, 1920-2000.* Population Studies, No. 44, Department of Economic and Social Affairs, New York, 1969, p. 30.